PEARSON

ALWAYS LEARNING

Tropical Island

TEACHER'S BOOK

Contents

Introduction

Our Discovery Island is a six-level course for children learning English as a foreign language in primary schools. It offers best practice methodology in the classroom whilst also offering teachers and pupils an innovative digital environment. *Our Discovery Island* can be used as a blended learning course and takes into account the current movement towards using an increased amount of technology in the classroom and also at home as more and more families have home computers and want safe, effective, educational material for their children. *Our Discovery Island* motivates children by introducing them to a group of characters in an Online Island that echoes the Island in their English book. Pupils follow the characters on a quest through their book whilst listening to stories, singing songs, communicating and playing games along the way. Most importantly, pupils will enjoy themselves and make their own discoveries in English. *Our Discovery Island* – where learning is an adventure!

On Tropical Island, Princess Emily was flying in her hot-air balloon and lost her precious treasure chest with all her favourite things and her friend Pippin the parrot tried to rescue them for her and got lost too. The pupils follow Grandad, Joe and Lindy on their quest to find all the items, find the princess and return her parrot.

Components for the pupil

PUPIL'S BOOK

The Pupil's Book provides materials to effectively present and practise the target language. It introduces new language in lively and engaging contexts. A wide variety of practice tasks lead from controlled language activities through to production and personalisation activities. Extensive further practice is provided in the Activity Book. Each unit includes listening, speaking, reading and writing activities, ensuring that pupils

develop their skills and are able to practise new language in a broad range of contexts. Additionally the Pupil's Book contains songs, chants, stories, games, listening and reading texts and communicative activities to ensure lessons are varied, motivating and effective. It is organised as follows:

- A Welcome unit introducing pupils to the group of characters and the island.
- Eight units divided into eight distinct lessons.
- Three festival lessons at the back of the book for use at Christmas, Valentine's Day and Easter.
- Cut out activities for use in skills Lesson 4 in alternate units.
- Five pages of stickers: Quest stickers for use in Lesson 2 when pupils find the Quest item, vocabulary stickers for use in Lesson 8 for further consolidation of the unit's target language and Look! stickers for use in the Activity Book which contain a target structure from the unit.

The access code printed at the back of the book gives pupils and parents unique and safe access to *Tropical Island Online* via the internet.

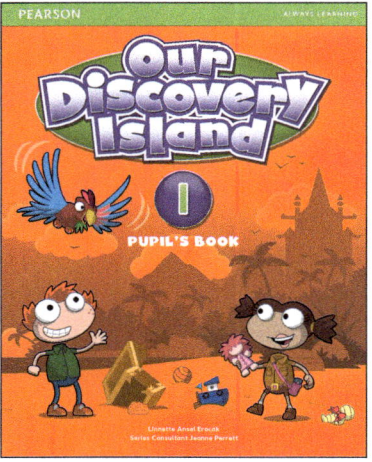

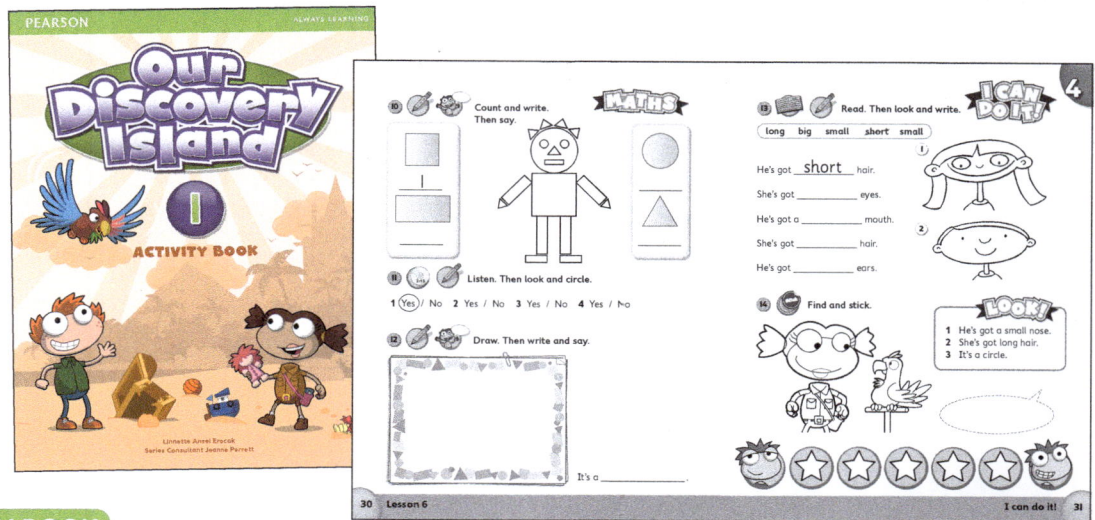

ACTIVITY BOOK

The Activity Book provides reinforcement and consolidation of the language presented in the Pupil's Book. It contains controlled and freer practice plus personalisation and further listening and reading texts. It is organised as follows:

- A Welcome unit introducing pupils to the group of characters and the island.
- Eight units divided into seven lessons for use after the corresponding Pupil's Book page, plus a photocopiable worksheet in the Teacher's Book for use at the end of Lesson 8.
- Three festival lessons at the back of the book for use at Christmas, Valentine's Day and Easter.
- A picture dictionary at the back of the book to aid pupils in remembering the target language.

Full details of when to use the Activity Book are given in the teaching notes.

ONLINE ISLAND

Our Discovery Island includes a unique Online Island component. This provides a safe, engaging, highly-motivating environment where pupils meet the characters from the Pupil's Book plus a host of other exciting characters and follow them on an adventure. Pupils encounter and practise target language from the course in a stimulating environment. They will engage in safe 'closed-chat' dialogues with the characters they meet and follow instructions and guidance to help them solve clues and puzzles and engage in supplementary language games along the way. It's a great way to make learning happen in an interactive environment and further consolidates and extends the language-learning process. Most of all, pupils will enjoy the experience of learning through play and will absorb English without realising it!

CD-ROM

The CD-ROM contains an 'offline' version of the Online Island adventure, games and puzzles for those pupils who don't have access to an internet connection. The CD-ROM also includes the songs and chants from the Pupil's Book.

Components for the teacher

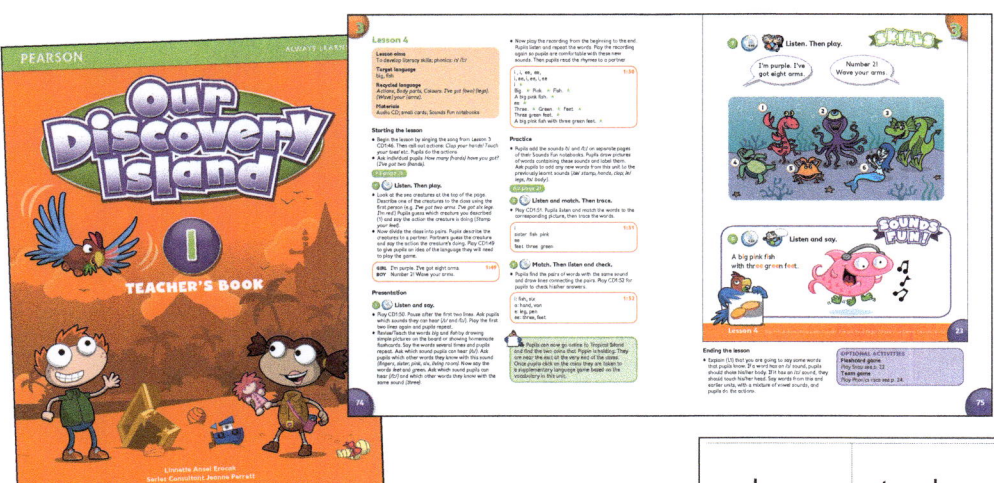

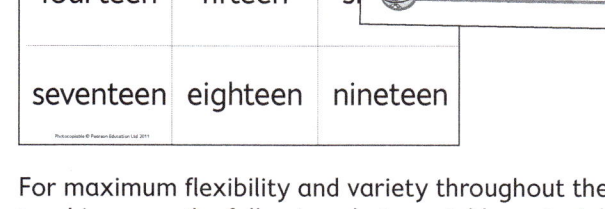

eleven	twelve	th
fourteen	fifteen	si
seventeen	eighteen	nineteen

TEACHER'S BOOK

The Teacher's Book provides step-by-step lesson plans covering all the course material. Each lesson is clearly structured into stages:
• Starting the lesson
• Presentation
• Practice
• Ending the lesson.

There are also further optional activities suggested for fast finishers. The lesson notes are designed to be flexible supporting all teachers, including those who may lack time for planning or have limited access to resources. The introduction includes recommended procedures for using games, classroom language and stories effectively and how the DVD, the Online Islands, and the posters can be best exploited in class.

ONLINE ISLAND

Teachers have special access to the Online Island using the access code provided in the Teacher's Book. This takes them into *Tropical Island Online* with their pupils plus gives access to an easy to use Progress Review System (PRS) where the teacher can monitor the progress of their pupils. There are step-by-step help guides detailing all aspects of game play, plus log in and classroom management through the PRS. These are available both on screen and as a download to print. Teachers will also find report cards showing each pupil's progress that they can print out for the class and parents. Teachers will find further information on pages 10–13.

For maximum flexibility and variety throughout the teaching year the following photocopiable materials can be found at the back of the book:
• Unit and end-of-year evaluations
• Worksheets
• A certificate
• Festival activities templates
• Word cards.
The access code printed at the back of the book gives the teacher special access to *Tropical Island Online* via the internet.

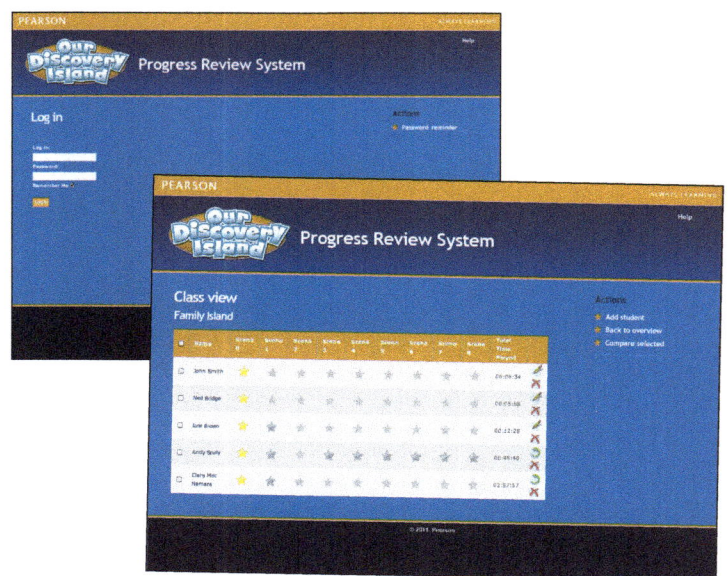

AUDIO CDs

The CDs contain all the chants, songs, stories and listening comprehension activities. There are also karaoke versions of the songs provided at the end of the third CD.

DVD

Each level of *Our Discovery Island* has a DVD with four episodes. Each episode can be used to reinforce and extend the language of the course, focussing on the topics and language of two units. There are songs presented by three young presenters, Sally, Jack and Albert. And there are animated stories, showing further adventures of the *Tropical Island* characters. Teachers will find further information on pages 16–19.

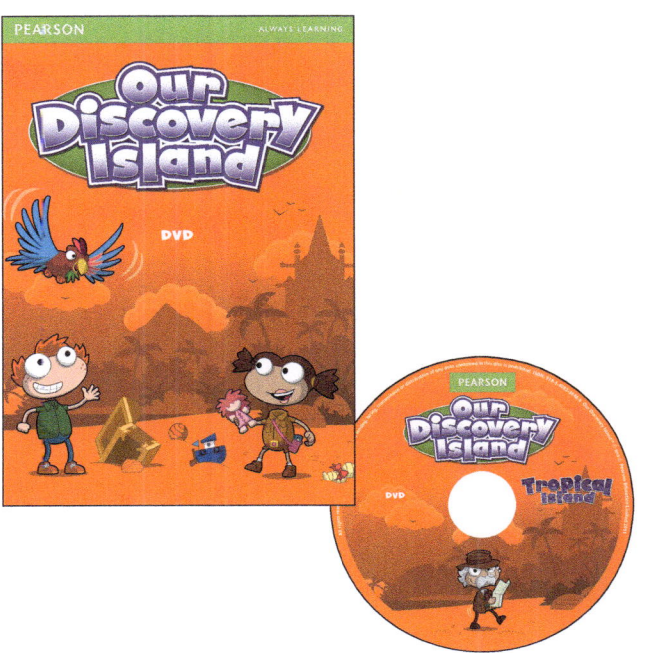

ACTIVE TEACH

Our Discovery Island Active Teach provides software for use on any Interactive Whiteboard (IWB) with integrated tools and a 'How to ...' DVD demonstration of use. It can also be used with just a computer and projector. It eases classroom management as it contains direct links to all of the Pupil's and Activity Book pages, digitally transformed to create more opportunities for interaction between the pupil, teacher and the material. It includes 'hide' and 'reveal' answers, links to further practice activities and games that recycle the language of the unit and previous units and links to audio and DVD content without the need of a separate CD or DVD player. It has stimulating and engaging digital board games with electronic spinners, flashcards and posters plus a special 'make a poster' feature where teachers can compose and print their own posters from a bank of images. Digital story cards are also included with 'hide' and 'reveal' speech bubbles and a 'make a story' feature where pupils' own stories can be made with their own speech bubbles for use in the classroom plus an internet link that takes teachers directly to the Online Islands.

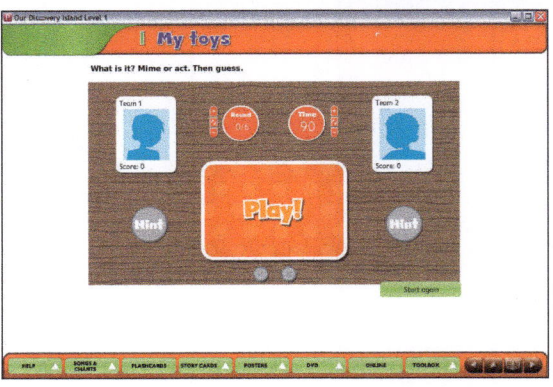

FLASHCARDS

There are 62 flashcards per level containing the main target language in each unit. The lesson plan and Games section in the Teacher's Books clearly explain how the flashcards can be used to present, practise and consolidate language through games and activities.

STORY CARDS

The story cards contain a frame from the *Tropical Island* story and teaching notes comprising 'Before listening' and 'After listening' activities plus the audioscript for the story frame. The story cards are on A4 cards, making them easy to use even in large classes. Teachers will find further information on page 15

POSTERS

There are three posters to accompany each level of *Our Discovery Island*. Teachers will find information on where best to use them in the main lesson notes both to extend the content of the course and to provide a new context for communication . Teachers will find further information on pages 20–21

Methodology and organisation

Our Discovery Island Level 1 assumes no previous knowledge of English and takes a '5P' approach to communication in order to provide support and encourage production from an early stage. The PPP (Presentation, Practice, Production) is a tried and tested approach which is favoured by many teachers in the primary classroom. The lesson sequence is clear and easy to follow and works in a structured way. The *Our Discovery Island* '5Ps' approach adds also Personalisation and Pronunciation.

Presentation is the first stage. The teacher demonstrates the key language (often in illustrated form or using gesture) while providing a model (on audio CD or Active Teach) for pupils to hear the correct pronunciation. When using *Our Discovery Island*, teachers can employ the flashcards at this stage of the lesson.

Practice is provided in the form of controlled and more open activities using the presented language. At early levels, this may involve reading and listening to the word and pointing to it in a picture.

Production activities encourage pupils to use the language either to speak or write something. These activities encourage pupils to become more autonomous and to manipulate the language in order to communicate.

Personalisation activities are also included in the lesson structure to engage the pupils further with the unit language and to help them with language recall.

Pronunciation of difficult sounds in English is a key literacy area which is addressed in the Sounds Fun feature in Lesson 4. *Our Discovery Island* also suggests that teachers encourage the creation of a Sounds Fun *notebook* (see page 8) in which pupils can make a record of the sounds learnt and identify words containing those sounds to aid memory.

ORGANISATION

At Level 1, there is an introductory unit (*Welcome*) followed by eight main teaching units, divided into eight lessons. The three Festival lessons can be used at Christmas, Valentine's Day and Easter. There are cut out activities at the back of the Pupil's Book to be used in skills Lesson 4 in alternate units. There are also five pages of stickers in the back of the Pupil's Books. It is advised that these are removed and kept by the teacher or school to avoid loss. There are three types of stickers, two are used in the Pupil's Books and one in the Activity Book.

The Activity Book provides opportunities for self-evaluation and there is a picture dictionary for reference and revision.

The eight main teaching units consist of eight lessons as follows:

Lesson 1

Presentation and practice of new vocabulary with audio support, pupils are reading, listening and associating the vocabulary with repetitive sounds. Pupils produce all the vocabulary before they move on to listening comprehension with the new vocabulary in context e.g. a dialogue between the characters.

Lesson 2

Chant. The new structure is presented in a chant and there is further practise of the new language. Pupils find the Quest sticker and sing the Quest song.

Lesson 3

Song. Vocabulary is extended and practised with further practice of vocabulary from previous lessons. Karaoke versions of the songs are present at the end of Class CD 3. A home-school link to encourage parental involvement appears in either this lesson, or Lesson 4 or 7 depending on the content of the unit.

The mascot, Pippin, appears in this lesson or Lessons 4, 6 or 7 depending on the content of the unit.

Pippin has a picture of an item from *Tropical Island Online*. Pupils have to find the item online, click on it and complete the supplementary language activity based on the vocabulary of the unit.

Lesson 4

Skills. Revision of unit language. Pupils practise reading, listening, speaking and interaction skills in the Pupil's Book and writing, listening and speaking in the Activity Book.

Sounds Fun. This pronunciation feature with audio support presents English sounds with comic characters.

Lesson 5

Story. The story is presented with speech bubbles for reading with audio support. It recycles vocabulary and structures from previous lessons and introduces some new language.

Lesson 6

CLIL. New language is presented through a cross curricular topic in English. This lesson practises new and recycled language from previous lessons. A *Mini project* encourages production of the unit language.

Lesson 7

Game. Pupils practise the unit language through a fun language game. There is also a TPR activity providing further practice of the unit language.

Lesson 8

Consolidation. Pupils use the vocabulary stickers to further consolidate the unit's target language. Pupils personalise the unit language and self-evaluate how well they feel they have done with the unit. The unit ends with a link to show teachers when to take pupils to *Tropical Island Online.*

LITERACY

In Level 1, reading is introduced in the Pupil's Book and Activity Book in the form of short sentences. In the Activity Book pupils practise tracing and copying single words to practise the new language.

The Sounds Fun notebook is something pupils prepare in class to be used at the end of Lesson 4 of each unit. Pupils record the sounds learnt in each unit in their Sounds Fun notebook and find or draw pictures of words with these sounds. More confident pupils could also write the words below their drawings. With the introduction of target vocabulary at the beginning of every unit, teachers should encourage pupils to add these new words to the appropriate page in their Sounds Fun notebook. In this way, pupils are consistently recycling the sounds introduced in this level. Pupils could use an exercise book as their Sounds Fun notebook and then carry it through into next year. Alternatively, you could help them to make their own mini book using the instructions below and three sheets of A4 paper.

Making a mini book

- Take one A4 sheet for every 8 pages needed in the book, i.e. three A4 sheets for a 24-page book.
- Put the sheets neatly one on top of the other. Fold the pile in half so that the short sides touch, and then in half again in the other direction. You should now have a small book shape.
- Cut along the folds at the top/bottom of the book so that the pages can turn, and staple at the top and bottom of the spine.

Join us at the Great Teachers Primary Place

Find inspiring ideas for your primary classroom, discover new techniques and solutions that work, connect with other primary teachers and share your own stories and creativity. The Great Teachers Primary Place is the place to go for free classroom resources and countless activities for primary teachers everywhere.

Go to www.pearsonelt.com/primaryplace and register for membership.

Members of The Great Teachers Primary Place will receive exclusive access to:

- Free articles on current trends in the primary classroom!
- Free reproducible activity sheets to download and use in your classroom!
- Free Teacher Primary Packs filled with posters, story cards and games to use in your classroom!
- Exclusive access to professional development via print materials and web conferences.

Pronunciation table

Consonants			Vowels	
Symbol	**Keyword**		**Symbol**	**Keyword**
p	**p**en	**short**	ɪ	b**i**t
b	**b**ack		e	b**e**d
t	**t**en		æ	c**a**t
d	**d**ay		ɒ	d**o**g
k	**k**ey		ʌ	c**u**t
g	**g**et		ʊ	p**u**t
f	**f**at		ə	**a**bout
v	**v**iew		i	happ**y**
θ	**th**ing		u	act**u**ality
ð	**th**en	**long**	iː	sh**ee**p
s	**s**oon		ɑː	f**a**ther
z	**z**ero		ɔː	f**ou**r
ʃ	**sh**ip		uː	b**oo**t
ʒ	plea**s**ure		ɜː	b**ir**d
h	**h**ot	**diphthongs**	eɪ	m**a**ke
x	lo**ch**		aɪ	l**ie**
tʃ	**ch**eer		ɔɪ	b**oy**
ʤ	**j**ump		əʊ	n**o**te
m	su**m**		aʊ	n**ow**
n	su**n**		ɪə	r**ea**l
ŋ	su**ng**		eə	h**air**
w	**w**et		ʊə	s**ure**
l	**l**et		uə	act**ua**l
r	**r**ed		iə	pecul**ia**r
j	**y**et			

Young learners and technology

Research shows that appropriate use of computer technology in education is beneficial for pupils (Clements and Sarama; Waxman, Connell, and Gray; Byrom and Bingham). Broadly speaking, pupils can learn *from* computers and *with* computers. Pupils learn *from* computers when the computer assumes the role of a tutor, with the goal of imparting and increasing basic knowledge and skills. Pupils learn *with* computers when the computer serves in the role of a facilitating tool, with the goal of developing critical thinking skills, research skills and the creative imagination (Ringstaff and Kelley).

Computer activities should be age-appropriate and foster instruction in ways that increase learning, motivation, personal productivity and creativity. For example, (Perry) noted that "Children three to five years old are natural 'manipulators' of the world – they learn through controlling the movement and interactions between objects in their world – dolls, blocks, toy cars, and their own bodies." Children are naturally curious and willing to interact with computers, and they enjoy their ability to control the type, pace and repetition of an activity. In some cases, children have even managed to learn how to use a computer with no instruction at all, through their own curiosity, fearlessness, and persistence. (Mitra).

Computers in the English language classroom

The decision to use computers in the language classroom, including the English language classroom, requires the establishment of both technological goals and language-learning goals. For young children, goals such as the following facilitate a path to focused learning.

Technology Objectives	Language Objectives
To become familiar with the parts of a computer (GPU, screen, keyboard, mouse, cursor, printer and so on).	To use English to interact in the classroom and to communicate in social situations.
To become familiar with approved software programs for the classroom.	To use English to describe self, family, community and country.
To become familiar with operations (select, drag, save, delete and so on).	To use learning strategies to increase communicative competence.
To become familiar with finding, filing, tracking and organising information.	To develop the four skills: listening, speaking, reading and writing.
To share information and collaborate with others.	To pronounce English words, phrases and sentences intelligibly.
To develop learner autonomy.	To use appropriate register.

International Society for Technology in Education. *National Educational Technology Standards for Students: Connecting Curriculum and Technology.*

Teachers of English to Speakers of Other Languages, Inc. *ESL Standards for Pre-K–12 Students.*

References

Byrom, E., and Bingham, M. "Factors Influencing the Effective Use of Technology for Teaching and Learning: Lessons Learned from SEIR-TEC Intensive Site Schools, 2nd Edition." Greensboro, NC: SERVE.

Clements, D. H., and Sarama, J. "Strip Mining for Gold: Research and Policy in Educational Technology – A Response to 'Fool's Gold.'" *Educational Technology Review,* 11(1), 7–69.

Kneas, K. M., and Perry, B. D. "Using Technology in the Early Childhood Classroom." *Early Childhood Today.* Scholastic.

Mitra, S. "Hole in the wall – can kids learn computer literacy by themselves?" Generation YES Blog.

Ringstaff, C., and Kelley, L. "The Learning Return on Our Educational Technology Investment." San Francisco, CA: WestEd.

Waxman, H. C., Connell, M. L., and Gray, J. "A Quantitative Synthesis of Recent Research on the Effects of Teaching and Learning with Technology on Student Outcomes." Naperville, IL: North Central Regional Educational Laboratory.

The Online Island is an immersive world which accompanies the *Our Discovery Island* series. It is a ground-breaking digital product, combining the methodologies of classroom-based ELT and games-based learning. It is a safe learning environment, suitable for young learners which, via an internet connection, can be:

- used on individual computers at school or at home
- used in groups at school
- used through the Active Teach IWB software.

It provides immediate feedback on performance; and contains features that appeal to young learners, such as colourful attractive visuals, clear audio providing excellent pronunciation models, animation, and game-like activities, all of which play a part in pupil motivation. It is carefully calibrated to appeal to children between the ages of 4 and 12. The target vocabulary and grammar directly reinforce the syllabus of the course. Because tasks are intuitive and clear, and because students receive immediate audio and visual feedback on their progress, the programme builds learner confidence and independence.

The Online Island was authored by a team of ELT specialists and multimedia games developers and offers rich and engaging digital worlds which build on the language and aims contained within the books. The main emphasis is on expanding vocabulary while the pupils learn through playing language games and achieving tasks. New language is introduced gradually and contextualised so that pupils feel confident and motivated to complete each level. The key concepts which have guided the design are:

- **Immersion**. The Online Island takes pupils out of their classroom or home environment and immerses them in a coherent and believable context. Engaging content and beautiful design hold the pupils' interest and motivate them to continue with the adventure. Research conducted with the Online Island indicates that even very young children are able to maintain concentration and enthusiasm for long periods of time.
- **Stealth learning**. The Online Island is enjoyable and learning takes place almost without the pupils being aware of it. Rather than mirroring the type of tasks in the Pupil's Book, pupils learn via interactions with characters in the adventure. They are presented with real-world-like tasks, giving them a sense of responsibility and active involvement which is extremely motivating. Learning takes place through listening and reading comprehension of speech bubbles, and through exposure to the target lexical sets via speech bubbles, dialogues, the Picture Dictionary and supplementary language games.

- **Mastery**. Striking the right balance of challenge and achievability is a key component in any game. The Online Island has been carefully designed to introduce the key skills needed to complete the task at the start of each level, and then by slowly building the complexity of the language pupils encounter. It is important that pupils find the tasks within the adventure sufficiently challenging. Children with prior exposure to digital games expect to fail at complex tasks several times before achieving them. This makes the tasks more, not less, satisfying, once achieved and encourages exploration and educational risk-taking. The model of 'try, fail, repeat, succeed' is also important because it gives repeated exposure to the target language, ensuring that pupils comprehend the language before they move on.
- **Control**. Pupils love immersive worlds because they feel free within them. They can move their avatar around at their own speed and in their own chosen direction. They are also free to experiment and to fail without censure or observation. This gives them confidence and motivation. The Online Island has been designed to allow children sufficient freedom to enjoy the adventure and games, but at the same time to carefully channel them towards the learning outcomes and to expose them gradually to the target language. A carefully controlled gating system means they must achieve certain tasks before progressing into new parts of the adventure. A starred report card system motivates them to complete all the tasks within a scene but gives them some freedom to determine when and how they do this.
- **Reward**. The Online Island includes many of the most popular features of existing games, such as collectible items, costumisation, avatar design and 'hidden' rewards such as new characters who appear once certain tasks are complete as well as audio and visual feedback to a task.

Teacher support

We recognise that many teachers are likely to be unfamiliar with this type of component and have developed a series of help guides both online and as a download to be printed to help teachers gain confidence in using the Online Island in the classroom, assisting pupils with queries about the tasks, or setting parts of the Online Island for home study.

In conjunction with this there are video walkthroughs of each level, to answer queries about specific sections of the adventure. These videos can also act as an introduction or provide quick support for teachers who can't spare the time to work through the Online Island themselves.

All teachers will receive an individual access code to the Online Island and, unlike the pupil version it will contain a map, allowing them to skip back and forward between scenes.

For ease of classroom management there is a Progress Review System (PRS) where teachers can register their classes and monitor their progress. Parents can also view pupils' progress via the Report Card online.

TROPICAL ISLAND ONLINE

Tropical Island Online is set on a fun island where the pupils visit a farm, a castle and some caves, among other locations. It's an island that is normally hot and sunny. However, Bob-a-Job, the villain, has created a special machine to turn the weather on *Tropical Island* cold and stormy. The main goal is to help the islanders find Bob-a-Job and his secret volcano lair and collect parts of a rainbow key which will turn off the weather machine, making the island hot and sunny again.

As they move around *Tropical Island* they will bump into and be able to interact with characters they recognise from the books, such as Princess Emily and Joe.

The adventure begins with an introductory tutorial *Scene Zero* with a simple activity. The aim is to familiarise the pupil with the layout and computer controls, and to provide some context for the following scenes. This also contains the chatroom, where the pupil can interact and play games with other pupils such as Spell Drop, etc. The chatroom contains sample dialogue matching the language aims of each unit at this level. The pupils can return to the chatroom at any stage during the adventure to test their mastery of the language.

The pupil then progresses to the first scene. Each scene contains one, two or three tasks (such as moving an object out of the way or finding the parts of a broken machine). Within each scene there are some supplementary activities such as Match Card or Hungry Shark to further test vocabulary. One of the supplementary activities in each scene is flagged by an image in the Pupil's Book, held by Pippin, the parrot. This is not linked in with the task and pupils can complete this at any time. Players can move freely through Scenes 1–3, but they cannot progress to Scenes 4–6 until they have completed all the tasks from Scenes 1–3. Progression to Scenes 7–8 is similarly dependent on the pupil having completed all the tasks in Scenes 4–6. The Level ends with an *Exit Scene*, which occurs automatically and doesn't require interaction from the pupil. The purpose of this scene is to 'round off' the Level, and to reward the pupil for completing all the tasks.

Tropical Island Unit 2 Lesson Plan

Tropical Island Online can be used safely by children at home if they have a computer and internet access or the *Tropical Island CD-ROM*. If you wish to incorporate *Tropical Island Online* into your lessons, below is an easy-to-follow lesson plan which shows how simple it is to manage it in class.

Lesson aims
- To distinguish between different family members (mum, dad, parents, brother, sister, aunt, uncle, cousin, granny, grandad) and to understand simple descriptions of location (Where's Lucy Lock-Picker? She's in the bedroom.)
- Receptive language: Here, take this umbrella to keep you dry. What are you looking for? Bob-a-Job wants the rainbow key. His friends are in this house.

- Carry this out as part of Lesson 8, after the pupils have completed the Pupil's Book and Activity Book activities. Pupils should have already found the book/online link item that Pippin is holding up on the Pupil's Book page at the end of Lesson 7 (bottle) and will have therefore completed the supplementary language activity based on the vocabulary in this unit. If not, the teacher can 'walk' the pupils through this now. The bottle is in the castle basement on a shelf.
- Online: Using the IWB or a computer screen visible to the class, go to *Tropical Island Online* and access Scene 2, the castle basement.
- Walk students through the first part of the quest. Find and talk to the butler. He will ask you to help him complete his word search. Ask the class to help you select the correct family vocabulary looking at the pictures of royal family members and find the words in the grid. Teach the new extended family vocabulary (aunt, uncle, parents, cousin), by sketching an example family tree on the board to illustrate.
- Ask a pupil to take over the mouse to find the jigsaw piece in this scene (apple).
- When the word search is complete, the butler will give pupils an umbrella that they can hold or put down, located in the inventory bag top right of screen.
- Exit the basement and talk to the police officer outside the manor house. She will give you a binoculars card which you must use to help her identify the location of some burglars (Bob-a-Job's friends/gang). Divide the class into four groups. Choose a pupil from each group to take over with the mouse, locating one of the burglars and calling out which room of the house they are in. To do this they may need to move between the binoculars and the picture of Bob-a-Job's friends/gang in the inventory bag at the top right of the screen.

- Ask a pupil to take over the mouse to find the jigsaw piece in this scene (nuts).
- Now talk to the delivery girl and ask her for a newspaper. The newspaper will be delivered into the inventory bag as a card (top right of screen). Open the card and read the news that you have just helped the police to capture Bob-a-Job's friends/gang.

- Alternatively, once you have completed an example online with the whole class, direct pupils to individual or shared computers, or have them access the task at home for homework.
- End the lesson as detailed in the main lesson notes.

Online Island access code record

Class: ....

Pupil's name	Access code

How to use stories

Stories are an essential part of language learning because they allow pupils to absorb information in a fun and stimulating way. Learning outside the normal boundaries of a teacher-based classroom environment creates the opportunity for pupils to develop their creative and communicative skills. Using stories in the classroom greatly enhances pupils' ability to listen and to actively respond to target language and structures in a fun and relaxed atmosphere. Stories increase motivation and encourage less confident pupils to contribute with their ideas and opinions because they are not confined to the limits of a certain structure. Stories provide larger chunks of language in a context and provide an opportunity for pupils to produce language.

There's a story in Lesson 5 of each unit featuring the *Tropical Island* characters. These stories serve to revise and reinforce the target language and structures of the unit. The artwork is visually stimulating and the audio effects ensure pupils listen avidly from start to finish. The story cards provided are an enormously versatile and useful tool for classroom learning. Story cards enable teachers to better utilise the story through an array of activities which would not be possible from the printed version alone in the Pupil's Book. All story cards are divided into three sections: questions to ask before listening to the story; the audioscript; and questions to ask after listening to the story. Below is a four-step method for using stories in the classroom that starts with L1 anticipation and ends with (assisted) performance.

Stage 1 – Anticipating the story
The questions to ask before listening to the story provide teachers with the opportunity to introduce any new vocabulary or to revise previously learnt language and structures. Pupils can begin to form an idea of the theme of the story and how it might develop. This allows teachers to assess how thoroughly pupils have absorbed the target language of the unit. At this stage, teachers should ask pupils questions or carry out a simple discussion in L1 to get the pupils thinking about the story. Teachers shouldn't provide answers at this stage, but rather allow pupils to think for themselves.

Stage 2 – Hearing and seeing the story
The fact that the full audioscript is printed on the back of each story card is extremely practical for the teacher in the classroom with young pupils. It saves precious time and doesn't allow the opportunity for pupils to stray from the subject at hand. If access to technology is limited or if that technology fails during the lesson, teachers can read from the story cards. At this stage, pupils listen to the story in English and work through it in English to find answers themselves.

Stage 3 – Checking the story
Questions to be asked after listening to the story are printed on the back of all story cards. This gives teachers the possibility to further assess the depth of pupils' comprehension of the story and of the language used. It also sparks pupils' creativity and imagination by encouraging them to visualise how the story develops.

Stage 4 – Acting the story
After listening to the story several times, pupils are ready to act it out in groups, providing them with the opportunity to say larger chunks of language. Props can be brought to class and used to make the experience even more stimulating. Teachers may play the recording or read the audioscript from the story cards while pupils act out, or pupils may read the story from their Pupil's Book.

Story activities
The story cards are greatly versatile and can be used in conjunction with a number of activities:
- Stick the story cards in random order on the board and pupils put them in the correct order.
- Stick the story cards on the board in order. Ask pupils to close their eyes while you remove one card. Pupils guess which card is missing.
- Hide the story cards around the classroom. Pupils find the cards and stick them in order on the board.
- Pupils invent a new script for one or all of the cards.
- Read the audioscript printed on the back of the story cards, making deliberate mistakes (e.g. say *red* instead of *yellow*). Pupils correct your mistakes.
- Hand each story card out to a different pupil. When you read the audioscript the pupil with the appropriate story card stands up and shows it to the class.
- Show any story card and pupils remember the audioscript.

Activities for the story not involving the story cards:
- While pupils listen to the story, they perform a specific action for target vocabulary (e.g. pupils clap when they hear the word *purple* or stamp their feet when they hear the word *blue*).
- Pupils draw a new picture for any frame of the story.
- Pupils create a new ending for the story.
- Pupils draw their favourite character.
- Pupils discuss real life situations with connotations to the story.
- Pupils comment on how they would feel or how they would behave if they were in a similar situation to one of the story characters.
- Write the story script on pieces of paper. Hold them up one by one. Pupils read them and say the name of the character who said the line in the story.
- Pupils keep a notebook of new words/expressions from the stories. Write any new words that are not part of the target language for the unit on the board and pupils copy the new words into their notebooks. Stronger pupils could also use the new words in a sentence.

How to use the DVD

Episode	Target language
1	May, I have ...? Please. Thank you. Excuse me. I'm sorry; Colours; Family
2	big, small, kite, pull; I'm ..., You're ...; Body parts
3	I like + (jump) +ing; Actions; Animals
4	put on, take off, wear; Clothes; Weather

The DVDs give the language of *Our Discovery Island* a new context and each episode is designed for use after every two units of the Pupil's Book. Sally, Jack and Albert provide a song and there is an animated story from *Tropical Island*. Each episode also contains a Last Word – a short focus on one language point.

• SONG
The pupils watch, listen and follow the actions. As they grow more confident, they can join in with the song.

• STORY
Watch the story. Ask the pupils (in L1) what happened in the story. Watch again, stopping at key points, and ask them about the language, the images or the story. Ask pupils to act out the story. Assign the roles of Joe and Lindy to confident speakers and let other pupils play the other parts. Encourage them to say as much of the dialogue as they can and prompt them where necessary.

• THE LAST WORD
These reinforce a common language point with short, humorous animation. Some Last Words are interactive, and pupils can use the DVD player controls to answer questions.

Episode 1

Song – Say 'please'

JACK	Hello, I'm Jack.
SALLY	Hello, I'm Sally.
ALBERT	Hello, Jack. Hello, Sally.
JACK AND SALLY	Hi, Albert!
JACK	May I have a grape?
	May I have a grape ... *please*?
SALLY	Ahem ...
JACK	Thank you.
SALLY	Albert?
ALBERT	Thank you!
SALLY	Say *please*.
JACK	Please!
SALLY	Say *thank you*.
JACK	Thank you!
JACK	Please! Thank you!
SALLY	Please! Thank you!

JACK	Please! Thank you!
SALLY	Please! Thank you!
ALBERT	May I have it?
	May I have it ... *please*?
ALBERT	Thank you!
JACK	Say *please*.
ALBERT	Please!
JACK	Say *thank you*.
ALBERT	Thank you!
JACK	Please! Thank you!
ALBERT	Please! Thank you!
JACK	Please! Thank you!
ALBERT	Please! Thank you!
JACK AND SALLY	Oops!
JACK AND SALLY	Sorry!
JACK AND SALLY	Excuse me.
JACK AND SALLY	Sorry!
SALLY	Please! Thank you!
ALBERT	Please! Thank you!
SALLY	Please! Thank you!
JACK	Please! Thank you!

Extra activity

Ask the pupils for various items on their desks using *May/Can I have ...?* Do this first without saying *please* and encourage the pupils to withhold the item and say *Say please!* until you repeat the request using *please*. With confident classes, get them to insist that you say *thank you*, too by saying *Say thank you!* Then get the pupils in pairs to practise asking for things using *please* and *thank you*.

Story – Pictures

JOE	Look. It's a car.
LINDY	Oh, that's good! Look at this. This is my grandad.
JOE	A train, a bike and a car.
LINDY	My house, my mum and my grandad.
PIPPIN	Red! Blue! Yellow!
JOE	Oh no! My pictures!
LINDY	Oh no!
	Urgh! I'm green! Pippin! Come here!
LINDY	Blue!
JOE	Yellow!
PIPPIN	Red!
LINDY	And green!

GRANDAD	Hello, Lindy. Oh dear!
LINDY	Hello, Grandad. Look.
GRANDAD	What's this?
LINDY	This is you.
GRANDAD	Oh, yes. This is good. Very good. Well done, Lindy.
PIPPIN	Pippin! Red, blue, green, yellow!
LINDY	Silly parrot!

The Last Word – A fat cat

ALBERT	A mat. A cat. A cat on a mat. A fat cat on a mat. Miaow!

Episode 2

Song – I'm big

SALLY	Hello!
JACK	Hello!
SALLY	Look, what's this?
JACK	It's a camera. Sally, look at this! I'm big!
SALLY	You're big! I'm small!
JACK	You're small!
SALLY	Your mouth is big!
JACK	Your head is small!
JACK	My feet are long!
SALLY	Your feet are long!
JACK	My eyes are big!
SALLY	Your eyes are big! My ears are small!
JACK	Your ears are small! My nose is long!
SALLY	Your nose is long!
SALLY	You're big!
JACK	You're small!

Extra activity

Ask pupils to draw a monster with a body, head, eyes, ears, mouth, nose, legs, arms, hands and feet. Tell them to make some of the features big, some small, some long and some short. Draw one yourself and then describe it. Say *I am a monster. My ears are long, my nose is short. My head is small. My body is big. My eyes are big. My mouth is small. My legs are long.*

Encourage pupils to describe his/her own monsters in a similar way.

Story – The kite

LINDY	Hello, Pippin!
PIPPIN	Hello!
LINDY	He's happy.
JOE	Look at this. I've got a kite.
LINDY	Wow, a kite! It's big. And it's lovely! Hmmm. Oh!
JOE	Look. Two small triangles and two big triangles.
LINDY	Aaah!
JOE	Come on!
LINDY	Yippee!
JOE	Help! Lindy, jump!
LINDY	Uh oh! It's OK. I've got you!
JOE	Hey! Help me! Help!
LINDY	Oh dear! Help!
JOE	Help!
LINDY	Good, Pippin. Pull! Pull!
LINDY	Thank you, Pippin! You're a good parrot.
PIPPIN	Joe's my friend! Lindy's my friend!
JOE	Oh no! Pippin!

The Last Word – Legs

ALBERT	How many legs can you see? Two legs. Four legs. Eight legs!

Episode 3

Song – I like dancing.

JACK	Hello! Do you like dancing? I like dancing.
SALLY	I like dancing.
JACK AND SALLY	I like dancing. I like dancing.
SALLY	I like jumping.
JACK	I like jumping.
JACK AND SALLY	I like dancing. I like jumping.
JACK AND SALLY	I like dancing. I like jumping.
JACK	I like clapping.
SALLY	I like clapping.
JACK AND SALLY	I like dancing. I like jumping. I like clapping.
SALLY	You like dancing.
JACK	You like jumping.
SALLY	You like clapping. I like stamping my feet.
JACK	I like stamping my feet.

JACK AND SALLY	I like dancing. I like jumping. I like clapping. And stamping my feet. You like dancing. You like jumping. You like clapping. And stamping your feet.
JACK	One more! I like moving my body!
SALLY	I like moving my body.
JACK AND SALLY	I like dancing. And jumping. And clapping. Stamping my feet. And moving my body. You like dancing. And jumping. And clapping. Stamping your feet. And moving your body. Dance! Jump! Clap! Stamp your feet! Move your body! Yeah, yeah, yeah!

Extra activity

Ask pupils what they like doing e.g., *Maria, do you like dancing?* Encourage them to reply with, *Yes, I like dancing* or *No, I don't like dancing.* Ask first about the things in the song, then expand it to include other verbs the children already know. For example, *Do you like singing?* Make sure they use the -*ing* form (the gerund) each time in their answers.

Story – The farm

LINDY	Hello, I'm Lindy.
JOE	Hello, I'm Joe.
FARMER	Hello, welcome to my farm!
LINDY	Look! I like sheep!
SHEEP	Baaa!
ELVIS SHEEP	Baaa!
PUNK STYLE SHEEP	Baaa!
AFRO STYLE SHEEP	Baaa!
LINDY	Look! Horses!
JOE	Urgh! Yuck! I don't like horses!
LINDY	Look! Hens!
JOE	I like hens!
JOE	Look! I like cows!
FARMER	Er … Joe …
LINDY	Look out!
JOE	Huh? I don't like cows!

The Last Word – Animals

FARMER	Where's the cow? No, that isn't the cow. Hurray! Yes, good! Where's the sheep? No, that isn't the sheep. Hurray! Yes, well done! Where's the hen? No, that isn't the hen.
FARMER	Hurray! Yes, good. Well done!

Episode 4

Song – Put on your T-shirt

SALLY	Hello!
JACK	Hello!
SALLY	Pyjamas!
JACK	Yes?
SALLY	It's time for school!
ABERT	It's time!
SALLY	It's time!
SALLY AND JACK	It's time for school!
SALLY	Put on your T-shirt!
JACK	T-shirt, T-shirt!
ALBERT	Put on your trousers!
JACK	Trousers, trousers!
SALLY	Put on your socks.
JACK	Socks, socks!
ALBERT	Put on your jumper!
JACK	Jumper, jumper!
SALLY	Put on your coat!
JACK	Coat, coat!
ALBERT	Put on your hat!
JACK	Hat, hat!
SALLY	Now you're dressed. It's time for school! Off you go!
JACK	Now I'm dressed. It's time for school. Off I go!
SALLY AND JACK	Pyjamas! T-shirt! Trousers! Socks! Jumper! Coat! Hat!
JACK	School's finished! Now it's time for bed.
SALLY	Take off your hat!
JACK	My hat, my hat!
ALBERT	Take off your coat!
JACK	My coat, my coat!
SALLY	Take off your jumper!
JACK	My jumper, my jumper!
ALBERT	Take off your trousers!
JACK	My trousers, my trousers!
SALLY	Take off your socks!
JACK	My socks, my socks!
ALBERT	Take off your T-shirt.
JACK	My T-shirt, my T-shirt!
SALLY	Put on your pyjamas!
JACK	I'm wearing my pyjamas!
ALBERT	It's time for bed! Off you go!

Story – Clothes

GRANDAD	Good morning!
JOE	Hello, Grandad!
LINDY	Let's go to the beach!
GRANDAD	Hmmm, what's the weather like?
JOE	It's sunny!
LINDY	What are you wearing?
GRANDAD	Oh dear. I'm wearing a big jumper.
JOE	Take off your jumper. Put on a T-shirt.
GRANDAD	I like my red T-shirt.
LINDY	Take off your shoes.
GRANDAD	Look at my old trousers!
JOE AND LINDY	Very nice, Grandad.
GRANDAD	Let's go to the beach!
JOE	We're here!
LINDY	It's sunny!
GRANDAD	I like sunny days!
JOE	Oh no! Look at the sky!
GRANDAD	Oh dear. It's rainy!

Extra activity

Play the story again, stop it at various points and ask pupils to say what the different characters are wearing. Encourage them to say the colours also e.g., *Joe is wearing a white T-shirt and blue trousers. Grandad is wearing a brown hat and a red T-shirt.* At the end, teach the word *umbrella* and ask what colour grandad's umbrella is (*blue and yellow*).

The Last Word – It's cold

FARMER	Brrr! Snow!
	Ah! A coat.
	Oh! It's rainy.
	Ah! A hat.
	Oh! It's cold.
	Ah! A scarf.
	Oh! It's sunny.
	Ah!

How to use posters

Posters can play a key role in the English language lesson as they are such a powerful visual tool. They can be a valuable way to focus pupils' attention, allowing for pupils to consolidate and extend the language already learnt. In addition, the *Our Discovery Island* posters help develop a pupil's speaking ability as they interact with visually appealing characters, authentic 'real-world' photos and captivating scenes. The interactive posters provide even greater scope as the interactive elements can be moved around and a wider variety of language can therefore be practised.

General poster activities

- Before displaying the poster for the first time, pupils can anticipate and predict who and what they will see within a topic area and then see how many items they guessed correctly once the poster is visible.
- Pupils can create their own posters, based on a similar topic.
- Using a large piece of paper placed over the top of the poster (with a 5 cm hole cut out), pupils can be asked to identify what they can see through the hole.
- Through description, pupils can identify objects that are being described orally, e.g. *It's fat. It's white. It's an animal. What is it? It's a cat.*
- With a time limit, pupils can look at the posters and try to remember as much language and content as possible and then in pairs or led by the teacher, they can try to recall the content through questions and answers, e.g. *Is there a hat? What colour is it?*
- By pointing to an object and making a statement, pupils can reply *Yes* or *No* if the information is correct or incorrect, e.g. *This is a library.*
- In teams or pairs, pupils can write down as many words as possible for the items in each poster.

Poster 1 Tropical Island Map

This is a visual representation of the *Online Island* for Level 1. It can be used to check pupils' progress through *Tropical Island Online*, to check where they have located the items presented in each unit of the Pupil's Book in order to play the supplementary vocabulary game and to stimulate language production. Pupils are taken further into *Tropical Island* as they meet new characters in new settings not represented in the stories in the Pupil's Book.

The map shows the nine main areas which the pupils will pass through:
- The courtyard
- The castle
- The manor house
- The mountain
- The prison
- The farm
- The supermarket
- The circus tent
- The volcano

Specific poster activities

New vocabulary: flags, police car, police van
Recycled vocabulary: *police officer, Animals, Food, Clothes, Colours*

- At the beginning of each lesson, unit or term ask pupils where they are in *Tropical Island Online* by asking them to point to the area on the map. This allows instant feedback as to which pupils are engaging with the *Online Island* and which pupils are perhaps progressing at a different speed to others.
- Ask pupils one by one to come up and point to a particular colour. *Point to orange.*
- Point to one of the orange flowers and ask *Is it orange?* Pupils answer *Yes* or *No.*

Unit 1 Lesson 7

- Focus pupils' attention on the circus tent. Ask pupils to count the number of flags from the tent to the lorry. If necessary, teach the word *flag.* Ask *How many flags? (6) What colours can you see? (orange, black, pink, blue, yellow and red).* Ask *How many blue flags? (two, one here and one on the castle).*

Unit 5 Lesson 7

- Play the animal chant CD2:19 to remind pupils the English words for the animals. Ask *Can you see a horse? Can you see a cow? Can you see a sheep? Can you see a goat? Ask a pupil to come and point to the sheep. Ask How many legs? (4) What colour is it? (white).*
- Play a guessing game, describe an animal and pupils must guess which one you are describing. Say *It's got four legs. It's big. It's grey. What is it? (It's a horse.)* This game can also be played by pupils in pairs as one chooses an animal and the other asks questions to guess which one it is. *Is it fat? Is it black and white? Is it a cow?*

Unit 6 Lesson 7

- In pairs, ask pupils to write down three food items. Ask pupils what food they can see on the poster (bananas, apples, eggs). See which pair thought of the three items that are visible.
- Pupils ask their friend questions about the food they can see in the poster, e.g. *Do you like (eggs)?* They can then create a survey to ask each other in class.

Unit 7 Lesson 7

- Ask pupils to find an item of clothing in the poster and mime putting it on and saying *I'm wearing (a hat).* This can be done in teams (hat, boots, coat).
- Check what other items they know. You can help by miming putting on the items (T-shirt, trousers, dress, skirt, shoes, socks, pyjamas, jumper, shirt).

Poster 2 Street scene

This is a cross section of a street scene with animals to be cut out of the interactive strip.

> **New vocabulary:** a shop, a library, a park, a café; mouse
> **Recycled vocabulary:** *a house, a garden; in; rabbit, cat, dog, cow, horse, duck, sheep, hen. It's (fat). It's (small). It's (white). Is it (brown)? Is it a (dog)?*

Unit 3 Lesson 7

- Focus pupils' attention on the poster and give them one minute to look and remember as many words as possible. See how many words they already know. (bedroom, living room, garden, hen) Teach the words library, park, cafe, shop house. Ask pupils to point to (the shop). Ask pupils to point to something (pink) etc.

Unit 5 Lesson 4

- Check pupils know the names of the six locations on the poster (garden, house, shop, library, café, park). Revise the names of the animals by holding them up and pupils say *hen, goat, cat, dog, mouse, cow, horse, duck, sheep.* Teach the word *rabbit.*
- Pupils can play a dictation game to direct a pupil at the front of the class to position the characters accordingly. Pupil A asks *Where's the hen?* Another pupil answers *It's in the (shop)* and Pupil A must place the hen into the shop on the poster. This can be turned into a team game and points can be awarded for correct positioning. Ask stronger pupils to stick (with blue tac or similar) the animal word cards in the correct places once the photos have been placed.

Unit 5 Lesson 8

- Place all the animals in the poster. Play a game asking pupils to point to items – first general and then specific. Teams can be created and points awarded. *Point to (green). Find the (thin dog).*
- Point to items and ask *Is it a (cow)?* to elicit *Yes* and *No* from the pupils.
- Place all the animals in the poster. Then make the animal noises and ask pupils to come and point to the animal and say what it is. *Miaow.* Pupil answers *It's a cat.*

Poster 3 Beach poster

This poster allows the pupils to revise the language both at moments throughout the course and as an end of year round up poster.

> **Recycled vocabulary:** *Clothes, Toys, Weather, like/ don't like...*

Unit 1 Lesson 4

- One pupil can sit with his/her back to the poster, then select a toy from the poster and the class can mime playing with the toy for the pupil to guess.
- Ask stronger pupils to stick (with blue tac or similar) the toy word cards in the correct places.

Unit 7 Lesson 6

- Describe the characters for pupils to guess, e.g. *I'm wearing (brown) (shorts). Who am I?* Pupils come to the poster and point to the correct character (Lindy).

Unit 8 Lesson 8

- Elicit the different weather in the poster: *sunny, cloudy, rainy, windy and snowy.* Get pupils to come and point to the different weather scenes. Teach actions for each of the weather types: rainy – holding an umbrella, windy – being blown around, sunny – sunbathing, cloudy – looking unhappy, snowy – making a snowball. Call out the weather types and ask pupils to act them out. This can be turned into a game to get pupils to respond quickly to the language. A stronger pupil can become the leader of the game, calling out the weather types.
- In pairs, pupils can try and write as many sentences as possible based on the poster. *I'm wearing (trousers). I like (sunny days). It's a (small) (boat).*
- Pupils can create a poster of clothes to wear in different weather types, drawing the items (or using items cut out from magazines) and labelling them.

Games

FLASHCARD GAMES

Correct order Call four to eight pupils to the front of the class (depending on the number of flashcards) and give them each a flashcard. Then call out four flashcards in random order. Pupils have to arrange themselves in the correct order.

Guess the card Cut out a small square in the centre of a piece of A4 paper. Hold the paper in front of a flashcard allowing pupils to see only a small bit of the card through the hole. Pupils guess the item.

Echo Explain (L1) the meaning of the word *echo*. Ask pupils to be your echo. Show them a card and say the item on it. Ask pupils to echo it by repeating several times, becoming quieter and quieter.

Collect the cards Hold up any flashcard. If a pupil can correctly identify it, he/she is allowed to keep it. The pupil with the most flashcards at the end of the game is the winner.

Memory Stick four or five flashcards on the board. After pupils memorise the cards, remove them from the board and pupils say the items. To make this more challenging, ask pupils to say the cards in the order they appeared on the board.

Snap Write a word on the board or say an item from a specific group of flashcards. Show several flashcards one by one. Pupils shout *Snap* when they see the corresponding flashcard.

Who's the fastest? Divide the class into two teams. Stick a number of flashcards on the board. Invite two pupils to stand facing the flashcards on different sides of the board. Call out one of the words and the pupil who is the fastest to touch the card wins a point for his/her team.

Name it Divide the class into two teams. Invite a pupil from each team to come to the front of the class and turn his/her back to you. Hold up a card and count to three and say *Turn around*. The first pupil to turn around and correctly identify the card is awarded a point for his/her team.

Pass the flashcards Choose five flashcards and pass them face down round the classroom at intervals so pupils can't see the cards. When you say stop, ask *Who's got the (sister)?* Pupils guess who's got the flashcard of the (sister) and get a point if his/her guess is correct.

Basketball Divide the class into teams. Show a pupil from Team 1 a flashcard. If he/she correctly states the content of the flashcard, he/she is allowed to 'shoot' at a specific target (e.g. the bin or a small box) with a ball of paper. If the 'ball' enters the target, he/she is awarded two points. If the 'ball' hits the target without going in, he/she is awarded one point.

Countdown Divide the class into small groups. Mix flashcards from different units together and divide into piles according to the number of groups. Pupils arrange them back into categories, e.g. Colours, Classroom objects, Family, etc. The first group to finish is the winner.

What's missing? Lay several flashcards facing upwards on the floor or a large table. Allow pupils a few minutes to study them. Tell pupils to close their eyes and remove a flashcard. Pupils have to correctly identify the missing card.

Noughts and crosses Divide the class into two teams. One is noughts and one crosses. Draw a large grid on the board with nine spaces. Stick one flashcard in each space facing towards the board. Pupils select a card, turn it over and say the word on the flashcard. If it's correct, remove the flashcard and write a nought or a cross accordingly.

Animal farm Call a pupil to the front of the class and secretly show him/her an animal flashcard, e.g. *a cat*. Blindfold the pupil. Give out several animal flashcards around the classroom including the one you've shown to the blindfolded pupil. Pupils make the appropriate sound for their given animal. The blindfolded pupil has to walk round the classroom listening to the different animal sounds until he or she finds the pupil making the correct animal noise, e.g. a cat sound. Be prepared for a lot of noise!

Who's got it? Invite several pupils to the board and give a different flashcard to each. Pupils hold their flashcards up to show the class. Ask *Who's got the (cat)?* Pupils answer *He's/She's got the cat*. Pupils have to say the name of the pupil who has that flashcard.

Sponge throw Place the flashcards on the floor facing upwards. Pupils throw a sponge or other soft object and identify the flashcard it lands on.

Easy or difficult Divide twenty flashcards into two piles, an easy pile and a difficult pile. Divide the class into two teams. Each team is awarded 5 points if they correctly name a flashcard from the difficult pile and one point for knowing a card from the easy pile. You could also use homemade flashcards of words from Lessons 4 and 6 to make this more challenging.

Flashcard mime Invite a pupil to the front of the classroom. Show him/her a card while hiding it from the rest of the class. He/she mimes the word. The pupil to correctly guess the word is the next one to come forward.

Spin the spinner Divide the class into several teams. Stick the flashcards on the board and number them from 1–10. Call out a word and pupils say the corresponding number. If it's correct, he/she spins the spinner and is awarded the amount shown.

Where is it? Stick the flashcards in different places around the classroom. Call out one of the items and pupils find it and point to the correct flashcard. Alternatively, say a sentence containing the item, e.g. *I like apples* and pupils point to or retrieve the flashcard of the apple.

Hit the card Stick all the flashcards of one vocabulary category on the board in mixed order. Call two pupils to the front of the room to stand a metre or two from the board. Call out a word. The first pupil to run to the board and 'hit' the correct flashcard wins. Play the game in teams and award points for each correct 'hit'.

Tick or cross Explain the meaning of a tick and a cross. Hand out two large squares of paper to each pupil. Ask them to draw a tick on one card and a cross on the other. Tell pupils you will show them one flashcard and one word card at the same time. If the flashcard corresponds with the word card, they hold up the 'tick' card. If it doesn't, they hold up the 'cross' card. Make lots of intentional mistakes. Stick the cards on the board when you make a match.

Mixed up flashcards Write the target vocabulary or stick the word cards on the board. Ask pupils to stick the appropriate flashcard next to each word. Then remove the flashcards and stick them back next to the wrong words. Call a group of four or five pupils to the board. Say Go! Time pupils to see how long it takes to put all the cards next to the correct words. Choose a second group and time them to see which group can do it the fastest.

Bluff Invite several pupils to the board and ask them to stand in a row. Give them each a flashcard and ask them to keep it secret from the class. The first pupil in the row says a word that might or might not correspond with the flashcard they are holding. Pupils guess whether or not they're bluffing. Pupils say *Bluff* if they think they're bluffing. Divide the class into teams and award points when pupils guess correctly.

Face race Give each pupil a number between 1 and 10. Stick the face flashcards on the board or draw a picture of a face. Say *Number 2 – Nose.* All pupils assigned number 2 race to the board and touch the nose. Alternatively, play the game with three or four teams. Assign each pupil from each team a number. Call out *Number 3 – Eyes.* The first pupil to touch the eyes wins a point for their team.

Same sounds Choose a vowel sound from any unit (e.g. /ɪ/). Stick a flashcard on the board of a word containing that sound (e.g. *sister*). Now say *dog, pen, boot, duck, pink*. Pupils say the word containing the same sound as *sister* (*pink*). Try with several other sounds.

Mix-matched flashcards Stick four flashcards on the board face down so pupils can't see the pictures. Divide the class into teams of four. Invite Team 1 to the board and give each person a word card. Pupils stick the word cards face up below the flashcards so they can be read. Now point to the first word card and pupils read out the word. Turn over the flashcard above it. The team receives one point if the flashcard corresponds with the word card below it. Continue with the remaining cards. Write the total number of points earned by each team on the board. Mix the cards and continue with the other teams.

TPR GAMES

Alternative Bingo Pupils each draw a simple picture of one of the items from a unit (e.g. Pets). Write the words on the board to remind them. Also include others from previous units of the same category (e.g. *bird, butterfly, frog*). As they draw, write the words on small slips of paper and put them in a small box or bag. Ask pupils to stand up. Pull out the slips of paper in turn and read the animal names. Pupils who have drawn that particular animal sit down. Continue until there's only one slip of paper remaining in the bag.

Number groups Play some lively music and ask pupils to perform a specific action (e.g. jump, walk, and hop) around the classroom. Stop the music and call out a number from 2–5. Pupils must quickly get together in groups of that number. The odd pupil must sit out until the next round. Start with the numbers 2–5 then move on to numbers 6–10 when pupils feel confident.

Guess the object Put an object in a bag for a pupil to feel (e.g. toy food or plastic animals). He/she must guess what the object is without looking.

Teacher says Give the pupils instructions but tell them to follow the instructions only if they are preceded by *Teacher says*. If you say *Pick up a pencil,* pupils should do nothing but if you say *Teacher says pick up a pencil*, pupils must pick up a pencil. They lose a point for doing an action when they shouldn't. Vary the speed of the instructions to make the game more interesting. You could also ask pupils in stronger classes to give the instructions.

Ball throw Pupils stand in a large circle. Make a paper ball, call out a category (e.g. Family) and throw the ball to a pupil. He/she must say a word in the category you mentioned. He/she then throws the ball to another pupil who says another word in the same category. If a pupil drops the ball or can't say a word in the category, he/she must sit down. Continue until one pupil remains.

Pass the ball Pupils sit in a circle. Make a paper ball. Choose a category and pupils pass the ball around the circle. Each pupil must say a word from the given category when he/she's got the ball. A pupil leaves the circle when he/she can't say a word from the given category. Alternatively, play music while pupils pass the ball and say words. Stop the music. The pupil holding the ball when the music stops leaves the game.

Drawing game Pupils draw pictures on the board of the target vocabulary. They must do this slowly, line by line. Pupils try and guess what he/she is drawing before he/she finishes the picture. The first pupil to guess draws the next item.

Grab it Pupils sit in a circle. Place some classroom objects (no sharp pencils or scissors, please) or flashcards in the middle of the circle. Pupils put their hands behind their backs. Call out an object and pupils race to find and touch it. Play this in teams and award points to the winner.

Drawing race Divide the class into two teams and invite a pupil from each team to the front of the class. Show a word card to each or whisper a word. Each pupil draws the word on the board. The first team to identify the picture correctly wins a point.

Phonics race Divide the class into several groups. Call out a phonics sound. Pupils write as many words with the same sound as possible during a given amount of time. Award pupils one point for each correct word.

Unscramble Divide the class into groups. Write a word on the board in jumbled order. The first group to guess the word wins a point.

Chair race Divide the class into two teams. Each team stands in a line with a chair at the front of the line and another chair a few metres across the room. A pupil from each team sits in the chair at the front of his/her line. Call out an action (e.g. *jump*). The pupils must jump to their team's chair on the other side of the room. The first pupil to sit on the chair after doing the correct action wins a point for his/her team.

Board game Draw a large race track on the board. Divide the class into two teams. Use small coloured circles as markers for each team. Ask questions, e.g. show flashcards/story cards and ask *What's this?* or show classroom objects in different numbers and ask *How many?* Pupils move ahead one space if they guess correctly. The winning team are the ones to reach the finish first.

Stop! Divide the class into two teams. Write the target vocabulary on small pieces of paper and put them in a bag or a small box. Write the word STOP on a few pieces of paper and add them to the others. Pupils reach into the bag/box without looking, choose a piece of paper and say the word. If he/she says the word correctly, his/her team wins a point. If a pupil chooses the word STOP, the team loses all of its points.

Spinner game Divide the class into two teams. Tell pupils to draw an item from the target vocabulary. If he/she draws correctly, he/she spins the spinner and wins that number of points for his/her team.

Parachute Play a guessing game in teams. Draw a large parachute on the board with three strings leading to a stick figure hanging from the parachute. Think of a word pupils have learnt and draw a dash inside the parachute for each letter in the word. Pupils from one team try to guess the word (*a car?*). For each incorrect guess, erase one of the parachute's strings. Award points to the team when they guess the word correctly. If all the parachute's strings are erased before pupils guess the word, then that team loses a point. To make it more interesting, draw a shark emerging from the sea below the stick figure. You can also draw a speech bubble near the figure and write *Hello! I'm (name)* using the names of the pupils.

Whoops! Write as many words as possible (from any unit or combination of units) on small pieces of paper. Fold them and put them in a box or a bag. Also write the word *Whoops!* on several pieces of paper and add them to your bag or box. Pupils come to the front of the class, choose a piece of paper and read the word. If they read it correctly, they keep the paper and receive one point for their team. If the word is read incorrectly, you keep the paper. If pupils choose the word *Whoops!* they sit down and don't receive any points. Alternatively, you could add some suspense by taking away all points when the *Whoops!* card is chosen.

Name the shape Cut out several shapes from coloured paper. Stick or carefully pin a shape to the back of a pupil's shirt without the pupil seeing the shape. The pupil turns around to reveal the shape to the class. The pupil tries to guess which shape and colour it is. Elicit *a blue triangle? a red square?* For stronger classes, suggest that when the volunteer guesses the correct shape but the wrong colour, the class shouts: *Shape!* Likewise, when the volunteer guesses the correct colour but the wrong shape, they shout: *Colour!* For example, if you stick a yellow circle on the pupil's back and they ask *a yellow square?*, the class should shout *Colour!* Do this game in teams and award points for correct answers.

Reading race Write sentences on long strips of paper describing a set of flashcards (e.g. Food, Toys, Family or Animals). *It's big. It's black and white. It's got four legs,* etc. Divide the class into two or more teams and ask each team to stand in a queue. Put a set of sentences face down at the front of the queue. Stick the flashcards on the board. When you say *go*, one pupil from each team picks up a sentence, sticks it below the appropriate flashcard on the board, and runs back to touch the hand of the next person in his team. Check that pupils are sticking the sentences in the correct place and call them back to the board if they make a mistake. The first team to stick up all its sentences is the winner.

Clothes line Cut out several clothes items from different colours of sturdy card. Draw a clothes line on the board and stick the clothes on the line (e.g. a pink skirt, a black T-shirt, a green shoe, and an orange dress). Alternatively, pin them to a real length of string hung to look like a clothes line. Give pupils a few minutes to study the order of the clothes. Remove the clothes cards. Now pupils draw and colour the clothes in the same order. Pupils could also label the clothes to make this more challenging. If you haven't got much time, pupils could simply recite the order. Do this game in teams and award points for correct answers.

Number spin Divide the class into teams. Invite a pupil from each team to the front of the classroom. Stick several flashcards on the board and write a number below each. Ask him/her to choose one of the flashcards from the board. Then spin the spinner and the pupil must say the word the appropriate number of times. He/she wins that number of points for his/her team.

Yes or no? Bring in several toys, classroom objects or toy animals of different colours and sizes. You may also use flashcards. Put them on a table at the front of the class. Explain that you will choose one of the items and pupils will guess the item, but you can only say *yes* or *no*. Pupils ask *Is it big? Is it red? Is it a duck?* Do this game in teams and award points for correct answers.

How to use classroom language

Using classroom language is a good way to get pupils to react in English rather than in L1. The more they use these new phrases and expressions, the more confident they become and the less they will need to rely on L1 to communicate with the teacher. If classroom language is used consistently, it becomes a natural part of pupils' vocabulary. It is important to teach both the classroom language the pupils have to understand as well as language they need to produce. The following is a list of common English expressions that could easily be introduced in the classroom and used on a daily basis. It's best to begin with a few expressions and increase the number gradually.

Greeting the class
Hello. Hi!
Good morning/afternoon.
Come in.
Sit down/stand up, please.
What day is it today?
How are you today?
Is everyone here?
Is anyone away today?
Where is (name)?

Starting the lesson
Are you ready?
Let's begin.
Listen (to me).
Look (at me/at the board).
Take out your books/notebooks/coloured pencils.
Give this/these out, please.
Have you got a (pencil)?
Open your books at page (4).
Turn to page (6).
Open the window/door.
Close the window/door.

Managing the Class
Be quiet, please.
Come to the front of the class.
Come to the board.
Come here, please.
Put your hands up/down.
Who's next?
Queue/Line up!
Repeat after me.
Wait a minute, please.
Hurry up.

During the lesson – instructions
Hold up your picture.
Show me (the class) your picture.
Draw/Colour/Stick/Cut out ...
Write the answer on the board/in your book.
Let's sing.
All together now.
It's break time/lunch time.
Wait a minute, please.
Be careful.
Sorry, guess/try again.
Next, please.
Again, please.

During the lesson – questions
Do you understand?
What do you think?
Anything else?
May/Can I help you?
Are you finished?
Who's finished?
Who would like to read?
What can you see?
Any questions?

Words of praise
Well done!
Excellent!
Fantastic!
That's nice.
Much better.
Good job.
Congratulations.
That's correct!
Great work!
Good luck!
Thank you.

Pair work/Group work
Find a partner.
Get into twos/threes.
Who's your partner?
Work in pairs/groups.
Make a circle.
Work with your partner/friend/group.
Show your partner/friend/group.
Tell your partner/friend/group.
Now ask your partner/friend/group.

Language used for playing games

It's my/your/his/her turn.
Whose turn is it?
You're out.
Don't look.
No cheating.
Turn around.
Shut your eyes.
Pass the (ball, cup) etc.
Wait outside.
Spin the spinner.
Move your/my counter (3) spaces.
Miss a turn.
Go back (2) spaces.
Spin again.
I've won!
You're the winner!

Online language

Move your mouse to the left/right/up/down.
Go left/right/up/down.
Go to (Scene 2, the school).
Enter (the chatroom).
Exit (the chatroom).
Jump (on the roof).
Click to collect (the card).
Click on the speech bubbles.
Click on the (Ticket Inspector).
Use your Picture Dictionary in your backpack.
Use.
Put on./Take off.
Pick up./Put down.
What's this/that?
Let's play a game.
Try again.
Come back later.
I'm busy now.
Bus stop.
Joy stick.
Map.
Costumiser.
Report card.

Active Teach language

Click on the tick/CD/game icon.
Find the sticker.
Look and sing.
Who wants to play a game?
You're in Team 1.
Spin the spinner.
Move the counters.
Let's start again.
You're out of time.
Team 1 get ready!
Team 1 wins!
It's a draw.
What's this in English?
Mime or act the word.
Make the sentence/question.
Move the wheel.
Find the pairs.
What's the answer to (number 2)?
I need a volunteer!
Touch the picture.
Compare your answers.
Are you right?
Is it right?

Ending the lesson

Put your books/notebooks/coloured pencils away.
Tidy up.
Put that in the bin/rubbish bin, please.
That's all for today.
Collect the stickers/ cards/ spinners / scissors, please.
The lesson is finished.
Goodbye!
See you tomorrow.
Have a nice weekend/holiday.

Useful phrases for the pupils

May/Can I go to the toilet?
I understand/I don't understand.
Excuse me/Pardon me?
I'm sorry.
Can you help me?
I'm finished.

Scope and sequence

Unit	New Vocabulary	New Structures
Welcome	1–10 red, orange, yellow, purple, blue, green, pink stand up, jump up, turn around, sit down treasure chest parrot	Hello, I'm (Lindy). What's your name? It's time to play. Come on a quest! Look for a (present) today. Find a (present) today.
1 My toys	bike, car, doll, train, boat, ball, toy present 11–20 hen, pen, box, frog friend, princess plus, minus, equals, sums	What's this? It's a (car). It's (orange). How many (dolls)? (Fifteen) (cars). I can see (fifteen cars). Let's go (to the princess)!
2 My family	mum, dad, sister, brother, granny, grandad, garden, house yes, no, photo bedroom, bathroom, living room, kitchen bus, bug, van, map horrible baby, young, old, poster	Where's my (dad)? In the (garden). He's/She's in the (kitchen). I love (Princess Emily). They're (young). This is my (granny).
3 My body	arms, legs, hands, feet, fingers, toes, head, body wave, stamp, clap, touch, move, shake, jump, dance, swim, key big, fish exercise routine	Wave your (arms). Stamp your feet. Clap your hands. Touch your (toes). Move your (legs). Shake your (body). I've got (two) (legs). I'm (purple). My name's Frank. I'm hot. Exercise is good for you.
4 My face	face, eyes, ears, nose, mouth, hair small, short, long sunglasses, clothes, play shapes, circle, triangle, square, rectangle	I've got a (small) (mouth). He's/She's got (long) (hair).

Recycled Language (vocabulary and structures)	Pronunciation	Cross Curricular focus	Values	DVD/Online/ Posters
				pipe, rope, climb, rainbow, key
Colours, 1–10	/e/ as in hen and /ɒ/ as in doll	Maths: Sums	Making new friends	teddy bear, kite, shield(s), jigsaw flags, police car, police van
Actions	/ʌ/ as in mum and /æ/ as in map	Social Science: Life processes	Caring for the young and the elderly	grape, picture, mat, aunt, uncle, cousin, parents, twins, wordsearch, butler, umbrella, knight, police officer, binoculars, newspaper
Actions, Numbers, Colours	/ɪ/ as in big and /iː/ as in green	PE: An exercise routine	Keeping fit	timer, code, bus, fix [v] a shop, a library, a park, a café
big, baby, old, Colours, Numbers I've got a (triangle). It's a (nose).	/əʊ/ as in nose and /eɪ/ as in baby	Maths: Shapes	Being kind	camera, pull curly, straight, blond, dark, prison, empty, cells, eye/ear test, glasses, email, photo

Unit	New Vocabulary	New Structures
5 Animals	cow, horse, goat, sheep, duck, cat, dog, animal, bat, fox, owl white, grey, black, brown thin, fat crown, torch bad, wings awake, day, night, farm	Is it a (cow)? Is it (white)? It's (brown). Is it (big)? It's (small). It's got (four) (legs). It's got (big ears).
6 Food	apple, banana, pizza, chicken, egg, fish, salad, rice, food, nuts, cheese, bread, cake, toast, cereal mice, bike breakfast, lunch, dinner, menu	I like (apples). How about you? I don't like (apples). It's very nice. Happy Birthday! I like (toast) for (breakfast).
7 Clothes	T-shirt, trousers, dress, skirt, shoe(s), socks, pyjamas, jumper, boots, shirt, hat, coat school, bed bird nurse, firefighter, chef, police officer	I'm wearing a (red) (dress). Take off your (shoes). Put on your (T-shirt). It's time for (bed). Put on a (red sock). It's the palace. We're here! Have you got (a shoe)? I'm a (nurse).
8 Weather	sunny, cloudy, windy, rainy, snowy umbrella mouse, picture moose, scooter Days of the week, weather chart, favourite	Do you like (snowy days)? It's a (sunny) day. It's (rainy). I'm sorry. Thank you. Are you hungry? It's (Thursday).
Goodbye	Goodbye	
Christmas	stocking, Christmas tree, Christmas Eve, Santa, star	Happy Christmas!
Valentine's Day	Valentine's Day, flowers, chocolates, heart, card, balloon	Let's (sing). Here's a card.
Easter	Easter Bunny, rabbit, egg, chick, flower	How are you?

Recycled Language (vocabulary and structures)	Pronunciation	Cross Curricular focus	Values	DVD/Online/Posters
hen, frog, parrot, yes, no, small, big, Colours, Body parts, Numbers What's this? It's a (goat).	/aʊ/ as in brown and /ɔː/ as in short	Science: Night and day animals	Caring for animals	turkey, chick, bat, owl, fox, letter, box, wash rabbit, mouse
Numbers	/aɪ/ as in bike	Social Science: Meals	Eating healthily	sandwich, fruit, beans, corn, soup, chef, computer dancing, jumping, clapping, stamping, moving
old, Colours I don't like (pink) (dresses). I've got (two shoes).	/ɜː/ as in bird	Social science: Jobs and uniforms	Being polite	jeans, trainers, parcel
big, small, yes, no, friend, Animals, Clothes, Colours, Food, Toys, Actions, Body parts, Family, Features, Numbers I like/don't like (sunny days). I've got a (small ball).	/uː/ as in moose	Science: The weather	Staying safe in different weather	beach hot, cold, centre, volcano, machine, prisoner, robot
duck, key, nuts, photo, present, shoe, sunglasses, treasure chest, umbrella Where's the (photo)?				
present, Colours				
Family				
wake up, jump, turn around				

Welcome

Lesson 1

Starting the lesson

- Greet pupils individually. Say *Hello, I'm (name).* Add some humour by changing your name each time. Use famous people, cartoon characters or just made-up funny names (e.g. Mr/Mrs Wabababadingdong). Pupils may also wish to respond with a made-up name.

PB pages 2–3

 **Listen and sing.**

- Ask pupils (L1) what they think is happening in the picture. Ask where they think the characters are and what they're doing. Introduce the characters. Point to each in turn and say *This is Lindy, Joe, Princess Emily and Pippin.* Draw attention (L1) to the fact that Pippin is a parrot. Encourage pupils to repeat the names several times.
- Point to each of the characters in turn and ask *Who's this? (Lindy)* Divide the class into pairs. Pupils say a name *(Joe)* and their partner points to the correct character.
- Play the song CD1:02. Pupils listen and point to each character as their name is mentioned. Play the song again and pupils sing along. You could also play the karaoke version of the song CD 3:41 for pupils to sing along to.

Practice

- Pupils make their own name tags by writing *Hello, I'm (name)* on squares of paper or shapes you've cut out before class. Write the sentence on the board to help them. Early finishers can decorate their name tags.

L = LINDY J = JOE E = EMILY P = PIPPIN	**1:02**
L	Hello. I'm Lindy.
	Hello. I'm Lindy.
	What's your name?
J	Hello. I'm Joe.
	Hello. I'm Joe.
	It's time to play!
E	Hello. I'm Emily.
	Hello. I'm Emily.
	What's your name?
P	Hello. I'm Pippin.
	Hello. I'm Pippin.
	It's time to play!
L	Lindy
E	Emily
J	Joe
L, E, J	Hello!
	Lindy, Emily, Joe
	Hello!
P	And Pippin, too!
ALL	Hello, hello!
P	And Pippin, too!
ALL	Hello, hello!
P	And Pippin, too!
ALL	Hello, hello!
P	And Pippin, too!
ALL	Hello, hello!

Listen and find. Then read.

- Play CD1:03. Pupils find the characters as they hear their voices or names. Play the recording a second time, pausing after each line so pupils can repeat. Then point to the labels of the characters' names in turn and pupils read them.

L = LINDY J = JOE P = PIPPIN E = EMILY	1:03
L	Hello, I'm Lindy. What's your name?
J	Hello, I'm Joe.
P	My princess. Princess Emily!
E	Pippin! Oh Pippin! Pippin! Pippin!

Presentation

- Count aloud to ten showing the correct number of fingers as you do so. Do this several times. Pupils join in, showing the correct number of fingers each time.

 **Listen and chant.**

- Count to ten with the class and point to each number on the page as it's mentioned. Play CD1:04. Pupils point to the numbers in his/her books as they hear them. Play it again. Pupils both point and repeat the words of the chant in time with the chorus.

J = JOE C = CHORUS P = PIPPIN E = EMILY	1:04
J	One.
C	One.
J	Two.
C	Two.
J	Three.
C	Three.
J	Four.
C	Four.
J	Five.
C	Five.
P	One, two, three, four, five.
	One, two, three, four, five.
L	Six.
C	Six.
L	Seven.
C	Seven.
L	Eight.
C	Eight.
L	Nine.
C	Nine.
L	Ten.
C	Ten.
E	Six, seven, eight, nine, ten.
	Six, seven, eight, nine, ten.

Practice

- Stick the word cards (numbers) in order on the board. Pupils read all the words. Ask pupils to close their eyes while you remove one card. Pupils say which card is missing.

AB page 2

Trace. Then read and match.

- Point to each character in turn and pupils say the name. Pupils trace the word *Hello* in each speech bubble. They then read and match each sentence to the correct character.

Write. Then draw and say.

- Pupils read the number words below each hot air balloon. They then write the number inside the box and draw the correct number of stars inside each balloon.

Ending the lesson

- Clap a beat with different numbers of claps. Pupils repeat the same rhythm and call out the number.

OPTIONAL ACTIVITIES
Welcome song
Play the karaoke version of the song CD3:41, using pupils' names instead of characters' names.
Flashcard game
Play Correct order see p. 22.

Lesson 2

Lesson aims
To revise the Lesson 1 vocabulary; to introduce new vocabulary; to introduce the Quest

Target language
blue, green, orange, parrot, pink, purple, red, treasure chest, yellow

Receptive language
stand up, jump up, sit down, turn around

Materials
Audio CD; Word cards (Colours)

Optional materials
Homemade colour flashcards; magazine pictures of items in various colours; seven sheets of paper labelled with the colour words

Starting the lesson

- Greet pupils in English. Say *Hello, I'm (name)*. Ask individual pupils *What's your name?* Play the song CD 1:02 from Lesson 1 and pupils sing along.
- Count from one to ten. Do this several times, varying the speed and the tone of your voice. Try speaking like a robot or with an echo. Hold up or point to various objects in the classroom (e.g. pencils, windows, etc.) and ask *How many?* Count the objects together.

PB pages 2–3

Presentation

- Introduce the colours by showing classroom items (e.g. pencils, rubbers, etc.) and saying the colour for each as pupils repeat. Teach the word *parrot* by pointing to Pippin.

4  Listen and chant.

- Play CD1:05. Pupils listen and point to the colours at the bottom of PB p. 2 as each colour is mentioned. Play it again and pupils join in with the words of the chant.

L = LINDY C = CHORUS	1:05

L   Paint a rainbow in the sky.
　　Red, orange, yellow.
C   Red, orange, yellow.
L   Red, orange, yellow.
C   Red, orange, yellow.
　　Red, orange, yellow.
L   Paint a rainbow in the sky.
　　Purple, blue, green, pink.
C   Purple, blue, green, pink.
L   Purple, blue, green, pink.
C   Purple, blue, green, pink.
　　Purple, blue, green, pink.

Practice

- Divide pupils into groups. Give each group a colour. Play the recording again and pupils stand when they hear their colour.
- Ask pupils to take out their coloured pencils. Show the word cards (colours) in turn and pupils hold up the appropriate coloured pencil as it is mentioned. Alternatively, pupils point to the colours in the Pupil's Book.

5 Look. Then listen and sing.

- Pupils look carefully at the main illustration. Ask (L1) how they think Princess Emily is feeling, and why. Explain that Princess Emily is flying home to her castle when a treasure chest filled with her favourite things falls out of her hot air balloon. Her naughty parrot, Pippin, flies down to collect the items. The princess is unhappy that Pippin has left her because he's her only friend.
- Teach the word *treasure chest* by pointing to it at the bottom of PB p. 3. Ask pupils to find it in the main illustration and to guess what things were inside. Explain (L1) that the items at the bottom of the page are the things that Princess Emily has lost and they are going to go on a Quest through the book to find the items. Tell them they are going to listen to a song about the quest to find Emily's things.

- Ask pupils to find the number 1 on the drawing of Pippin. Now point to the number 1 at the top of the page and ask *What colour is it?* Pupils colour Pippin's body red. Continue with the remaining numbers/colours.

Ending the lesson

- Call out a colour (*pink*) and pupils find and point to it on PB pp. 2–3. You could also point to different coloured things around the room or pupils' clothes and ask *What colour is it? (red)*.

OPTIONAL ACTIVITIES

Make a colour collage

Pupils cut out pictures from magazines of things in different colours. Stick sheets of paper on the board and label each with a different colour name. Make a collage by sticking the pictures on the appropriate piece of paper.

Flashcard game

Play Hit the card see p. 23, with homemade colour flashcards.

NOTES

- Play the Quest song CD 1:06. Pupils point to the treasure chest in the main illustration every time they hear the word.

> Stand up, jump up, come on a quest,   **1:06**
> Come on a quest today.
> Turn around, sit down, come on a quest.
> Look for a treasure chest today.
> A treasure chest.
> Find a treasure chest today.

- Teach the actions from the song (*stand up, jump up, sit down, turn around*) by miming them. Play CD 1:06 again and pupils mime the actions as they listen.
- Pupils find the sticker of the treasure chest in the back of the Pupil's Book and stick it on the grey image of the treasure chest in the main illustration on PB p. 3. Play the recording again and pupils sing along.

AB page 3

3 **Trace. Then find and colour.**

- Pupils read the colour words next to each number and trace them. In pairs, pupils call out a number and partners call out the colour of that particular number.

Lesson 1

Lesson aims
To present and practise new vocabulary

Target language
ball, bike, boat, car, doll, toy, train

Receptive language
What's this? It's a car.

Materials
Audio CD; Flashcards (Toys); Word cards (Toys); three small pieces of paper for each pupil

Optional materials
Small box or bag

Starting the lesson

- Greet pupils by saying *Hello, I'm (name).* Ask a few individual pupils *What's your name? I'm (name).*
- Sing the song CD1:02 from the Welcome unit.

PB pages 4–5

- Ask pupils (L1) to remember what was happening in the main illustration of the Welcome unit. (Princess Emily was in a hot air balloon. Her parrot Pippin went to find the contents of the treasure chest that fell out of the balloon. Lindy and Joe were there.)
- Pupils describe (L1) what they think is happening in the picture on PB pp. 4–5. (Lindy and Joe are playing with their toys. Pippin sees a present and is flying in to get a closer look.) Ask pupils (L1) what they think is inside the present.
- Say the names of the characters (*Pippin, Lindy* and *Joe*) and pupils point to them on the page.

Presentation

- Ask pupils (L1) to guess what they think they're going to learn in this unit (*toys*). Teach the toy words by showing the flashcards (toys) in turn. Say the word and pupils repeat. Stick the flashcards on the board as you say each word.
- Now say the words again and pupils find the toys in the main illustration. Indicate the cards on the board and say *My Toys*. Have a short discussion (L1) about the toys pupils play with at home.

1 🔵 Listen and say.

- Point to each of the toys in Activity 1 in turn and ask for each *What's this? (bike)*
- Play CD1:07. Pupils listen, point to the toys and repeat the words. Then pupils say the missing words in each line until at the end they are saying all the words.

Each word is associated with a sound to indicate when the pupil should say the word. The association of word and sound will also help them to memorise the words. Encourage them to use the pictures at the bottom of PB p. 4 for reference.

bike ★ car ★ doll ★ train ★ boat ★ ball ★   **1:07**

Listen and say the missing words.
bike, car, doll, train, boat ★
bike, car, doll, train ★ ★
bike, car, doll ★ ★ ★
bike, car ★ ★ ★ ★
bike ★ ★ ★ ★ ★
★ ★ ★ ★ ★ ★

Game

- Pupils use small squares of paper to cover three of the toys in Activity 1. Call out the toys in turn. When you say a toy that pupils have covered, they write an X on the paper. A pupil wins when all three toys they covered have been said.

3 1:09 Listen and chant.

bike ☐

train ✓

4 1:10 Listen and colour. Then say.

① ② ③ ④

- Play the recording again. Pause after each line so pupils can repeat.
- Focus on the labels next to each toy. Read them to the class one by one. Pupils find the words as they hear them and repeat. Pupils continue in pairs.

Practice

- Stick the word cards (toys) on the board or write the toy words. Hand out the flashcards (toys) to several pupils. Point to the (bike) word card and pupils read it aloud. The pupil with the bike flashcard stands up, shows the flashcard to the class and says *a bike*.

AB page 4

1 **Match. Then trace and say.**

- Look at the puzzle pieces. Point to the ball and ask *What's this?* Say *It's a ball* as you point to the puzzle piece with the correct sentence written on it. Pupils match the pictures to the correct sentences, then trace the toy words and say them out loud.

Ending the lesson

- Ask pupils to stand up. Call out the toy words in turn. Pupils turn around if a toy is mentioned that they've got at home or sit down if they haven't got the toy.

OPTIONAL ACTIVITIES

Word card game
Stick the flashcards (toys) on the board. Put the word cards (toys) in a small bag or box. Invite pupils to choose one of the word cards, read it and stick it next to the appropriate flashcard on the board.
Flashcard game
Play Tick or cross see p. 23.

NOTES

Pairwork

- Divide the class into pairs. One pupil covers a toy with a piece of paper and the other tries to guess which toy is covered. *A bike? (Yes/No.)* Pupils then switch roles.

2 **Listen and ✓.**

- Point to the bike in the main illustration and ask *What's this? (It's a bike.)* Repeat with the remaining toys. Play CD1:08 and pupils write a tick in the box next to the words as they are mentioned.

L = LINDY　J = JOE　　　　　　　**1:08**
L　Look! A train. Choo! Choo!
J　Oh. And a boat.
　　A ball!
　　Lindy! Look! It's a bike.
L　What's this, Joe?
J　It's a car.
L　Look, Joe! A doll.
J　I love toys!
L　Me, too!

37

Lesson 2

Lesson aims
To revise the Lesson 1 vocabulary with a chant;
to present the new structure

Target language
present. What's this? It's red. It's a (car).

Recycled language
Colours, Toys

Materials
Audio CD; Flashcards (Toys); Word cards (Toys);
Word cards (Colours); some toys

Optional materials
A4 blank paper

Starting the lesson

- Divide the class into groups. Give each group a toy
  flashcard or word card or, alternatively, use real toys
  that you've brought to class. Say the toys in turn *(It's
  a train).* Groups with the (train) stand up, turn around
  and sit down when his/her toy is mentioned.
- Divide the class into groups. Give each group a word
  card (colours) or homemade colour flashcard. Say a
  colour (e.g. *green),* then call out an action (e.g. *turn
  around).* Pupils in the group with the green card
  turn around.

Presentation

- Hold up one of the flashcards (toys) or indicate one
  of the toys from the Pupil's Book. Ask *What's this?
  (ball)* Then say *It's a (ball). It's (orange).* Continue with
  other toys.

PB pages 4–5

3 **Listen and chant.**

- Play CD1:09. Pupils point to the toys as they hear
  them in the chant. Play the recording again. Pause
  after each colour word and challenge pupils to guess
  which toy is being described before it's mentioned.

V = VOICE J = JOE L = LINDY	1:09

V   What's this? It's red.
J   It's a car!
V   Oh.
V   What's this? It's blue.
L   It's a boat!
V   Oh.
V   What's this? It's pink.
J   It's a doll!
V   What's this? It's green.
L   It's a train!
V   What's this? It's orange.
J   It's a ball!
V   What's this? It's yellow.
L   It's a bike!

Practice

- Point to the boat and ask *What's this? (It's a boat.)*
  Ask *What colour is it? (It's blue.)* Continue for a few
  rounds. Now say *It's blue. What is it?* Pupils say the
  correct toy *(It's a boat).* Pupils continue in pairs.

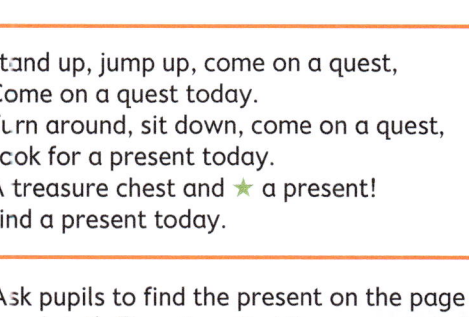

3 Listen and chant.

train ✓

bike

4 Listen and colour. Then say.

1 2 3 4

Lesson 2

present. What's this? It's red. It's a (car). Colours, Toys

5

Stand up, jump up, come on a quest,
Come on a quest today.
Turn around, sit down, come on a quest,
Look for a present today.
A treasure chest and ★ a present!
Find a present today.

1:11

- Ask pupils to find the present on the page (under the word *doll*). They then find the present sticker at the back of the Pupil's Book and stick it on the grey image of the present in the main illustration. Ask pupils what they think might be inside the present. Ask pupils to look through Unit 1 and find the present again (Hint: PB p. 8, in the story)
- Play the recording again and pupils sing along.

AB page 5

2 Listen and ✓ or X. Then colour.

- Play CD1:12. Pupils listen and write a tick in the box if the toy mentioned is correct and a cross if it isn't. Pupils then colour the toys in pairs. One pupil says *It's a (bike). It's (green)* and his/her partner colours the toys accordingly. They then change roles.

1 It's a bike.
2 It's a ball.
3 It's a boat.

1:12

3 Trace. Then draw and colour.

- Pupils read the sentences in the boxes and trace the colour words. They then read the sentences again and draw the toys and colour them accordingly.

Ending the lesson

- End the lesson by imitating the sounds from the chant CD1:09. Pupils guess which toy it is by saying *It's a (car)*. Pupils play the game in pairs or small groups.

 4 Listen and colour. Then say.

- Play CD1:10. Pupils listen and colour the toys the correct colour. Play the recording again. Pupils then check their answers in pairs. One pupil says *It's a ball. His/Her partner says the colour (It's red.)*

W = WOMAN   L = LINDY   J = JOE   **1:10**
1 W   What's this?
   L   It's a ball. It's red.
2 W   What's this?
   J   It's a boat. It's orange.
3 W   What's this?
   L   It's a car. It's purple.
4 W   What's this?
   J   It's a doll. It's blue.

Quest sticker and song

- Ask pupils (L1) to remember the treasure chest from the Welcome spread and the items the characters have to find for Princess Emily. Ask pupils to guess which item could be found here. Play the Quest Song CD1:11 so pupils learn the name of the Quest item *(a present)*.

Lesson 3

Lesson aims
To extend the unit vocabulary set; to practise the vocabulary with a song

Target language
11–20. How many …? I can see …

Recycled language
1–10, Colours, Toys

Receptive language
dolls

Materials
Audio CD; Flashcards (Toys); homemade number flashcards; Poster 1

Starting the lesson

- Revise numbers 1–10. Write the numbers on the board and point to each as you count to ten several times.

> PB page 6

Presentation

- Teach numbers 11–20 by using homemade flashcards. Show the cards in turn and say the numbers.

5 **Listen and point. Then say.**

- Play CD1:13. Pupils follow in their books and point to the numbers as they hear them. Play the recording again and pupils repeat the words they hear.

> One. ★ Two. ★ Three. ★ Four. ★ Five. ★ Six. ★ **1:13**
> Seven. ★ Eight. ★ Nine. ★ Ten. ★ Eleven. ★ Twelve. ★
> Thirteen. ★ Fourteen. ★ Fifteen. ★ Sixteen. ★
> Seventeen. ★ Eighteen. ★ Nineteen. ★ Twenty. ★

Practice

- Invite ten pupils to the board and give them each a homemade number flashcard. Put the pupils in order and count from 11–20. Ask pupils to hold up the correct number as you count. Now arrange the pupils in mixed order. Point to each flashcard in turn and pupils call out the numbers. Then pupils arrange themselves in the correct order.

Presentation

- Teach the plural form of nouns. Draw a ball on the board and ask *How many balls?* (1 ball) Now draw three balls and ask *How many balls?* (3 balls) Say *three balls* emphasising the 's' sound. Now add three more balls and ask *How many balls?* (6 balls)

6 **Listen and find. Then sing.**

- Focus on the song illustration. Ask pupils which toys they can see in the picture. Indicate the two balls in the bottom left of the picture and ask *How many (balls)?* (2 balls)
- Play CD1:14 and ask pupils to point to the correct type of toy for each verse. Then play the recording again and pupils join in with the words. You could also play the karaoke version of the song CD3:42 for pupils to sing along to.

> Trains, trains. How many trains? **1:14**
> How many trains can you see?
> Seven trains. Seven trains.
> I can see seven trains.
> Cars, cars. How many cars?
> How many cars can you see?
> Fifteen cars. Fifteen cars.
> I can see fifteen cars.
> Balls, balls. How many balls?
> How many balls can you see?
> Sixteen balls. Sixteen balls.
> I can see sixteen balls.

7 **Listen and say. Then ask and answer.**

- Pupils use the song illustration to play a game. Play CD1:15 to give pupils an idea of the language they will need. One pupil asks *How many (cars)?* His/her partner counts the (cars) and answers (15 cars).

> How many dolls? **1:15**
> Eleven dolls.

> AB page 6

4 **Match and say.**

- Pupils match the numbers written on each car to their written form. They then say the numbers to a partner.

5 **Find and count. Then write.**

- Pupils follow the maze and count the number of toys they collect on the path. They then read the sentence at the bottom of the activity and write the number of balls (16 balls).

Pupils can now go online to Tropical Island and find the teddy bear that Pippin is holding on the Pupil's Book page. It is on the second window sill on the top floor inside the castle. Once pupils click on the teddy bear they are taken to a supplementary language game based on the vocabulary in this unit. Use Poster 1 to talk about the different parts of the island (see the notes on p. 20).

5 1:13 Listen and point. Then say.

SONG

1 2 3 4 5 6 7 8 9 10 11 12 13 14 15 16 17 18 19 20

6 1:14 ♪ Listen and find. Then sing.

7 1:15 Listen and say. Then ask and answer.

How many dolls?

Eleven dolls.

---

6 **Lesson 3**   11–20. How many...? I can see... (Eleven) (dolls). 1–10, Colours, Toys

Ending the lesson

- Write the numbers 11–20 on the board in written form. Pupils stick homemade number flashcards next to the correct number.

OPTIONAL ACTIVITIES
TPR game
Play Grab it see p. 24.
Team game
Play Spinner game see p. 24.

Lesson 4

Lesson aims
To develop literacy skills; phonics: /e/ /ɒ/

Target language
box, frog, hen, pen

Recycled language
doll, Colours, Toys. It's a (car). It's (red).

Materials
Audio CD; Flashcards (Toys); Poster 3; A4 paper and stapler to make a Sounds Fun booklet

Starting the lesson

- Use Poster 3 see p.21.
- Play the recording of the song CD1:14 from Lesson 3, and pupils sing along. Revise plural nouns by drawing some toys on the board or showing real toys or classroom objects in various numbers. Ask *How many (boats)? (2 boats).*

 **PB page 7**

8 **Say and colour. Then play Bingo.**

- Point to the picture of the red car on the Bingo board. Ask *What's this? (It's a car.) What colour is it? (It's red.)* Now say *It's a car. It's red.* Do the same with the green train. Pupils continue in pairs.
- Focus pupils' attention on the last row of toys on the board (train, boat and car). In pairs, pupils dictate the colours of the toys to a partner *(It's a train. It's yellow.)*
- After all the toys have been coloured, pupils play a game of Bingo in groups or as a class. Pupils choose four toys and circle them. Call out the toys and his/her colours in turn. Say *It's a ball. It's purple.* Pupils draw a large X over a toy they've circled or cover it with a small piece of paper when it's called out in the correct colour. They win when all the circled toys have been called.

Presentation

9 **Listen and say.**

- Play CD1:16. Pause after the first two lines. Ask pupils which sounds they can hear (/e/ and /ɒ/). Play the first two lines again and pupils repeat.
- Point to something red and say *red.* Ask pupils which sound they can hear (/e/). Then teach the words *pen* and *hen* by drawing them on the board or pointing to the pictures in the Pupil's Book. Say the words several times, emphasising the /e/ sound. Do the same with the words *doll, frog* and *box*, emphasising the

/ɒ/ sound. Ask pupils which other words they know with these sounds and write them on the board (*ten, orange, yellow*).

- Now play the recording from the beginning to the end. Pupils listen and repeat the words. Play the recording again so pupils are comfortable with these new sounds, then read the rhymes to a partner.

> e, e, o, o   **1:16**
> e, o, e, o, e, o
> e ★
> Hen. ★
> Red. ★
> Pen. ★
> A hen with a red pen. ★
> o ★
> Doll. ★
> Box. ★
> Frog. ★
> A doll in a box with a frog. ★
> A hen with a red pen. ★
> A doll in a box with a frog. ★

Practice

Pupils create a Sounds Fun notebook. Pupils write the sounds /e/ and /ɒ/ on separate pages and draw pictures of things containing these sounds on the appropriate pages (*frog, doll, box, orange, ten, pen, hen, red, yellow, chest, present, twenty,* etc). Encourage stronger pupils to write the words next to each picture.

 **AB page 7**

6 **Listen and number. Then trace and match.**

- Point to the words in turn and ask pupils to read them aloud.
- Play CD1:17. Pupils listen and number the words correctly. Pupils then trace the words and match them to the correct pictures.

> o   **1:17**
> e
> **1** frog   **2** doll   **3** box   **4** ten   **5** pen   **6** hen

7 **Find and colour.**

- Point to the colour words below the hen and the frog and ask pupils to read them. They then colour the animals the correct colour. Pupils colour the objects in the picture containing the /e/ sound red and objects containing the /ɒ/ sound orange.

8 Say and colour.
Then play Bingo.

SKILLS

It's a car.
It's red.

9 1:16 Listen and say.

SOUNDS FUN!

A h**e**n with a r**e**d p**e**n.

A d**o**ll in a b**o**x with a fr**o**g.

Lesson 4 box, frog, hen, pen, *doll, Colours, Toys. It's a (car). It's (red).* Sounds: /e/ /ɒ/ **7**

Ending the lesson

- Ask pupils to stand up if you say a word with the /e/ sound and sit down for a word with the /ɒ/ sound. Say words from CD1:17. If pupils are standing when they should be sitting, or vice versa, they continue the game with their hands on their heads. The winner is the last pupil without hands on head.

OPTIONAL ACTIVITIES
Flashcard Game
Play Sponge throw see p. 22.
Team game
Play Phonics race see p. 24.

Lesson 5

Lesson aims
To consolidate the unit language with a story

Values
Making new friends

Target language
friend, princess. Let's go …

Recycled language
What's this? It's a doll.

Materials
Audio CD; Unit 1 Story cards; props for acting out the story, e.g. a doll wrapped up as a present

Optional materials
Blank paper

Starting the lesson

- Play the song CD1:02 from the Welcome unit to remind pupils of the characters' names. Pupils sing along and point to the characters on PB pp. 2–3.
- Remind pupils (L1) that Princess Emily lost her treasure chest containing her special things and her naughty parrot, Pippin, flew away. The Princess is very sad because she lost her only friend. Pippin then flew to the island to collect Princess Emily's belongings. Teach the word *friend* using L1 if necessary.

PB page 8

- Ask pupils to recall the picture in the main illustration in Lesson 1 of Unit 1. Ask (L1) Where were Lindy and Joe? (on the island). What were they doing? (playing with their toys). What was Pippin looking at? (a present). Ask pupils to guess what might be inside the present.
- Before pupils open their books, show the story cards in turn and ask the questions from the 'Before reading the story' section written on the back of each card.

10 Listen and read. Then act.

- Play the recording of the story CD1:18 and pupils follow along in their books. Play the recording again, pausing after each line for pupils to repeat.
- Call on pupils to read the story. Stop after each frame and ask the questions from the 'After reading the story' section on the back of each story card to check pupils' understanding. Be sure that pupils understand that Lindy and Joe are meeting Pippin for the first time.

- After pupils have a clear understanding of the story, invite three pupils to the board to act it out. You may wish to play the recording, pause after each line and have them repeat the lines. Alternatively, you could have other pupils read the lines while the pupils act it out or have them say the lines from memory. When acting out, encourage tone of voice and expressions to match those in the pictures. Use props that you've brought to class if you wish.
- Read the audioscript on the back of the story cards in mixed order. Pupils follow in their books and say the number of the frame from which you are reading. Pupils continue in small groups or pairs.

Values

- Have a discussion (L1) about making new friends. Ask pupils to describe situations in which they've met new friends. Ask pupils what's important in finding a friend and how they like their friends to treat them. Discuss the importance of treating others with kindness.

AB page 8

8 Write.

- Point to the words in the word bank and ask pupils to read them. Now point to the pictures in turn and ask *What's this? It's a (ball).* Pupils write the correct words from the word bank below each picture to complete the sentences.

9 Draw. Then number and say.

- Pupils complete the drawings of Princess Emily and Pippin by tracing over the right halves of the pictures. They then read the sentences below the drawings and write the correct number in each box.

For the next lesson

- Pupils could bring in beans, buttons, bottle caps, etc. to make a project relating to sums.

Ending the lesson

• Hand out the story cards to six different pupils. Read the sentences from the story. The pupil with the appropriate card stands up and shows it to the class. Alternatively, read the sentences from the story in mixed order. Pupils stand up and show his/her card to the class when you read the sentences from his/her card.

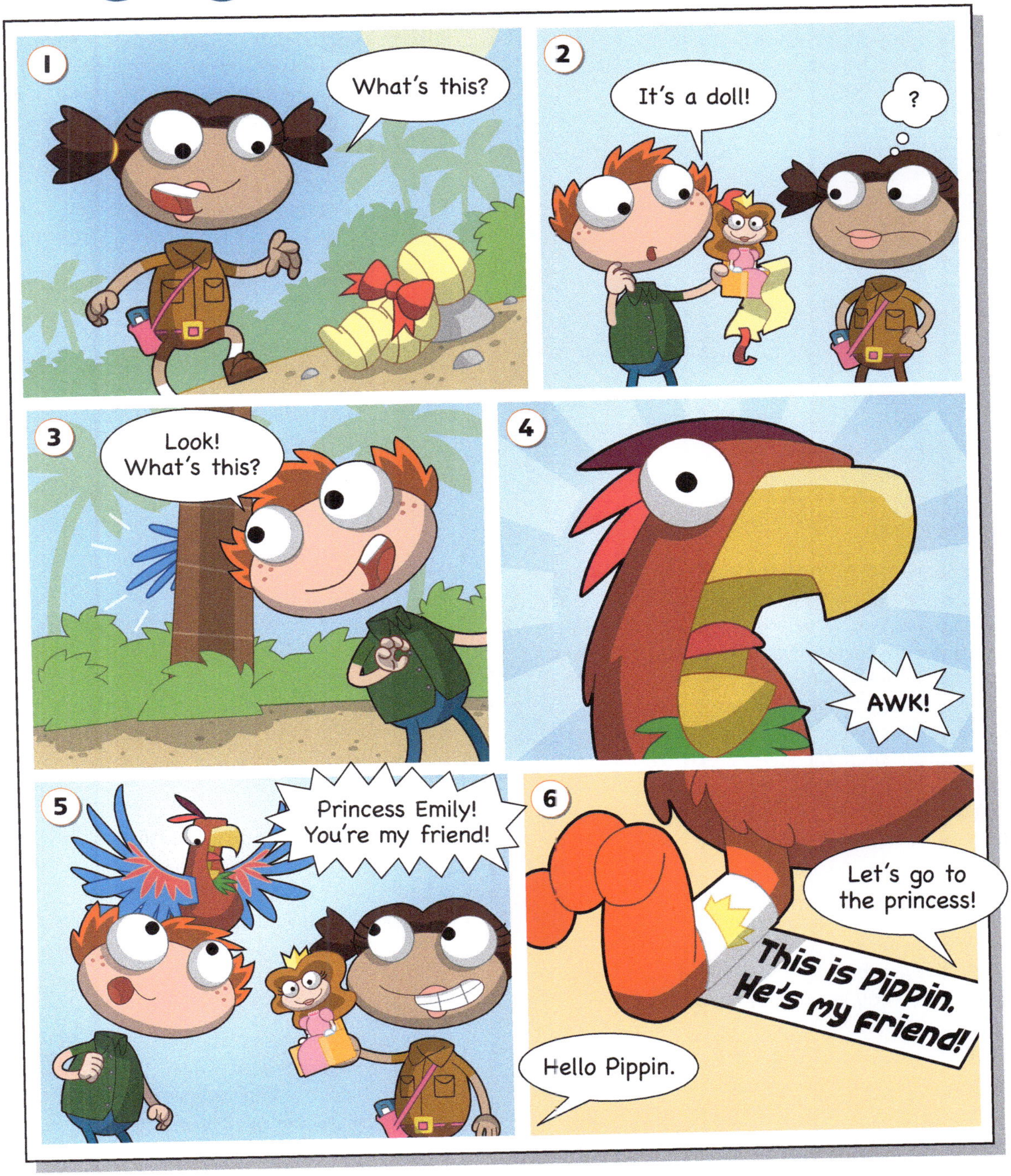

45

Lesson 6

Starting the lesson

- Revise numbers 1–20. Write the numbers in numerical form across the board. Count to 20, pointing to each number as you do so. Now erase one or more of the numbers and pupils say which number(s) you erased.
- Practise plural nouns by playing a game. Say some phrases like *one bike, two dolls*, etc. Make some intentional mistakes (e.g. *one boats, ten train*, etc). Pupils clap once when you say it correctly and three times when you make a mistake. Call on pupils to correct your mistakes.

PB page 9

11 Look and write.

- Pupils write the missing numbers on the number chart. Now write the numbers on the board. Pupils check their answers by counting to 20 in pairs.

Presentation

- Explain (L1) that pupils are going to learn to do sums in English. Write a large plus sign, minus sign and equals sign on the board. Write the words *plus, minus* and *equals* below each symbol. Point to each in turn and say the words several times.

12 Listen and point. Then look and draw.

- Pupils look at the Maths symbols on the page and read the words next to each to a partner. Identify each of the toys by pointing to them and asking *What's this?*

- Play CD1:19 and pupils point to the corresponding pictures and symbols in their books. Play the recording again and pupils say the equations along with the recording.

> One boat plus one boat equals two boats. **1:19**
> Three balls minus two balls equals one ball.

- Pupils complete the next two sums in pairs. They say the sums aloud and draw the answers in the boxes provided. Check pupils' answers by asking *How many cars? (3 cars) How many dolls? (1 doll)*

Practice

- Do some more sums on the board. Use pictures you brought from home, draw pictures of toys or use numbers as in traditional equations (e.g. 4 + 5 = 9). Be sure to do an equal number of addition and subtraction problems.

AB page 9

10 Listen and write.

- Point to each of the toys and ask *What's this?* Now ask *How many (dolls)? (4)* Play CD1:20. Pupils listen and write a plus sign or a minus sign in each box. They then complete the sums by writing a number in the space provided. Pause the recording if pupils need more time. Play the recording again and pupils check their answers in pairs.

> **1:20**
> 1 Two dolls plus two dolls equals ★ four dolls!
> 2 Three trains minus one train equals ★ two trains!
> 3 Four bikes minus three bikes equals ★ one bike!
> 4 Six boats plus four boats equals ★ ten boats!

11 Write. Then say.

- Pupils complete the sums by writing the correct number in the space provided. Ask some pupils to read out his/her completed sums. Pupils then practise reading out his/her sums in pairs.

Mini project

13 Draw some sums for a friend.

- Give each pupil a blank sheet of paper. Pupils draw three or four sums like the ones in PB Activity 12 for a friend to complete. Pupils share his/her sums with the class and read them aloud (e.g. *2 trains + 5 trains = 7 trains*).

11 Look and write.

1	2	3	4	5	6	7	8		10
11		13		15		17	18		20

12 1:19 Listen and point. Then look and draw.

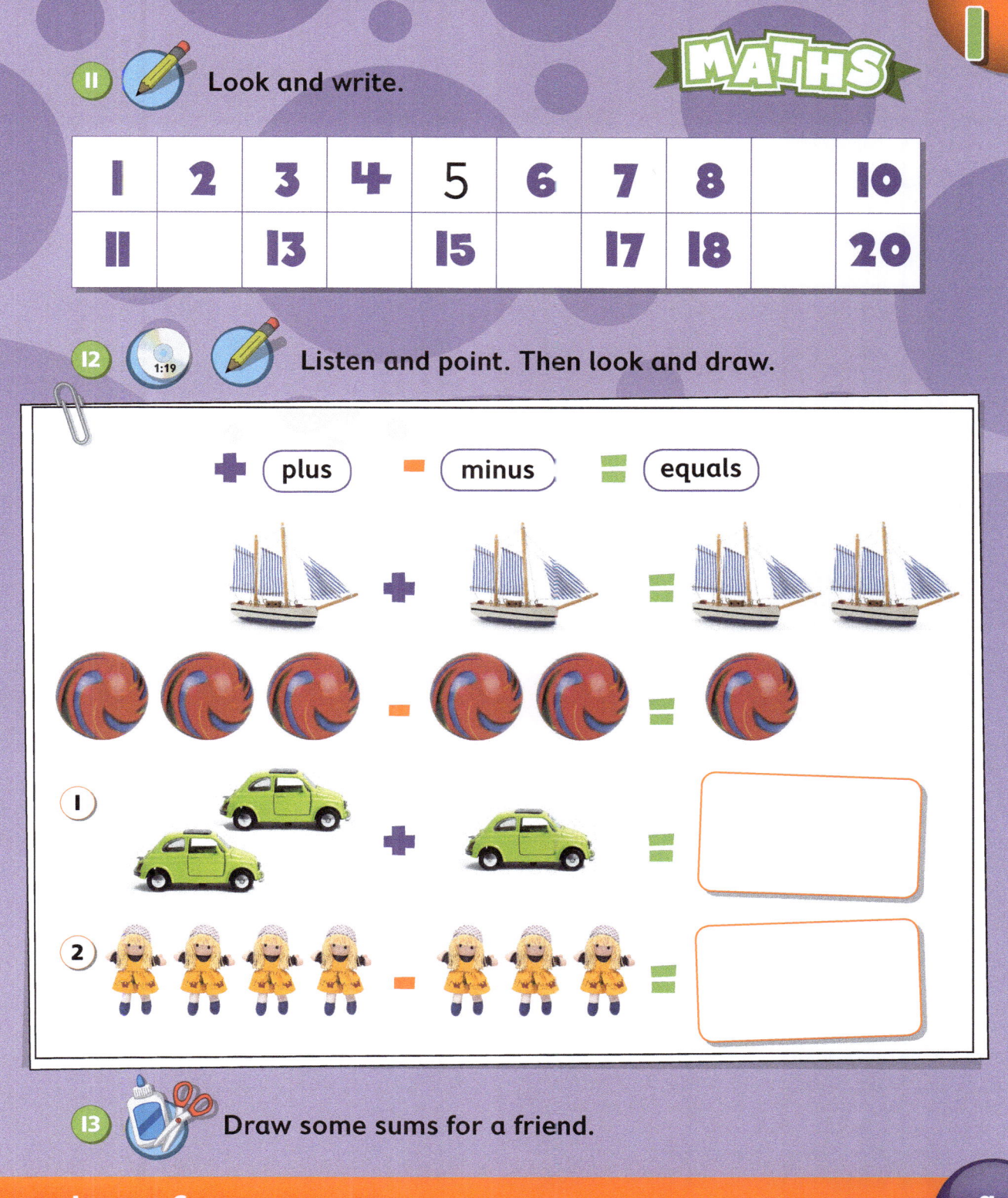

➕ (plus)   ➖ (minus)   🟩 (equals)

13 Draw some sums for a friend.

Lesson 6

equals, minus, plus. 1–20, Toys

9

Ending the lesson

- Write some sums on the board with a gap instead of a plus or minus sign (e.g. 7 __ 8 = 15). Invite pupils to the board to write in the missing signs and say the sums (7 + 8 = 15).

OPTIONAL ACTIVITIES
Sums display
Pupils create a sums display. Suggest using beans, bottle caps, buttons, etc. Pupils stick the items on heavy card and display them around the classroom.
Flashcard game
Play What's missing? see p. 22.

Lesson 7

Lesson aims
To review the unit language with a game

Recycled language
Colours, Numbers, Toys. It's a (doll). It's (pink). (Three) (balls).

Receptive language
Point to something ...

Materials
Audio CD; Poster 1; Word cards (Toys, Colours, Numbers); Flashcards (Toys); a spinner for each pair of pupils (see the template at the back of the book); counters; Numbers 1–20 written on small cards; small bag, Worksheet 1

Starting the lesson

- Use Poster 1 see p.20.
- Write the following headings on the board: Colours, Numbers and Toys. Hand out the word cards for these word categories to several pupils. Each pupil says which word card he's/she's got, then sticks it under the appropriate heading. Alternatively, do this activity verbally. Say a number, colour or toy word and pupils say which category it belongs to.

PB page 10

14 **Listen. Then play.**

- Teach the word *game*. Indicate the board game in the book and say *Let's play a game!* Point to various objects along the path of the game and ask *What is it? (It's a boat.) What colour is it? (It's purple.)*
- Give each pair of pupils a spinner. Each pupil will also need a counter (or a small piece of paper or coin).
- Explain (L1) how to play the game. In pairs, pupils take turns to spin the spinner and move his/her counter, beginning at START and following the squares to reach the castle at FINISH. Pupils receive a point for every correct action/answer and lose a point for every mistake. The pupil with the highest number of points at the end of the game wins.
- There are three different types of square:
  1) a drawing of a toy with a sentence below it; pupils colour the toy and say the toy and its colour. *(It's a train. It's green.)* 2) multiple numbers of toys; pupils say the number of that particular toy *(two boats).* 3) a blank square with a sentence written in it; pupils read the sentence, draw the correct toy, colour it and then describe it. *(It's a doll. It's red.)*

- Play CD1:21 as an example of the language pupils may find helpful while playing the game. Pairs then play the game. Monitor each pair to help with pronunciation.

> 1! **1:21**
> 1. It's a doll. It's pink.

- Collect in any spinners at the end of the game, for use in future lessons.

15 **Listen and do.**

- Stick the flashcards (toys) in different places around the classroom. Say *Point to the (boat).* Demonstrate by pointing to the boat flashcard. Continue with a few more and then say *Point to something (green).* Play CD1:22 and pupils point as instructed on the recording.

> Point to something green. **1:22**
> Point to something red.
> Point to something pink.
> Point to something blue.
> Point to something yellow.
> Point to something orange.

Practice

- Pupils can now complete Worksheet 1.

1 **Read. Then find and colour.**

- Pupils read sentences about the toys and colour them accordingly.

2 **Draw. Then write.**

- Pupils complete the partial drawings of toys, then complete the sentence below the drawing by writing the name of the toy in the gap.

> Pupils create his/her own board game at home. Draw a simple outline of a game board with nine or ten squares. Pupils complete the board by drawing toys in different numbers, writing sentences (*It's a train*), or drawing toys and writing colours (*It's yellow*). You may wish to begin the activity in class to be sure pupils understand the task.
>
> Pupils use his/her game boards to play the game at home. Ask pupils to bring his/her games to the next lesson and give them time to play with a partner.

For the next lesson

- Ask pupils to bring his/her favourite toy from home to the next lesson.

14 🔵 1:21 🎲 Listen. Then play. **ROUND-UP**

It's a doll.
It's pink.

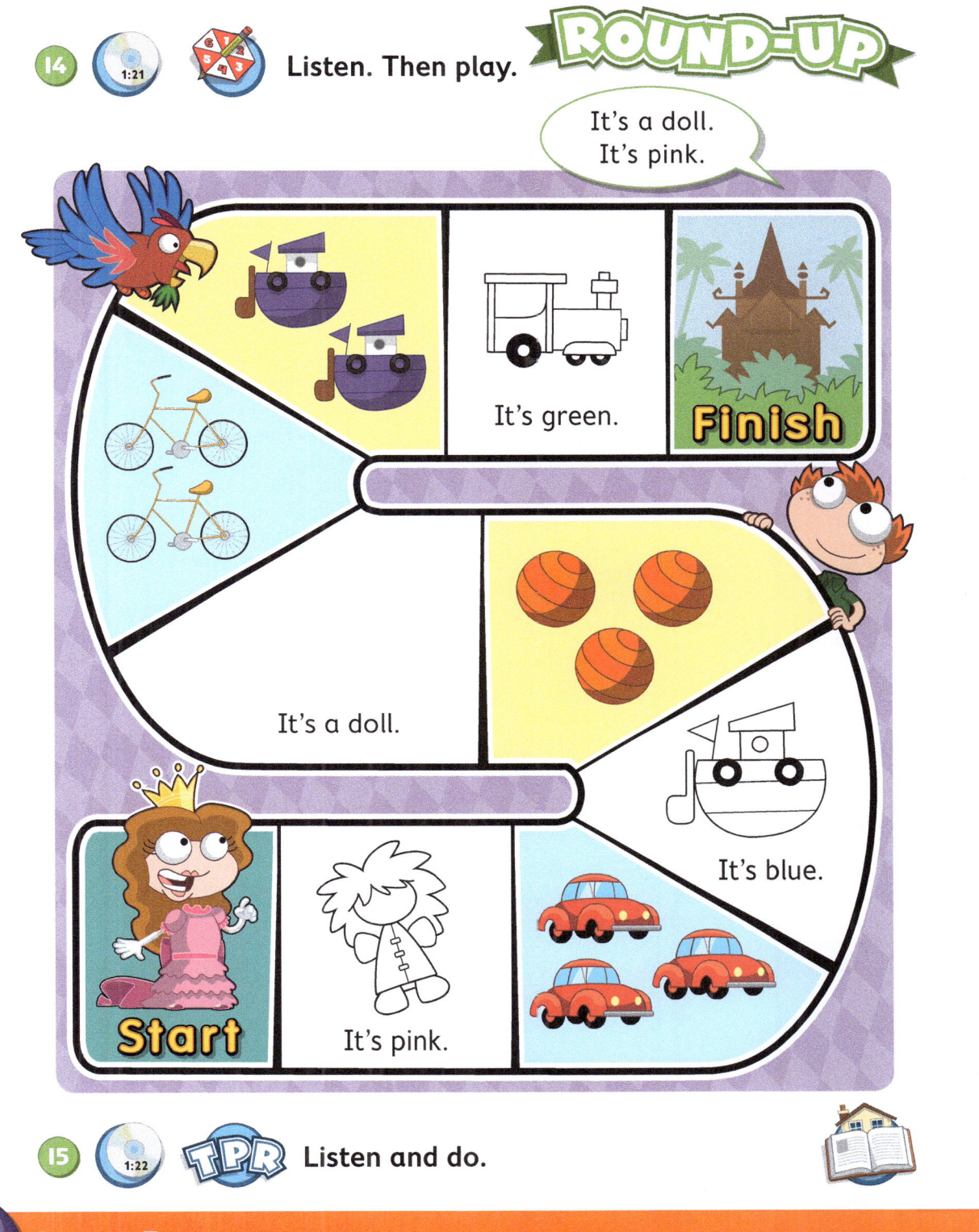

It's green.

Finish

It's a doll.

It's blue.

Start

It's pink.

15 🔵 1:22 **TPR** Listen and do.

Ending the lesson

- Choose a toy word and write it in jumbled form on the board. Ask a volunteer to the board to unscramble the letters and write, then say the word correctly. Continue with other words. Pupils could then write scrambled words on a piece of paper for a partner to guess.

OPTIONAL ACTIVITIES
Flashcard game
Play Who's the fastest? see p. 22.
Team game
Play Parachute see p. 25.

Lesson 8

Lesson aims
To personalise the unit language; to provide an opportunity for self-evaluation

Recycled language
Toys. It's a (boat).

Materials
Audio CD; Unit 1 stickers; Flashcards (Toys); Word cards (Toys, Numbers); pupils' toys from home; paper to make Project book; Evaluation sheet 1

Starting the lesson

- Stick the flashcards (toys) on the board. Stick a word card below each but make some intentional mistakes. Teach the words *right* and *wrong* (L1 translation). Point to each in turn and ask *right* or *wrong?* Invite pupils to the board to correct your mistakes.
- Give each pupil of piece of paper. Do a drawing dictation by sticking a word card (numbers) next to a word card (toys), e.g. *six cars*. Pupils draw six cars.
- Ask pupils to bring in a favourite toy from home. Give them time for 'show and tell' and to share the toys with friends. Ask stronger pupils to describe his/her toys to his/her classmates. You could also play some music to create a relaxing atmosphere.

PB page 11

16 Listen, stick, then trace.

- Pupils read the toy words on the page, then find the stickers at the back of their Pupil's Books and say the names. Play CD1:23 and pupils stick the stickers in place. Finally they trace the words below each.

1 It's a boat.	**1:23**
2 It's a train.	
3 It's a doll.	
4 It's a bike.	
5 It's a ball.	
6 It's a car.	

17 Draw two of your toys. Then write.

- Pupils draw two of his/her favourite toys inside the frame. They then complete the sentence next to the frame by writing the names of the toys they've drawn in the gap. Call pupils to the board to present his/her artwork and read the completed text to the class.

AB page 10

12 Read and colour.

- Pupils read the sentences below each square. They then colour the areas containing a dot the correct colour to reveal the toy. Pupils check his/her answers in pairs.

13 Find and stick. Then colour.

- Pupils find the Unit 1 sticker in the back of his/her Pupil's Book and stick the speech bubble sticker in the correct place to complete the picture. They read the sentences on the sticker and colour the car the correct colour.
- Pupils read the three sentences in the Look! Box and tick the ones they can understand and use correctly. Note that the Look! Box in this level moves the pupils on from the sticker activity in Starter Level and prepares them for the way that they will look at language in their subsequent years of English.
- Explain (L1) that pupils should colour in the stars at the bottom of the page to correspond with how well they think they completed the unit. If they completed and understood everything very well, they should colour all five stars.

AB page 60

- Pupils colour the number and toy pictures in the Picture Dictionary. They can then play a game in pairs. Each pupil takes turns to say a word and his/her partner points to the correct picture. Stronger pupils may wish to cover the written words below each picture and try writing the words themselves.

Practice

- Help pupils to make an 8-page booklet as an end of unit project. They write the title *My Unit 1 Project Book* on the cover and draw pictures on each page, of toys in different numbers and colours. Pupils write sentences below each drawing (e.g. *It's a (boat).* etc). Pupils decorate the book with stickers and drawings of the characters, etc.

Evaluation

You can check your pupils' progress using Evaluation sheet 1. See also Teacher's notes p. 176.

Pupils can now go online to Tropical Island and enjoy the fun and games.

16 🔊 1:23 ✏️ **Listen, stick, then trace.**

1 **boat**

2 train

3 doll

4 bike

5 ball

6 car

Stick

17 ✏️ **Draw two of your toys. Then write.**

Look at my _____**toys**_____!

A _____

and a _____.

🖱️ **Now go to Tropical Island.**

Lesson 8   *Toys. It's a (boat).*   II

Ending the lesson

- End the lesson by handing out the flashcards and word cards (toys) to twelve different pupils. Tell pupils to keep his/her cards secret. Say *Go!* Pupils have to find his/her partner by showing their cards to each other without speaking. When they find their partners they should say the name of the toy.

OPTIONAL ACTIVITIES
TPR Game
Play Drawing game see p. 24.
Team Game
Play Unscramble see p. 24.

2 My family

Lesson 1

> **Lesson aims**
> To present and practise new vocabulary
>
> **Target language**
> brother, dad, family, garden, grandad, granny, house, mum, sister
>
> **Receptive language**
> This is my mum.
>
> **Materials**
> Audio CD; Flashcards (Family); Word cards (Family); a coin or small piece of paper for each pupil

Starting the lesson

- Sing the song CD1:02 from the Welcome unit. Divide the class into four groups and give each group a character (Lindy, Emily, Joe or Pippin). Groups stand up and sing their part of the song.

> **PB pages 12–13**

- Ask pupils to describe (L1) what they remember about the Quest so far. Remind pupils that Pippin wants to find Emily's belongings and return them to the castle, and on his quest he has met Lindy and Joe.
- Discuss (L1) the main illustration. Ask pupils whose family we can see here (Lindy's family). Ask what Lindy's grandad is giving her. Point to the map and say *It's a map.* Ask why they think he's giving them a map. What do they think the map shows? Explain that Lindy and Joe are now enlisting grandad's help in finding the castle. He's giving them a map to help them find their way.

Presentation

- Ask pupils what they think they'll be learning in this unit. Indicate the family members and say *family.* Ask which family members they can see. Point to each in turn and say *mum, dad, granny, grandad, sister, brother.* Point to the dog and say *This is a dog.* Point to the house and the garden and say *This is the house. This is the garden.*

1 🔵 Listen and say.

- Play CD1:24. Pupils listen, point to the family members and repeat the words. Then pupils say the missing words in each line until at the end they are saying all the words. Each word is associated with a sound to indicate when the pupil should say the word. The association of word and sound will also help them to memorise the words. Encourage them to use the pictures at the bottom of PB p. 12 for reference.

2 My family

house · granny · dad · grandad

Listen and say. 1:24 · Listen and ✓. 1:25

12 Lesson 1 · brother, dad, family, garden, grandad, granny, house, mum, sister. (This is my mum.)

---

mum ★ dad ★ sister ★ brother ★ granny ★   **1:24**
grandad ★ garden ★ house ★

Listen and say the missing words.
mum, dad, sister, brother, granny, grandad, garden, ★
mum, dad, sister, brother, granny, grandad, ★ ★
mum, dad, sister, brother, granny, ★ ★ ★
mum, dad, sister, brother, ★ ★ ★ ★
mum, dad, sister, ★ ★ ★ ★ ★
mum, dad, ★ ★ ★ ★ ★ ★
mum, ★ ★ ★ ★ ★ ★ ★
★ ★ ★ ★ ★ ★ ★ ★

Game

- Pupils use small squares of paper to cover three of the family members in Activity 1. Call out the words in turn. When you say a family member that a pupil covered, they write an X on the paper. A pupil wins when all three family members they covered have been said.

Pairwork

- Divide the class into pairs. One pupil covers a family member with a coin or piece of paper and the other tries to guess which is covered. Pupils then switch roles.

- Focus on the labels next to each family member. Encourage pupils to read the labels one by one. Sound out the words slowly and ask pupils to repeat. Pupils point to each label and read it to a partner.

Practice

- Stick the word cards (family) on the board or write the family words. Hand out the flashcards (family) to several pupils. Point to the (granny) word card and pupils read it aloud. The pupil with the granny flashcard stands up, shows it to the class and says *granny*.

AB page II

① Match. Then trace and say.

- Pupils draw lines from the words to the corresponding family members. They then trace the family words below the portrait. Pupils say the family words to a partner, who points to the correct person in the portrait.

Ending the lesson

- Discuss (L1) things pupils do together with their families.

OPTIONAL ACTIVITIES

Who is it?
Send one volunteer out of the room. Choose a group of six pupils and give each pupil a word (*mum, dad, sister, brother, granny* and *grandad*). Invite the volunteer back into the room. Call out the word *mum* and the pupil given that word stands up, then sits down again. After you've called out all words, the volunteer tries to remember each pupil's word.
Flashcard game
Play Mixed up flashcards see p. 23.

② 🔵 Listen and ✓.

- Point to mum in the main illustration and ask *Who's this? (mum)* Repeat with the remaining family members.
- Play CD1:25 and pupils write a tick in the box next to the words as they are mentioned. Play the recording again. Pause after each line so pupils can repeat.

L = LINDY GD = GRANDAD GY = GRANNY	1:25
D = DAD M = MUM S = SISTER B = BROTHER	

L	Joe, this is my family. This is my grandad. Hello Grandad!
GD	Hello Lindy. Hello Joe.
L	This is my granny and this is my dad.
GY, D	Hello!
D	I'm in the house.
L	This is my mum.
M	Oh! Hello! Look at my garden.
L	My sister …
S	Hello!
L	And my brother.
B	Hello!
L	And my dog, Rufus! Hello, Rufus! I love my family.

NOTES

Lesson 2

Lesson aims
To revise the Lesson 1 vocabulary with a chant; to present the new structure

Target language
no, photo, yes. Where's my (mum)? In the (garden).

Recycled language
Family

Materials
Audio CD; Flashcards (Family); Word cards (Family); props or costumes to represent the house, garden and characters, e.g. a leafy branch, a hat, a moustache, etc.

Optional materials
Photocopied house and family cards for the Family squares game

Starting the lesson

• Revise family vocabulary by showing the flashcards one by one. Reveal the picture slowly and ask *Who's this?* Now choose one of the characters from the Pupil's Book. Stick a small piece of paper on the character and ask pupils to guess who you've chosen.

PB pages 12–13

Presentation

• Draw a large house on the board with a garden next to it represented by grass and some trees/flowers. Point to the house and ask *What's this? (It's a house.)* Do the same with the garden. Say *I'm Lindy.* Show the mum flashcard and ask *Who's this? (my mum.)* Now stick the flashcard inside the drawing of the house and ask *Where's my mum?* Say *In the house.* Continue with other family flashcards and alternate between the house and the garden.

Practice

3 **Listen and chant.**

• Play CD1:26. Pupils find the family members as they hear them in the chant. Play the recording again, pausing it after each line so pupils can repeat.

L = LINDY	1:26
L Where's my mum? In the garden. (x 3) In the garden today.	
L Where's my dad? In the house. (x 3) In the house today.	

4 **Listen and find. Then say *Yes* or *No*.**

• Point to the silhouettes of the characters at the bottom of the page. Elicit who they are (granny,

sister, etc.) Point to the silhouette of *Grandad* and ask *Who's this? (Grandad.)* Now point at Grandad in the main illustration and ask *Where's the grandad? (In the garden.)* Play CD1:27 and pupils find the location of each character in the main illustration and answer *yes* or *no* accordingly. Pause the recording after each question to give pupils time to answer.

L = LINDY J = JOE	1:27
L Where's my granny?	
J In the house.	
L Yes.	
L Where's my sister?	
J In the garden.	
L Yes.	
L Where's my dad?	
J In the garden.	
L No.	
L Where's my brother?	
J In the house.	
L No.	
L Where's my grandad?	
J In the garden.	
L Yes.	
L Where's my mum?	
J In the house.	
L No.	

Lesson 2   no, photo, yes. Where's my (mum)? In the (garden). *Family*   **13**

Game

- Choose several pupils to be trees, flowers, etc. (representing a garden) and position them on one side of the classroom. Position another group at the opposite side of the room. Ask them to put their arms together to form a large square (representing a house). Hand out the word cards (family) to six pupils and position them in the 'garden' or in the 'house'. Now ask *Where's (the grandad)? (In the house.)* You may also use costumes or props (hats, moustaches, etc.) rather than word cards to add more fun.

Quest sticker and song

- Ask pupils (L1) to remember which of Princess Emily's things they found in Unit 1 (the present). Explain that they are now going to find the second Quest item. Ask pupils to guess which item can be found here. Play the Quest Song CD1:28 so pupils learn the name of the Quest item *(a photo)*.

Stand up, jump up, come on a quest,   **1:28**
Come on a quest today.
Turn around, sit down, come on a quest,
Look for a photo today.
A treasure chest, a present and ★ a photo ...
Find a photo today.

- Ask pupils to find the photo on the page (it's in the bush on the far left). They then find the photo sticker at the back of the Pupil's Book and stick it over the grey image of the photo in the main illustration. Ask pupils who they can see in the photo (It's Pippin).
- Play the recording again and pupils sing along.

AB page 12

2 Read. Then look and write.

- Remind pupils of the written form of *house* and *garden* by pointing to the word bank and reading the words aloud. Pupils read the questions and answers below each picture of Lindy's family. They then complete the answers by writing *house* or *garden* in the gap. Pupils check his/her answers in pairs.

Ending the lesson

- Play the chant CD1:26 again. Girls sing the first verse and boys sing the second.

OPTIONAL ACTIVITIES
Family squares
Draw a house with a garden on a sheet of paper. Also draw a face representing each family member on a grid of six small squares. Photocopy the house/garden and the family cards for every two pupils. Pupils cut out the squares and play a game. One pupil arranges the squares around the drawing of the house/garden and then asks a partner *Where's (the dad)? In the (garden.)*
Team game
Play Stop! see p. 24.

NOTES

Lesson 3

Lesson aims
To extend the unit vocabulary set; to practise the vocabulary with a song

Target language
bathroom, bedroom, kitchen, living room. She's in the (bathroom).

Recycled language
Family. Where's my (granny)?

Materials
Audio CD; Flashcards (Family); pictures of people from famous families from film or TV

Starting the lesson

- Play the chant from Lesson 2 CD1:26. Pupils join in with the words.
- Give the flashcards (family) to different pupils, revising the words as you do so. Say *I'm Lindy. Where's my (brother)?* Pupils point to the pupil with the correct flashcard. You could also do this with pictures of people from famous families from film or TV.

PB page 14

Presentation

- Stick the house and garden flashcards on opposite sides of the board. Draw a large circle around each. Stick some of the family flashcards inside the circle with the house flashcard and some inside the circle with the garden flashcard. Say *I'm Lindy* and ask *Where's (my mum)? (In the house.)* Say *My mum's in the house. She's in the house.* Now ask *Where's my dad? (In the garden.)* Say *My dad's in the garden. He's in the garden.*
- Focus on the cross-section of the house (Activity 5). Teach the rooms of the house (*living room, kitchen, bathroom* and *bedroom*) by pointing to each and saying the words several times. Now ask *Where's (my granny)? (She's in the bathroom.)* Continue with other family members and rooms.

5  **Listen and find. Then sing.**

- Play CD1:29. Pupils listen and find the family members in the rooms in the illustration. Play the song again and create actions to go along with the sound effects. Mime having a bath, sleeping, cooking and dancing. Finally, play the song again and pupils sing as they do the actions. You could also play the karaoke version of the song CD3:43 for pupils to sing along to.

Where's my granny? (x2) She's in the bathroom. **1:29**
Splash, splash, splash. Where's my granny? (x2)
She's in the bathroom. Splash, granny, splash!
Where's my sister? (x2) She's in the bedroom.
Snore, snore, snore. Where's my sister? (x2)
She's in the bedroom. Snore, sister, snore!
Where's my grandad? (x2) He's in the living room.
Dance, dance, dance. Where's my grandad? (x2)
He's in the living room. Dance, grandad, dance!
Where's my brother? Where's my brother?
He's in the kitchen. Yum, yum, yum!

6 **Listen. Then ask and answer.**

- Divide the class into pairs. Explain that pupils have to look at the cross-section of a house and ask a partner *Where's the brother?* His/Her partner finds the brother in the illustration and says *He's in the bedroom.* Pupils continue with the other family members in the house, and then swap roles. Play CD1:30 to give pupils an idea of the language they'll need. They then ask and answer in pairs.

Where's the mum? **1:30**
She's in the living room.

AB page 13

3 **Listen and match.**

- Play CD1:31. Pupils listen and match the family members to the rooms.

1 Where's my mum? **1:31**
  She's in the living room.
2 Where's my dad?
  He's in the kitchen.
3 Where's my sister?
  She's in the bedroom.
4 Where's my brother?
  He's in the bathroom.
5 Where's my granny?
  She's in the kitchen.
6 Where's my grandad?
  He's in the living room.

4 **Now circle and write. Then say.**

- Pupils read the questions and find which room each family member is in from the previous activity. Pupils circle *He's* or *She's* and write the correct room from the word bank to complete the sentences. He/She then reads his/her sentences to a partner.

KEY 2 He's/bathroom, **3** She's/kitchen, **4** He's/living room

5 🔵 1:29 🎵 Listen and find. Then sing. **SONG**

bedroom

bathroom

living room

kitchen

6 🔵 1:30 Listen. Then ask and answer.

Where's the mum?

She's in the living room.

Lesson 3 bathroom, bedroom, kitchen, living room. She's in the (bathroom). *Family. Where's my (granny)?*

Ending the lesson

● Give each pupil a flashcard of a member of the family. Play the song CD1:29. Suggest actions to do (L1) when each person is mentioned (e.g. Granny walking with a cane, sister skipping rope, brother riding a bike, etc). Play the recording again and pupils stand up and mime his/her family members. Everyone does the actions for the sound effects as well.

OPTIONAL ACTIVITIES
My dream house
Pupils create a drawing of his/her dream house. They label the rooms and other items inside the rooms, e.g. family members, toys, etc.
Flashcard game
Play Easy or difficult see p. 23.

Lesson 4

Lesson aims
To develop literacy skills; phonics: /ʌ/ /æ/

Target language
bug, bus, map, van

Recycled language
Family, Rooms. Where's my (dad)? He's in the (kitchen).

Materials
Audio CD; Flashcards (Family); Unit 2 Cut outs; Sounds Fun notebooks

Starting the lesson

● Stick the flashcards (family) on the board. Pupils write the correct family members next to each flashcard in turn. Alternatively, pupils stick the family word cards next to the correct flashcard.
● Invite pupils to the front of the classroom to mime actions like brushing your teeth, having a shower, cooking, eating, sleeping, watching TV, etc. After each pupil's mime, ask *Where's (name)? (He/She's in the bathroom.)*

PB page 15

7 Play the game (page 73).

● Pupils cut out the photo cards of the rooms from p. 73 of the Pupil's Book and arrange them in the drawing of the house. Pupils then cut out the cards of the family members.
● Pupils play the game in pairs. One pupil puts the family cards in different rooms of the house and asks a partner *Where's (my granny)? (She's in the bedroom.)*

Presentation

8 **Listen and say.**

● Play CD1:32. Pause after the first two lines. Ask pupils which sounds they can hear (/ʌ/ and /æ/). Play the first two lines again and pupils repeat.
● Teach the words *bus* and *bug* by drawing simple pictures on the board or showing homemade flashcards. Say the words several times and pupils repeat. Ask which sound pupils can hear (/ʌ/) and which other words they know with the same sound *(plus, mum)*. Now teach the word *van* and recycle the word *map*. Ask which sound pupils can hear *(æ/)* and which other words they know with the same sound *(black, parrot, dad, granny, grandad* and *family).*

● Now play the recording from the beginning to the end. Pupils listen and repeat the words. Play the recording again so pupils are comfortable with these new sounds. Then pupils read the rhymes to a partner.

	1:32
u, u, a, a	
u, a, u, a, u, a	
u ★	
Mum. ★ Bus. ★ Bug. ★	
Mum's on a bus. ★	
Mum's on a bus with a bug. ★	
a ★	
Dad. ★ Van. ★ Map. ★	
Dad's in a van. ★	
Dad's in a van with a map. ★	
Mum's on a bus with a bug. ★	
Dad's in a van with a map. ★	

Practice

● Pupils add the sounds /ʌ/ and /æ/ to separate pages of his/her Sounds Fun notebooks. Pupils draw pictures of words containing these sounds and label them. Ask pupils to add any new words from this unit to the previously learnt sounds (/e/ *bedroom*).
● Explain (L1) that you want pupils to be your echo. Say a short sentence taken from the recording and pupils repeat the last word several times, becoming quieter and quieter, e.g. *Dad's in a van (van, van, van, van …) Mum's with a bug (bug, bug, bug, bug …)*

AB page 14

5 **Listen and match. Then trace.**

● Play CD1:33. Pupils listen and match the words to the correct pictures, then trace over the words.

/u /	/a /	1:33
mum	dad	
bus	van	
bug	map	

6 **Listen and circle the odd one out.**

● Play CD1:34. Pupils listen and decide which word contains a different sound than the others. Pause the recording before hearing the correct answer to give pupils a chance to answer.

	1:34
1 Mum ★ bus ★ van ★ bug. Van!	
2 Map ★ van ★ dad ★ frog. Frog!	
3 Doll ★ bus ★ frog ★ box. Bus!	
4 Hen ★ pen ★ bug ★ ten. Bug!	

7 Play the game (page 73).

SKILLS

My house

8 Listen and say.

SOUNDS FUN!

Mum's on a bus with a bug.

Dad's in a van with a map.

Lesson 4   bug, bus, map, van. *Family. Rooms. Where's my (dad)? He's in the (kitchen).* Sounds: /ʌ/ /æ/   **15**

Ending the lesson

- Divide the class into two teams. Write the words *van* and *bug* on the board. Begin with the /ʌ/ sound and teams take turns calling out other words containing the same sound. Write the words on the board below the word *bug* as they are mentioned. Award points for correct answers. Continue with the /e/ and /ɒ/ sounds.

OPTIONAL ACTIVITIES

Phonics rhymes
Challenge pupils to create his/her own rhymes using words with any of the phonics sounds.

TPR game
Play Ball throw see p. 24.

Lesson 5

Lesson aims
To consolidate the unit language with a story

Target language
horrible. I love …

Recycled language
brother, dad, grandad, granny, mum, sister

Materials
Audio CD; Unit 2 Story cards; props for acting out the story, e.g. three crowns, a small mirror, a book, a rocking horse or toy horse

Optional materials
Blank paper to create new story cards

Starting the lesson

- Ask pupils to recall the story from the previous unit. Ask what Lindy and Joe found (a present). What was inside the present? (a doll that looked like Princess Emily). Who did Lindy and Joe meet? (Pippin). Where are Lindy, Joe and Pippin going now? (to the castle) Remind pupils that the characters are now on a Quest to collect Princess Emily's belongings and take them to her. Ask which Quest items they have found so far (the present and the photo).

PB page I6

Presentation

- Before pupils open their books, show the story cards in turn and ask the questions from the 'Before reading the story' section written on the back of each card. Teach the word *horrible* and the phrase *I love …*, using L1 if necessary.

9 **Listen and read. Then act.**

- Play the recording of the story CD1:35 and pupils follow along in their books. Play the recording again, pausing after each line for pupils to repeat.
- Call on pupils to read the story. Stop after each frame and ask the questions from the 'After reading the story' section on the back of each Story card to check pupils' understanding. Be sure that pupils understand that at the end, Princess Emily is upset because Pippin is missing.

- After pupils have a clear understanding of the story, invite seven pupils to the board to act it out. You may wish to play the recording and pause after each line for pupils to repeat. Alternatively, you could have other pupils read the lines while the pupils act it out or have them say the lines from memory. When acting out, encourage tone of voice and expressions to match those in the pictures. Use props that you've brought to class if you wish.
- Call six pupils to the board and give them each one story card. Give them a few minutes to arrange themselves in the correct order according to the story. Play the story again to check pupils are in the right order.

Game

- Choose six words from the story and assign each word an action (e.g. ride a rocking horse for *brother*, read a book for *sister*, wave your arms for *granny*, etc.) Read the story slowly and pupils do the actions when they hear the words.

AB page I5

7 **Listen and number.**

- Point to each of Princess Emily's family members in turn and ask *Who's this? (mum).* Play CD1:36. Pupils listen and number the family members accordingly.

> 1 This is my sister, Elizabeth.   **1:36**
> 2 This is my dad.
> 3 This is my mum.
> 4 This is my granny.
> 5 This is my brother, Eric.
> 6 This is my grandad.

8 Write. Then match and say.

- Pupils find the missing person in each picture, looking back at the story in the Pupil's Book to help them if necessary. Pupils match the correct people pictures with the gapped sentences and pictures on the left, then write the missing names. To check the activity, they read the completed sentences to a partner.

For the next lesson

- Ask pupils (L1) to bring some photos to class of people who are distinctly young or old (be sure to include babies and children). You might also want them to bring in a photo of themselves as a baby, and a more recent photo, for a baby photo collage. Explain that pupils will be using the pictures for sticking activities, and that they must have their parents' permission.

  **Listen and read. Then act.**

1 Ah! I **love** Princess Emily.

2 My mum and dad! Huh!

Hello Emily.

3 My **horrible** brother and my **horrible** sister.

4 Grandad and Granny!

5 Family! Huh! And how many friends? One!

6 PIPPIN! WHERE ARE YOU?!

horrible. I love... *brother, dad, grandad, granny, mum, sister*

Ending the lesson

- Read the audioscript printed on the back of the story cards, making deliberate mistakes (e.g. say *granny* instead of *mum* in Frame 2). Pupils correct your mistakes.

OPTIONAL ACTIVITIES

New characters

Add some new characters to the story. Decide on the dialogue and where they will appear. Pupils then create story cards with the new characters.

Flashcard game

Play Flashcard mime see p. 23.

Lesson 6

Lesson aims
To integrate other areas of the curriculum into the English class; to develop the cross-curricular topic through a short project

Cross-Curricular focus
Social Science – Stages of life

Values
Caring for the young and the elderly

Target language
baby, old, young. They're (young).

Recycled language
Family. This is my (granny).

Materials
Audio CD; Flashcards (Family); pupils' family pictures of young and old people; sturdy card for posters

Optional materials
Pupils' photos of themselves as babies and as older children

Starting the lesson

- Ask (L1) how many pupils have a baby brother or sister. Ask how many live with their grandparents. Explain that they will learn about the different stages of life in this lesson.
- Arrange four of the family flashcards on the board in mixed order (granny or grandad, mum or dad, sister or brother and baby). Pupils arrange them in order from youngest to oldest.

PB page 17

Presentation

- Teach the word *baby* using the flashcard. Ask pupils to repeat the word several times. Then read the words *young* and *old* at the top of the page. Pupils repeat the words several times. Choose a pupil to mime an old person walking with a cane and say *He's/she's old.* Choose another pupil to mime a toddler learning to walk and making baby sounds, and say *He's/she's young.* Ask pupils (L1) who in their families are young and who are old.

Practice

10 🔵 Listen and point. Then say.

- Point to the labels below the photos and pupils read them aloud.
- Play CD1:37. Pupils listen and point to each person as they are mentioned. Listen again and pause after each line so pupils can repeat.

> This is my family. **1:37**
> Look at the baby. She's young.
> This is my brother and sister. They're young, too.
> Look at my mum and dad.
> This is my granny. She's old.
> And this is my grandad. He's old, too.
> I love my family.

- Show the family flashcards or some of the pupils' pictures of old and young people one by one. Pupils clap when they see a young person and stamp his/her feet when they see an old person.

11 Number the pictures.

- Point to each photo in turn and ask *Who's this? (Granny). Is (she) old? Is (he) young?* Pupils number the photos in age order.

Values

- Discuss (L1) some of the things that we are able to do which babies can't do (e.g. feed themselves, walk, dress themselves, etc). Now discuss things that some elderly people may find it difficult to do (walking, carrying heavy things, reading without glasses, etc). Discuss ways that we can help the young and the elderly.

AB page 16

9 Number. Then write and say.

- Pupils number the pictures in age order. They then choose words from the word bank and write captions below the pictures.

10 Read and ✓. Then trace and say.

- Pupils read the sentences and tick the box of the person it best describes. Pupils then trace the words *young* and *old* and read the sentences to a partner.

Mini project

12 Make a poster about your family.

- Divide the class into pairs or small groups. Pupils take out the pictures they brought to class of old and young people in their family. Give each group/ pair a large sheet of sturdy card. Write the headings *Young* and *Old* on the board. Pupils divide the card into two sections and label one section *Young* and the other *Old* and stick his/her picture below the correct heading. Pupils then label the people in the collage (granny, baby, etc).

> Pupils create a family tree or draw pictures of his/her family members in order of their ages. Ask pupils to bring his/her pictures to the lesson to share with the class.

10 1:37 Listen and point. Then say.

SOCIAL SCIENCE

old

young

baby

sister   brother

dad   mum

grandad

granny

11 Number the pictures.

12 Make a poster about your family.

Lesson 6

baby, old, young. They're (young). *Family. This is my (granny).*

17

Ending the lesson

- Discuss (L1) some of the things that young people are best at (e.g. running, computer games, being flexible, learning new things) and other things that older people such as grandparents are best at (e.g. cooking, listening, being patient, general knowledge). Talk about the advantages and disadvantages of being older and younger.

OPTIONAL ACTIVITIES
Baby photo collage
Ask pupils to bring one baby photo and one recent photo to class. Make a collage of the photos and display it in the classroom.
Flashcard game
Play Where is it? see p. 23.

Lesson 7

Lesson aims
To review the unit language with a game

Recycled language
garden, house, Actions, Family, Rooms. Where's the (dad)? He's in the (kitchen).

Materials
Audio CD; Word cards (Family); spinners; blank paper; Worksheet 2

Starting the lesson

• Write the words *house* and *garden* on the board. Choose pupils to mime some actions that you do in the house and others that you do outside or in the garden (e.g. ride a bike, eat, pick flowers, climb a tree, vacuum the floor, have a bath, etc). Explain in L1 if necessary. Other pupils guess where he/she is (*He/she's in the house/garden)*. Pupils continue in groups or pairs.

PB page 18

13 **Listen. Then play.**

• Divide the class into pairs and give each pair one spinner. Explain (L1) the rules of the game. Pupils begin at START and move through Lindy's tree house. Pupil A spins the spinner and moves the correct number of spaces. Pupil A lands on a character (e.g. *mum*). Pupil B asks *Where's the (mum)?* Pupil A answers *She's in the bathroom/garden.* Each pupil receives one point for asking the correct question and giving the correct answer. Pupils can keep score on blank paper. The pupil with the most points at the end of the game wins.

• Play CD1:38 as an example of the language pupils may find helpful while playing the game. Pairs then play the game. Monitor each pair to help with pronunciation.

A	5!	**1:38**
	1, 2, 3, 4, 5 ...	
B	Where's the dad?	
A	He's in the kitchen.	
B	My turn!	

Practice

• Stick the word cards (family) on the board with a generous amount of space below each. Now write the name of a room below each word card. Ask *Where's mum?* Pupils find the *mum* word card and the room written below it and say the correct sentence *(She's in the living room).*

• Extend the activity by giving each pupil a blank sheet of paper. Pupils draw a cross section of a house and label each of the rooms. You may wish to draw this in advance and photocopy one for each pupil. Stick a family word card on the board and write the name of a room below it. Pupils draw the family members in the correct rooms. Pupils then check his/her answers in pairs by asking a partner *Where's my granny? (She's in the bedroom.)* Fast finishers may complete his/her drawing by adding furniture and colouring the rooms.

14 **Listen and do.**

• Explain that pupils will listen to some actions. Play CD1:39 and pupils do as instructed on the CD. Ask pupils where they've learned these actions (in the Quest song).

Stand up.	**1:39**
Jump up.	
Turn around.	
Sit down. (x 2)	

Practice

• Pupils can now complete Worksheet 2.

1 **Write.**

• Pupils write the names of the family members on the line below each character.

2 **Draw and write.**

• Pupils read the questions and draw the family members in any room they wish. Pupils then complete the sentences.

Game

• Divide the class into groups of seven. Choose a strong pupil from each group to be the speaker. Pupils sit together with the members of his/her group and each pupil chooses a family member they wish to be (granny, grandad, mum, dad, sister or brother). Smaller groups may omit certain family members. Groups come to the board in turn and the speaker introduces the family members *(This is my mum, this is my dad,* etc). Now say *Go!* and the (mums) from each group find each other. The (mums) hold hands and walk round the classroom looking for other (mums).

 Pupils can now go online to Tropical Island and find the blue bottle that Pippin is holding. It is the smallest blue bottle on the top shelf in the basement of the castle. Once pupils click on the blue bottle they are taken to a supplementary language game based on the vocabulary in this unit.

13 **1:38** Listen. Then play.

Where's the dad?

He's in the kitchen.

Where's my family?

14 **1:39** **TPR** Listen and do.

18 **Lesson 7** *garden. house. Actions. Family. Rooms. Where's the (dad)? He's in the (kitchen).*

Ending the lesson

- Divide the class into two teams. Call out a category, e.g. family, toys, colours, numbers, words with the /a/ sound, etc. Teams take turns saying words from these categories. Give each team one point for each correct answer. Alternatively, pupils write the words on the board or on a sheet of paper rather than calling them out.

OPTIONAL ACTIVITIES
Game
Pupils do the actions from CD1:39 in pairs. One pupil calls out an action and his/her partner follows the instruction. Pupils then switch roles.
Flashcard game
Play Correct order see p. 22.

Lesson 8

Lesson aims
To personalise the unit language; to provide an opportunity for self-evaluation

Recycled language
Family, Rooms. This is my (mum). She's in the (living room).

Materials
Audio CD; Unit 2 Stickers ; Flashcards (all); Word cards (all); DVD; paper to make project book; Evaluation sheet 2

Starting the lesson

- Ask pupils (L1) to recall all the new words they've learnt in this unit. Ask which activity or lesson they found most interesting. Ask what they found easy and what was difficult.
- Flip through the family flashcards, colour flashcards, numbers, etc. Pupils call out the words as quickly as possible.

PB page 19

15  **Listen, stick, then trace.**

- Pupils look at the missing faces and find the stickers needed to complete them at the back of the Pupil's Book. Play CD1:40. Pupils listen and stick the stickers of each family member in place as they are mentioned in the recording. Alternatively, pupils work in pairs, calling out the family members and sticking the stickers. Finally, they trace over the words.

This is me and my family.	1:40
1 This is my grandad.	
2 This is my granny.	
3 This is my mum.	
4 This is my dad.	
5 This is my brother.	
6 This is my sister.	

16 **Draw. Then write.**

- Pupils draw his/her house or a room in his/her house in the frame. They then draw a family member in the picture. Pupils read the sentences next to the frame and fill in the gaps with the appropriate words. Call on individual pupils to read his/her sentences and share the drawings with the class.

Practice

- Pupils choose a member of his/her family and draw pictures of activities they enjoy doing in the house and things they enjoy doing in the garden. Pupils write captions below his/her drawing: *He's/She's in the (house).*

AB page 17

11 **Read and look. Then write.**

- Pupils read the questions and answers below the cross section of the house. Pupils then find the characters in the house and complete the questions with the correct words from the word bank.

12 **Find and stick.**

- Pupils find the Unit 2 stickers in the back of his/her Pupil's Book and stick the speech bubble stickers in the correct place to complete the picture. Pupils read the sentences on the stickers to a partner.
- Pupils read the three sentences in the Look! Box and tick the ones they can understand and use correctly.
- Explain (L1) that pupils should colour in the stars at the bottom of the page to correspond with how well they think they completed the unit.

AB page 60

- Pupils colour the pictures (my home) in the Picture Dictionary. They can then play a game in pairs. They take turns to say a word and his/her partner points to the correct picture. Stronger pupils may wish to cover the written words below each picture and try writing the words themselves.

Practice

- Help pupils to make an 8-page booklet as an end of unit project. They write the title *My Unit 2 Project Book* on the cover and draw pictures on each page, of his/her family members. Pupils write sentences below each drawing (e.g. *This is my mum.*) Pupils should decorate the book. If you have pupils in the class with special circumstances, you might suggest pupils draw pictures of Lindy's or Emily's family for this project.

 Now watch the DVD.

Evaluation

You can check your pupils' progress using Evaluation sheet 2. See also Teacher's notes p. 176.

Pupils can now go online to Tropical Island and enjoy the fun and games.

15   **Listen, stick, then trace.**

 I CAN DO IT!

granny   mum

grandad

1   2   3   4

dad

5   6

brother

sister   me

Stick

16  **Draw. Then write.**

This is my house.

This is my _____.

He's/She's in the _____.

 **Now go to Tropical Island.**

Lesson 8   *Family, Rooms. This is my (mum). She's in the (living room).*   **19**

Ending the lesson

- Divide the class into two teams. Ask each team questions in turn and give a point for each correct answer. Hold up various flashcards and ask *Who/ What's this?* Point to things around the room and ask *What colour is it?* Hold up pencils in different numbers and ask *How many?* Hold up various word cards and pupils read the words, etc.

OPTIONAL ACTIVITIES
Flashcard game
Play Collect the cards see p. 22.
TPR game
Play Number groups see p. 24.

3 My body

Lesson 1

Lesson aims
To present and practise new vocabulary

Target language
arms, body, feet, fingers, hands, head, legs, toes

Recycled language
Numbers

Materials
Audio CD; Flashcards (Body); Word cards (Body); small squares of paper or coins

Optional materials
Sticky notes or small pieces of paper

Starting the lesson

- Revise the actions from the Quest song. Then play CD1:39 from Lesson 7 in Unit 2 and pupils do the actions.
- Revise numbers 1–20. Write a number on the board (e.g. 7). Pupils say the word, then the numbers that come before and after the number you've written (e.g. 6 and 8).

PB pages 20–21

- Ask questions about the main illustration. Where's Pippin? Who's this? What's this? Explain that Lindy, Joe and Pippin are on their way to the castle now. Grandad has joined them and is using the map to guide them. They have come across some other children enjoying a beach party and have decided to join in the fun.

Presentation

- Ask pupils (L1) what they think they're going to learn in this unit (parts of the body). Read the heading of the unit, then indicate your body and say *My body*.
- Teach the parts of the body using your own body as a model or the flashcards (body). Wave your arms and say *arms*. Pupils do the action and repeat the word. Continue doing an action to teach each word.

1 🔊 Listen and say.

- Point to each body part at the bottom of the page (and in the main illustration in the case of *body)* and ask *What's this? (arms).* Play CD1:41. Pupils listen, point to the parts of the body and repeat the words. Then pupils say the missing words in each line until at the end they are saying all the words. Each word is associated with a sound to indicate when the pupil should say the word. The association of word and sound will also help them to memorise the words. Encourage them to use the pictures at the bottom of PB p. 20 for reference.

arms ★ legs ★ hands ★ feet ★ fingers ★   **1:41**
toes ★ head ★ body ★

Listen and say the missing words.
arms, legs, hands, feet, fingers, toes, head, ★
arms, legs, hands, feet, fingers, toes, ★ ★
arms, legs, hands, feet, fingers, ★ ★ ★
arms, legs, hands, feet, ★ ★ ★ ★
arms, legs, hands, ★ ★ ★ ★ ★
arms, legs, ★ ★ ★ ★ ★ ★
arms, ★ ★ ★ ★ ★ ★ ★
★ ★ ★ ★ ★ ★ ★ ★

Game

- Pupils use small squares of paper to cover three of the body parts in Activity 1. Call out the words in turn. When you say a part of the body that a pupil covered, they write an X on the paper. A pupil wins when all three of the body parts they covered have been said.

Pairwork

- Divide the class into pairs. One pupil covers a part of the body with a coin or piece of paper and the other tries to guess which is covered. Pupils then switch roles.

68

D One head!
F Move your body!
G Come on. Let's go!

Practice

- Pupils read the labels in the main illustration to a partner. The partner moves the part of the body as it is read out.

AB page 18

1 Match. Then trace and say.

- Pupils write the numbers in the boxes that correspond with the correct part of the body. Pupils then trace the words and check his/her answers in pairs.

Ending the lesson

- Wave your arms and pupils say the part of the body you're moving. Continue with legs, feet, hands, toes fingers, body and head. Pupils continue the game in groups or pairs. You could use a puppet for some variety.

OPTIONAL ACTIVITIES
Sticky note labelling
Write the parts of the body on sticky notes. Ask one pupil to come to the front of the class. Pupils stick the sticky notes on the appropriate part of the body.
Action song
Teach the song 'Head, shoulders, knees and toes', but with the words *Heads, fingers, legs and toes*. Pupils do the actions as they sing.

NOTES

---

2  Listen and ✓.

- Play CD1:42 and pupils write a tick in the box next to the words in the main illustration as they are mentioned. Play the recording again and pupils join in the dance.

G = GRANDAD J = JOE L = LINDY F = FRANK   1:42
D = DANCERS
G Come on. This way.
J Look! A party!
G Come on!
L Wait Grandad!
F Two legs!
D Two legs!
F Two arms!
D Two arms!
F Two feet!
D Two feet!
F Two hands!
D Two hands!
F Ten fingers!
D Ten fingers!
F Ten toes!
D Ten toes!
F One head!

Lesson 2

Lesson aims
To extend the unit vocabulary set; to practise the vocabulary with a chant

Target language
clap, key, move, shake, stamp, touch, wave. (Move) your (legs).

Recycled language
Body parts

Materials
Audio CD; music CDs

Optional materials
Word cards (Body); small box or bag

Starting the lesson

- Revise parts of the body. Say *fingers.* Pupils move his/ her fingers. Continue with other body parts.
- Bring a few music CDs to class. Play the music and call out parts of the body. Pupils move the part you've mentioned to the rhythm of the music.

PB pages 20–21

Presentation

3  **Listen and chant.**

- Tell pupils they will learn some new actions in a chant. Encourage them to move their bodies along with the recording. Play CD1:43 several times, miming the new actions. Then encourage them to join in with the words, too.

Arms, arms, wave your arms, **1:43** Wave your arms with me. Feet, feet, stamp your feet, Stamp your feet with me. Hands, hands, clap your hands, Clap your hands with me. Toes, toes, touch your toes, Touch your toes with me. Legs, legs, move your legs, Move your legs with me. Body, body, shake your body, Shake your body with me. Stamp, stamp, stamp. Mooooove, Waaaaave, Shaaaaake Clap, clap, clap!!!

head · arms

body

legs

1 1:41 Listen and say. 2 1:42 Listen and ✔.

20 Lesson 1   arms, body, feet, fingers, hands, head, legs, toes, *Numbers*

Practice

- Use the actions from the chant to play a game of 'Teacher says'. Explain that pupils should perform an action only when you say 'Teacher says ...' at the beginning of the sentence. Say *Teacher says clap your hands* and pupils clap his/her hands. Say *Touch your toes* and pupils should do nothing. Try variations like *move your legs*, *shake your hands*, etc.

4 **Listen and number. Then say.**

- Say the actions from the chant and pupils point to the picture of the child doing that action. Play CD1:44. Pupils write the number in the correct box. Play the recording again and pupils check answers in pairs.

1 Stamp your feet. **1:44** 2 Clap your hands. 3 Wave your arms. 4 Move your legs. 5 Touch your toes. 6 Shake your body.

Listen and chant.

CASTLE THIS WAY

fingers ☐

hands ☐

feet ☐

toes ☐

Listen and number. Then say.

☐ ☐ ☐ ☐ ☐ ☐

Lesson 2   clap, key, move, shake, stamp, touch, wave. (Move) your (legs). Body parts   21

AB page 19

2 Look and write. Then trace and say.

- Say a part of the body (e.g. *body*) and pupils say an action that you can do with that part (e.g. *shake your body*). Continue with several other body parts and actions.
- Pupils read the words in the word bank. They then look at the pictures, read the sentences below them and choose a word from the word bank that best completes the sentence. They then trace the action words. Finally, they read out their completed sentences to a partner to check answers.

Ending the lesson

- Write the parts of the body on the board. Choose one pupil to leave the room and erase one of the words. When you are ready, call out one of the phrases from the chant to signal the pupil to come back into the room, e.g. *Shake your body, shake your body!* The pupil walks into the room performing the action, then tries to guess which word was erased. Play the game in teams and award points for correct answers.

OPTIONAL ACTIVITIES

Choose a card

Put the word cards (*body*) in a small box or bag. Pupils choose a card from the bag and read the part of the body written on the card. Pupils move, touch, or shake the part of the body referred to. Pupils may do this activity in pairs or groups.

Team game

Play Chair race see p. 24.

NOTES

Quest sticker and song

- Ask pupils (L1) to recall which of Princess Emily's things they found in Units 1 and 2 (the present and the photo). Explain that they are now going to find the third Quest item. Ask them to look at the main illustration and guess what the item might be. Then play the Quest Song CD1:45 so pupils learn the name of the Quest item (*a key*).

> Stand up, jump up, come on a quest,   **1:45**
> Come on a quest today.
> Turn around, sit down, come on a quest,
> Look for a key today.
> A treasure chest, a present, a photo and ★ a key …
> Find a key today!

- Ask pupils to find the key sticker at the back of the Pupil's Book and stick it over the grey image of the key in the main illustration. Discuss (L1) whose key it might be. Ask pupils to guess what the key opens. Play the recording again and pupils sing along.

Lesson 3

Lesson aims
To revise the unit vocabulary with a song; to present the new structure; to practice the unit vocabulary with a song

Target language
I've got (two) (legs).

Recycled language
Actions, Body parts, Numbers

Materials
Audio CD; spinners

Optional materials
Pictures of children doing different actions

Starting the lesson

- Ask pupils to vote on which song/chant from the previous units is his/her favourite. Choose a class favourite and play it once or twice to get them moving!
- Do a TPR activity using the sentences from the chant CD1:43 in Lesson 2. Try different variations like *touch your legs* or *move your feet*.

PB page 22

Presentation

- Hold up two hands and say *I've got two hands.* Ask pupils to repeat. Continue with *I've got ten fingers,* etc. Now draw a sea creature, monster or alien on the board. Make a statement about it using the *I've got* structure as you draw each body part (e.g. draw four arms on your monster and say *I've got (four arms)*).

 5 **Listen and find. Then sing.**

- Ask pupils (L1) where they think the children are in the illustration. (They're at a kids' club on the beach.) Point out that the turtle mascot is leading the children in a dance and the children are doing different actions. Say *Clap your hands* and pupils point to the child doing that action. Continue with *wave your arms, stamp your feet* and *touch your toes.*
- Pupils listen to the song CD1:46 and point to the correct children as they are mentioned. Play the song again and pupils sing along and do the actions. You could also play the karaoke version of the song CD3:44 for pupils to sing along to.

I've got two hands. Clap your hands. (x 3)　**1:46**
Clap your hands with me.
I've got two arms. Wave, wave, wave. (x 3)
Wave, wave, wave with me.
I've got ten toes. Touch your toes. (x 3)
Touch your toes with me.
I've got two feet. Stamp your feet. (x 3)
Stamp your feet with me.

Pairwork

- Pupils say *I've got (two hands)* to a partner who shows his/her (two hands). They continue with other parts of the body.

6 **Listen. Then say and do.**

- Explain (L1) that pupils are going to play a game in pairs. Pupil A spins the spinner and makes a sentence using the corresponding body part and the *I've got* structure (e.g. if the spinner lands on number 1, he/she says *I've got two feet*). Pupil B then makes a sentence with an action that matches the body part (e.g. *Stamp your feet*). Pupil A then performs the action. Play CD1:47 to give pupils an idea of the language they'll need. They then play the game in pairs.

BOY　I've got two feet.　**1:47**
GIRL　Stamp your feet.

AB page 20

3 **Read and find. Then colour.**

- Pupils read the sentences and find the monster it describes (number 1). They then colour it as specified in the description (green). Pupils could colour the other monsters by doing a colour dictation in pairs (e.g. *(green) (body), (red) (legs)*, etc.).

4 **Listen and write. Then draw.**

- Play CD1:48. Pupils listen to the number of body parts and complete the sentences by writing a number in the gap. They then draw a monster in the frame with the correct number of body parts. Fast finishers could draw his/her own monster and dictate colours for a partner to colour in.

1 I've got four arms.　**1:48**
2 I've got three legs.
3 I've got eight hands.
4 I've got six feet.
5 I've got eight fingers.
6 I've got twelve toes.
7 I'm red.

5    **Listen and find. Then sing.**

6 **Listen. Then say and do.**

I've got two feet.

Stamp your feet.

I've got (two) (legs). *Actions, Body parts, Numbers*

Ending the lesson

• Write numbers 1–6 across the top of the board, and underneath each number write an action: *stamp your feet, shake your body, clap your hands, wave your arms, touch your toes* and *move your legs.* Say a number and pupils do the corresponding action. Say numbers quickly to make the activity more challenging.

OPTIONAL ACTIVITIES
Action collages
Bring in pictures from magazines/the internet of children doing the actions learnt in this unit. Pupils stick the pictures on paper and label them.
Flashcard game
Play Basketball see p. 22.

Lesson 4

Lesson aims
To develop literacy skills; phonics: /ɪ/ /iː/

Target language
big, fish

Recycled language
Actions, Body parts, Colours. I've got (two) (legs).
(Wave) your (arms).

Materials
Audio CD; small cards; Sounds Fun notebooks

Starting the lesson

- Begin the lesson by singing the song from Lesson 3 CD1:46. Then call out actions: *Clap your hands! Touch your toes!* etc. Pupils do the actions.
- Ask individual pupils *How many (hands) have you got?* (*I've got two (hands).*

 **PB page 23**

7 **Listen. Then play.**

- Look at the sea creatures at the top of the page. Describe one of the creatures to the class using the first person (e.g. *I've got two arms. I've got six legs. I'm red.*) Pupils guess which creature you described (1) and say the action the creature is doing (*Stamp your feet*).
- Now divide the class into pairs. Pupils describe the creatures to a partner. Partners guess the creature and say the action the creature's doing. Play CD1:49 to give pupils an idea of the language they will need to play the game.

GIRL I'm purple. I've got eight arms.	**1:49**
BOY Number 2! Wave your arms.	

Presentation

8 **Listen and say.**

- Play CD1:50. Pause after the first two lines. Ask pupils which sounds they can hear (/ɪ/ and /iː/). Play the first two lines again and pupils repeat.
- Revise/Teach the words *big* and *fish* by drawing simple pictures on the board or showing homemade flashcards. Say the words several times and pupils repeat. Ask which sound pupils can hear (/ɪ/). Ask pupils which other words they know with this sound (*fingers, sister, pink, six, living room*). Now say the words *feet* and *green*. Ask which sound pupils can hear (/iː/) and which other words they know with the same sound (*three*).

- Now play the recording from the beginning to the end. Pupils listen and repeat the words. Play the recording again so pupils are comfortable with these new sounds. Then pupils read the rhymes to a partner.

i , i, ee, ee,	**1:50**
i, ee, i, ee, i, ee	
i ★	
Big. ★ Pink. ★ Fish. ★	
A big pink fish. ★	
ee ★	
Three. ★ Green. ★ Feet. ★	
Three green feet. ★	
A big pink fish with three green feet. ★	

Practice

- Pupils add the sounds /ɪ/ and /iː/ on separate pages of their Sounds Fun notebooks. Pupils draw pictures of words containing these sounds and label them. Ask pupils to add any new words from this unit to the previously learnt sounds (/æ/ *stamp, hands, clap*; /e/ *legs*, /ɒ/ *body*).

AB page 21

5 **Listen and match. Then trace.**

- Play CD1:51. Pupils listen and match the words to the corresponding picture, then trace the words.

i	**1:51**
sister fish pink	
ee	
feet three green	

6 **Match. Then listen and check.**

- Pupils find the pairs of words with the same sound and draw lines connecting the pairs. Play CD1:52 for pupils to check his/her answers.

i: fish, six	**1:52**
a: hand, van	
e: leg, pen	
ee: three, feet	

Pupils can now go online to Tropical Island and find the two coins that Pippin is holding. They are near the exit at the very end of the caves. Once pupils click on the coins they are taken to a supplementary language game based on the vocabulary in this unit.

7  **Listen. Then play.**

> I'm purple. I've got eight arms.

> Number 2! Wave your arms.

8 1:50 **Listen and say.**

SOUNDS FUN!

A big pink fish
with three green feet.

Lesson 4   big, fish. *Actions, Body parts. Colours. I've got (two) (legs). (Wave) your (arms). Sounds: /ɪ/ /iː/*   **23**

Ending the lesson

- Explain (L1) that you are going to say some words that pupils know. If a word has an /ɪ/ sound, pupils should shake his/her body. If it has an /iː/ sound, they should touch his/her head. Say words from this and earlier units, with a mixture of vowel sounds, and pupils do the actions.

OPTIONAL ACTIVITIES
Flashcard game
Play Snap see p. 22.
Team game
Play Phonics race see p. 24.

Lesson 5

Lesson aims
To consolidate the unit language with a story

Target language
jump. Exercise is good for you. I'm hot. My name's Frank.

Recycled language
Actions

Materials
Audio CD; Unit 3 Story cards

Optional materials
Music CDs

Starting the lesson

- Draw a sea creature on the board. Call on pupils to describe the creature in first person (*I've got four arms*, etc).
- Ask pupils to remember (L1) what happened in the story from Unit 2. Who was the main character in the story? (Princess Emily). Who else did we meet in the story? (The princess' family). Who did Princess Emily call out for at the end of the story? (Pippin).

PB page 24

Presentation

- Remind pupils (L1) that Lindy, Joe and Pippin have now set out on their Quest to find Princess Emily's castle along with Lindy's grandad. Ask pupils to remember where the characters were in Lesson 1 of this unit (at a beach party).
- Before pupils open their books, show the story cards for Unit 3 in turn and ask the questions from the 'Before reading the story' section written on the back of each card. Teach the action *jump* and the sentences *I'm hot* and *Exercise is good for you*, using mime and L1 as appropriate.

9 **Listen and read. Then act.**

- Play the recording of the story CD1:53 and pupils follow along in their books. Play the recording again, pausing after each line for pupils to repeat.

- Call on pupils to read the story. Stop after each frame and check pupils' understanding of the story by asking the questions from the 'After reading the story' section on the back of each story card. Be sure that pupils understand that Pippin was being naughty by pretending to be Frank.
- After pupils have a clear understanding of the story, invite four or more pupils to the board to act it out. You may wish to play the recording, pause after each line and have them repeat the lines. Alternatively, you could have other pupils read the lines while the pupils act it out or have them say the lines from memory. When acting out, encourage tone of voice and expressions to match those in the pictures. Use props that you've brought to class if you wish.

Practice

- Hand out the story cards to six pupils. Play the recording of the story again. When his/her part of the story is playing, they jump up and show his/her card to the class.
- Now call six different pupils to the board and hand out the cards in mixed order. Ask all pupils to close their books and just listen to the story. Play the recording, pausing after each line, and pupils say who's holding the correct card.

AB page 22

7 **Listen and match.**

- Point to each of the characters in turn and ask *Who's this?* (Frank/Lindy/Pippin) Play CD1:54. Pupils listen and find the character who says the sentences in the story and draw lines matching the speech bubbles to the correct character.

F = FRANK P = PIPPIN L = LINDY	1:54
F Hello. My name's Frank.	
P Jump! Jump!	
L I'm hot.	

8 **Read and number.**

- Point to each of the characters and elicit the action the character is performing. Pupils read the sentences and write the correct number in each box.

 **Listen and read. Then act.**

Ending the lesson

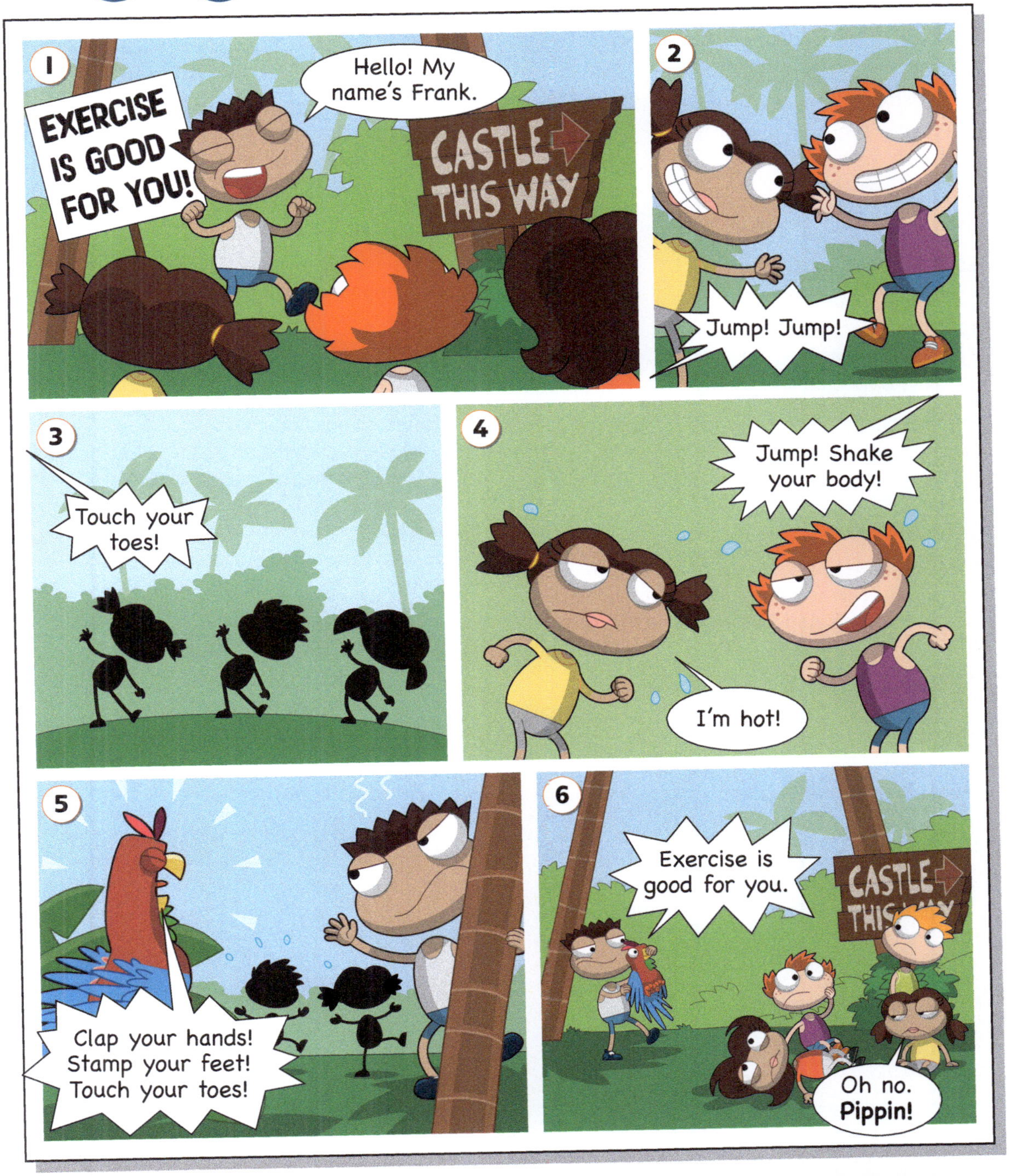

- Stick the story cards on the board in mixed order. Pupils order the story cards by writing a number from 1–6 below each. Play the recording of the story CD1:53 to check pupils' answers.

OPTIONAL ACTIVITIES

Have a class party!
Play some music and create some interesting moves to teach the class. Call out actions while you're dancing (move your arms, shake your body, etc).

Flashcard game
Play Hit the card see p. 23.

Lesson 6

Lesson aims
To integrate other areas of the curriculum into the English class; to develop the cross-curricular topic through a short project

Cross-Curricular focus
PE – Exercise routines

Target language
dance, swim

Recycled language
Actions, Body parts

Materials
Audio CD; homemade word cards (jump, dance and swim); pictures of people exercising

Optional materials
Skipping ropes; music CDs

Starting the lesson

- Play a miming game to review the actions from Lessons 2 and 3. Now say *I've got two hands.* Pupils add in an action that's done with your hands: *Clap, clap, clap.*

PB page 25

Presentation

10 **Listen and say.**

- Teach the words *dance* and *swim* by miming the words. Revise *jump*. Ask pupils to repeat and say the words several times. Play CD1:55 and pupils repeat and do the actions. Pupils then read the words below the pictures.

1 Jump.	**1:55**
2 Dance.	
3 Swim.	

Practice

- Make word cards of the new actions (*jump, dance* and *swim*) by writing the words on strips of paper. Make three or four of each word. Also write an X on several pieces of the same paper. Put the papers into a bag. Divide the class into two teams. Invite a pupil from one team to choose a paper from the bag. They receive one point for reading it out correctly and another point for doing the correct action. If they choose a paper with an X written on it, no points are awarded and the next team has a go.

11 **Listen and number. Then do.**

- Read the actions below each photo. Mime the action as you read and ask pupils to repeat. Play CD1:56 of children doing an exercise routine. Pupils listen and write a number in the correct box.

Exercise is good for you!	**1:56**
Exercise is good for you!	
Are you ready?	
Yes! Yes!	
Let's begin!	
1 Move your head. (x 2)	
2 Stamp your feet. (x 2)	
3 Swim, swim, swim. (x 2)	
4 Touch your toes. (x 2)	
5 Clap your hands. (x 2)	
6 Jump, jump, jump. (x 2)	
7 Shake your body. (x 2)	
8 Wave your arms. (x 2)	
9 Dance, dance, dance. (x 2)	
Exercise is good for you!	
Exercise is good for you!	

AB page 23

9 **Look and write. Then say.**

- Pupils find the words from the word bank that match each picture and write them in the gaps. They then read out the words to a partner.

10 **Read and find. Then number.**

- Pupils find the children with numbers written next to them in the picture. They write the numbers next to the correct action.

Mini project

12 **Make your own exercise routine.**

- Divide the class into small groups or pairs. Each group/pair creates an exercise routine for the class of at least six different actions. Call the groups/pairs to the board one by one to lead the class in their routine. You may wish to have a different group/pair begin the class each day with their exercises rather than doing them all at once.

Pupils make a collage using pictures or drawings of people doing different exercises. They could make this into the form of an exercise routine if they wish, and call out the instructions while members of their family do the routine. Pupils should label their drawings with the actions. Ask them to bring their collages to the next lesson to share with the class.

10 1:55 **Listen and say.**

1 **jump**

2 **dance**

3 **swim**

11 1:56 **Listen and number. Then do.**

Clap your hands.

Jump.

Stamp your feet.

Wave your arms.

Move your head.

Swim.

Dance.

Touch your toes.

Shake your body.

12 Make your own exercise routine.

Lesson 6

dance, swim, *Actions, Body parts* **25**

Ending the lesson

- Talk about (L1) different types of exercise people do to keep fit. Bring pictures to class of people exercising. Discuss ways that people keep fit like football, yoga, Pilates, jogging, climbing, aerobics, etc.

OPTIONAL ACTIVITIES
TPR game
Play Number groups see p. 24.
'Exercise is good for you' day
Have an exercise day. Make stations in the classroom. One station could contain skipping ropes, in another music for dancing, etc.

Lesson 7

Lesson aims
To review the unit language with a game

Values
Keeping fit

Recycled language
Actions, Body parts, Numbers. I've got (four) (legs). (Move) your (legs).

Materials
Audio CD; Flashcards (Body); spinners; pictures of monsters, aliens, animals, etc; Worksheet 3

Optional materials
Poster 2

Starting the lesson

- Revise actions and parts of the body. Call out an action (e.g. *jump*) and pupils say which part of the body they use to perform the activity (*legs*).
- Play the recording from Lesson 6 CD1:56 to remind pupils of the actions. Now call pupils to the board to lead the class in a TPR activity using the actions from the chant. Pupils say an action (e.g. *Move your head*) and the class repeats.

PB page 26

  Listen. Then play.

- Divide the class into small groups or pairs. Each group will need a spinner. Explain (L1) that pupils should begin at START and travel around the board. Pupils spin the spinner and move the correct number of squares following the arrows on the board. When pupils land on a square, they read the word, then say the action the character on the square is doing (e.g. *toes; touch your toes*). The first pupil to reach FINISH wins.
- Play CD1:57 to give pupils an idea of the language they should use. They then start the game.

> **BOY** 3!   **1:57**
> 1, 2, 3 …
> Feet. I've got two feet.
> **GIRL** Stamp your feet.

Game

- Play a game to give pupils more practice of the *I've got* structure. Divide the class into two to four teams depending on the size. Ask each team to draw a circle on the board and explain (L1) that this is a body. They will make sentences in order to win more body parts for his/her body. Specify which body parts they will need to win the game (e.g. two arms, two legs and one head).

- Each team stands in a row facing the board. Show each team a picture of an animal, alien, monster, etc. in turn. You may bring these pictures from home, or use pictures from the Pupil's Book. Pupils say one sentence to the class about the picture (e.g. *I've got four legs; I'm blue*). For each correct answer, pupils draw a part of the body on the board until a team has completed their drawing.

 Listen and do.

- Explain that pupils will listen to some actions. Play CD1:58 and pupils do the actions as instructed on the CD.

> Jump.   **1:58**
> Dance.
> Swim.
> Touch your toes.
> Wave your arms.
> Shake your body.
> Move your legs.
> Stamp your feet.
> Clap your hands.

Practice

- Put the flashcards (body) in a pile. Invite a pupil to choose one of the flashcards and stick it on the board (e.g. *arms*). He/She now spins the spinner and writes the number (e.g. *four*) on the board next to the flashcard. Pupils create a sentence (e.g. *I've got four arms*). Write the sentence next to the (arm) flashcard. Continue until all the body flashcards have been used.

Values

- Ask pupils (L1) which types of exercise they enjoy. Ask which parts of the body they use when they exercise. Discuss the benefits of exercising regularly and the importance of exercise in our lives. Discuss how we feel when we don't exercise and how this affects our bodies. Talk about things we can do in our daily routines to help us keep fit.

Practice

- Pupils can now complete Worksheet 3.

1 **Read and draw.**

- Pupils read the sentences and complete the drawings of the monsters.

2 **Read and ✓ or ✗.**

- Pupils read the sentences about the monsters in Activity 1 and write a tick or a cross in the box accordingly.

13 🔵 1:57 🎲 Listen. Then play.

ROUND-UP

I've got two feet.

Stamp your feet.

14 🔵 1:58 **TPR** Listen and do.

Ending the lesson

- Write partial sentences on the board. Write *I've got two ...* Pupils complete the sentences with a part of the body to make true sentences. Alternatively, say the sentences rather than writing them.

OPTIONAL ACTIVITIES
Flashcard game
Play Bluff see p. 23.
Poster activity
See the notes on Poster 2 on p. 21.

Lesson 8

Lesson aims
To personalise the unit language; to provide an opportunity for self-evaluation

Recycled language
Actions, Body parts, Numbers. I've got (two) (arms). (Touch) your (toes).

Materials
Audio CD; Flashcards (Toys); Flashcards (Body); Unit 3 Stickers; paper to make Project book; Evaluation sheet 3

Starting the lesson

- Revise the *I've got* sentence structure by handing out flashcards of toys (or use real toys). Pupils hold up his/her flashcards and say *I've got a (boat).*

PB page 27

15 **Listen, stick, then trace.**

- Read out the sentences and pupils point to the words on the page.
- Pupils look at the pictures and find the matching stickers at the back of the Pupil's Book. Play CD1:59. Pupils listen and stick the stickers of each action in place as they are mentioned in the recording. Alternatively, pupils work in pairs, calling out the actions and sticking the stickers. Finally, they trace over the words.

1 Wave your arms.	**1:59**
2 Move your legs.	
3 Touch your toes.	
4 Jump.	
5 Clap your hands.	
6 Dance.	

16 **Draw your body. Then write.**

- Pupils draw a picture of his/her body in the frame. They then complete the sentences by writing suitable words in the gaps. Call on individual pupils to read his/her sentences and share the drawings with the class.

Practice

- Give each pupil a blank sheet of paper. Pupils dictate a monster/sea creature to a friend (e.g. *I've got three legs. I've got two heads*, etc). Stronger pupils should also dictate an action for his/her monster to be doing (e.g. *I'm waving my arms*). Pupils give his/her creature a name and describe them to the class in the first person. *Hello. I'm Lulu. I've got three arms. I've got one head*, etc.

- Alternatively, you could divide the class into groups of four. You might want to do this activity in the school hall and give each group a mat to stand on. Say *I've got four heads.* Pupils all get on the mat and join together to become a four-headed monster. Say *I've got five arms.* Three pupils join together and one hides an arm, to become a monster with five arms, Continue with other body parts.

AB page 24

11 **Look and write. Then say.**

- Pupils fill in the gaps below each creature with number and body words from the word bank. Pupils then say a sentence and a partner points to the correct creature.

12 **Find and stick.**

- Pupils find the Unit 3 sticker in the back of their Pupil's Book and stick the speech bubble sticker in the correct place to complete the picture. Pupils read the sentence on the sticker to a partner.
- Pupils read the three sentences in the Look! Box and tick the ones they can understand and use correctly.
- Explain (L1) that pupils should colour in the stars at the bottom of the page to correspond with how well they think they completed the unit.

AB page 60

- Pupils play a game in pairs with the pictures (my body) in the Picture Dictionary. They take turns to say a word and his/her partner points to the correct picture. Then do a colour dictation. Say *Colour the (feet) blue,* etc. and pupils colour the pictures accordingly. Alternatively, pupils dictate the colours in pairs. Stronger pupils may wish to cover the written words below each picture and try writing the words themselves.

Practice

- Help pupils to make an 8-page booklet as an end of unit project. They write the title *My Unit 3 Project Book* on the cover and draw pictures on each page, of parts of the body or an exercise routine. Pupils write captions below each drawing (e.g. *Wave your arms, I've got two hands, jump,* etc).

Evaluation

You can check your pupils' progress using Evaluation sheet 3. See also Teacher's notes p. 176.

 Pupils can now go online to Tropical Island and enjoy the fun and games.

15 🔊 1:59 ✏️ **Listen, stick, then trace.**

1 Wave your _arms_ .

2 Move your _legs_ .

3 Touch your _toes_ .

4 Jump.

5 Clap your _hands_ .

6 Dance.

Stick

16 ✏️ **Draw your body. Then write.**

I've got two _____

and two _____.

I've got ten _____

and one _____.

Now go to Tropical Island.

| **Lesson 8** | Actions. Body parts. Numbers. I've got (two) (arms). (Touch) your (toes). | 27 |

Ending the lesson

• Play a chain game using parts of the body. Invite eight pupils to the board and put them in a single line. The first pupil says *I've got four arms*. The second pupil repeats and adds *I've got four arms and three legs*. The third pupil repeats and adds *I've got four arms, three legs and ten heads* and so on.

OPTIONAL ACTIVITIES
Flashcard game
Play Who's the fastest? see p. 22.
TPR game
Play Teacher says see p. 24.

4 My face

Lesson 1

Lesson aims
To present and practise new vocabulary

Target language
ears, eyes, face, hair, mouth, nose

Recycled language
Colours

Materials
Audio CD; Word cards (Face); small squares of paper

Optional materials
Four pieces of paper for each pupil to play Bingo

Starting the lesson

- Draw a monster with a multiple number of body parts on the board. Say some true sentences about the monster (e.g. *I've got four arms*) and then some false ones. Pupils wave his/her arms if the sentence correctly describes the monster and stamp his/her feet if it's incorrect.

> **PB pages 28–29**

- Ask pupils (L1) what they remember from the Quest so far. Remind them that Lindy, Joe, Pippin and Grandad just passed a party on the beach and are closer to the castle.
- Ask questions (L1) about the main illustration. Ask which character they can see (Princess Emily). Ask Where's Princess Emily? (She's in the garden.) Point to the empty cage and ask pupils who they think the cage belongs to (it's Pippin's cage). Focus on the differences between the princess's appearance and the artist's portrait of her. Ask if they think the princess is going to be pleased with the portrait.

Presentation

- Ask (L1) what pupils think they are going to learn in this unit (parts of the face). Indicate your face and say *This is my face.*
- Teach the parts of the face. Touch various parts of your face and say *Touch your (ears).* Continue with *eyes, hair, mouth* and *nose.* Then begin again but make intentional mistakes (e.g. touch your nose, but say *Touch your mouth.*) Ask pupils to correct your mistakes.

① 🔵 Listen and say.

- Play CD2:01. Pupils listen, point to the parts of the face and repeat the words. Then pupils say the

missing words in each line until at the end they are saying all the words. Each word is associated with a sound to indicate when the pupil should say the word. The association of word and sound will also help them to memorise the words. Encourage them to use the pictures at the bottom of PB p. 28 for reference.

> face ★ eyes ★ ears ★ nose ★ mouth ★ hair ★   **2:01**
> **Listen and say the missing words.**
> face, eyes, ears, nose, mouth, ★
> face, eyes, ears, nose, ★ ★
> face, eyes, ears, ★ ★ ★
> face, eyes, ★ ★ ★ ★
> face, ★ ★ ★ ★ ★
> ★ ★ ★ ★ ★ ★

Game

- Pupils use small squares of paper to cover three of the facial features in Activity 1. Call out the words in turn. When you say a part of the face that a pupil covered, they write an X on the paper. A pupil wins when all three facial features they covered have been said.

Practice

- Divide the class into two teams. Stick the word cards (face) on the board. Call two pupils to the board to draw the correct picture below each word. The pupil who draws the fastest/best wins a point for his/her team.

AB page 25

1 Look and write. Then say.

- Point to each of the facial features in turn and ask *What's this?* Pupils create labels by writing the parts of the face in the appropriate boxes.

Ending the lesson

- Divide the class into pairs. Tell pupils to pretend they are looking into a mirror. Say *Touch your nose.* Pupils touch his/her partner's nose.

OPTIONAL ACTIVITIES

Alternative Bingo
Give each pupil four pieces of paper and ask them to draw one facial feature on each piece. Call out the facial features one by one. Pupils turn the pieces of paper face down when they are mentioned. A pupil wins when all his/her pieces of paper are face down.

Flashcard game
Play What's missing? see p. 22.

NOTES

Focus on the labels next to each part of the face. Encourage pupils to read the labels one by one. Sound out the words slowly and ask pupils to repeat. Pupils point to each label and read it to a partner, who points to the corresponding part of his/her face.

Pairwork

- Divide the class into pairs. One pupil covers a facial feature with a coin or piece of paper and the other tries to guess which is covered. Pupils then switch roles.

2  **Listen and ✓.**

- Point to the parts of the face in the main illustration in turn and ask *What's this? (nose)* Play CD2:02 and pupils tick the box next to the words as they are mentioned. Play the recording again and pupils touch the corresponding parts of his/her own face.

A = ARTIST   E = EMILY   2:02
A   Red. Yes, yes. And yellow. Some pink.
    Ah! It's finished!
    Look, Princess Emily! It's lovely!
E   What?!? Look at my face!!
    I've got small eyes!
    I've got a big nose!
    I've got big ears!
    I've got a small mouth!
    And look at my hair! It's red!!
A   Oh, dear ...

Lesson 2

Starting the lesson

- Show the flashcards (face) in turn and say a word, either the correct word or one that does not correspond with the picture. For example, show the *eye* flashcard and say *a nose.* Pupils say *right* or *wrong* using a 'thumbs up/down' motion at the same time.

PB pages 28–29

Presentation

- Draw two faces on the board with hair and eyes only. One face has got long hair and big eyes; the other has got short hair and small eyes. Point to the big eyes and say *big eyes.* Now point to the small eyes and say *small eyes.* Do the same with long/short hair. Continue by drawing the remaining facial features saying, *big ears/small ears* as you draw. Now point to the features individually and say *I've got (small) eyes.*
- Note: Teachers need to be sensitive when talking about facial features, e.g. big and small noses, so that pupils with larger features are not made to feel uncomfortable. It's best to describe illustrations and to avoid asking pupils to describe others in the classroom.

3 🔵 Listen and chant.

- Explain that Princess Emily is very angry at the artist because the painting doesn't look anything like her. Play CD2:03. Pupils point to the features in the painting as they listen to the first verse, then point to Princess Emily's features as they listen to the second verse. Play the recording again and pupils join in with the words.

A = ARTIST E = EMILY	2:03

A Princess. Look!.
E I've got small eyes.
  I've got a big nose.
  I've got a small mouth.
  And I've got short hair.
  Short, short hair.
  Short, short hair.
  Aarrrggghhh!
E I've got big eyes.
  I've got a small nose.
  I've got a big mouth.
  And I've got long hair.
  Long, long, hair.
  Long, long, hair.
  Aaaaaah!

Practice

- Say a sentence, either about Princess Emily or about the painting. Say *I've got small eyes.* Pupils wave his/her arms when you describe the painting and clap his/her hands when you describe the princess. Pupils continue in pairs.

4  Listen and draw.

- Focus pupils' attention on the outline of face 1. Play CD2:04. Pupils listen and complete the picture by drawing the facial features. Pupils then choose facial features for face 2 and dictate them to a partner.

I've got big eyes.	2:04
I've got a small nose.	
I've got a big mouth.	
I've got small ears.	
I've got short hair.	

Quest sticker and song

- Ask pupils to recall which of Princess Emily's things they found in the first three units (the present, the photo and the key). Explain that they are now going to find the fourth Quest item. Ask them to look at the main illustration and guess what the item might be. Then play the Quest Song CD2:05 so pupils learn the name of the Quest item *(sunglasses)*.

Stand up, jump up, come on a quest,	2:05
Come on a quest today.	
Turn around, sit down, come on a quest,	
Look for sunglasses today.	
A treasure chest, a present, a photo, a key and ★	
sunglasses ...	
Find sunglasses today!	

- Ask pupils to find the sunglasses sticker at the back of the Pupil's Book and stick it over the grey image of the sunglasses, on the wall on the left in the main illustration. Play the recording again and pupils sing along.

Game

Stick the nose on the face
For this activity you will need a blindfold and large cardboard cut outs of eyes, a nose, a mouth, hair, ears. Draw a large outline of a face on the board. Call a volunteer to the board. Blindfold the pupil and put the nose in his/her hand. They have to guess which facial feature it is and then try to stick in on the face in the correct place. Invite a different pupil to the board and hand them an eye. Continue until all the features have been used and look what a funny face you now have.

AB page 26

2 Read and match.

- Pupils read the words on the page and match them to the correct picture. Pupils then check his/her answers with a partner.

3 Read. Then look and write.

- Pupils read the sentences and write the number of the child they describe in the boxes provided.

Ending the lesson

- Draw a large face on the board with eyes, nose, etc. Make sentences about the face using *big/small/long/short*. Say *I've got big eyes*. Pupils say *right* or *wrong*.

OPTIONAL ACTIVITIES
Silly faces
Ask pupils to draw a silly face on a sheet of blank paper and label the parts of the face. Display their work in the classroom. Alternatively, make silly faces by dictating the number of eyes, ears, noses, etc. using *big/small/long/short*. Pupils then dictate a second face for a partner to draw.
International masks
Bring pictures or prepare a short presentation about masks from Africa, Asia, Venice, Native American cultures, etc. You may wish to decorate small eye masks and conduct a masquerade ball.

(Text within image 1:)

3 2:03 Listen and chant.

4 2:04 Listen and draw.

1   2

Lesson 2   *long, short, small, sunglasses, big, Features. I've got (big) (eyes).*   29

Lesson 3

Lesson aims
To revise the unit vocabulary with a song; to present the new structure

Target language
He's/She's got (big) (ears). Who is it?

Recycled language
big, long, short, small, Colours, Features

Materials
Audio CD; sentences written on big strips of paper; large sheet of paper

Optional materials
Materials to make a sock puppet or mask

Starting the lesson

- Write sentences on big strips of paper before class (e.g. *I've got long hair*). Draw two faces on the board with different facial features. Show the sentences to the class in turn and pupils stick them under the correct face on the board.

PB page 30

Presentation

- Point to something brown and say *What colour is it? It's brown.* Pupils repeat *It's brown* several times. Point to someone's brown hair and say *brown hair.* Pupils find other things around the classroom that are brown.

  Listen and find. Then sing.

- Ask pupils (L1) what they see in the picture (a puppet theatre with three puppets, performing the story *Hansel and Gretel*). Play CD2:06. Pause after each verse and pupils find the puppet being described. Play the recording again and pupils sing along. You could also play the karaoke version of the song CD3:45.

Who is it? Who can it be? Who is it?	**2:06**
Listen to me!	
She's got blue eyes, blue eyes	
And a small nose, a small nose.	
She's got small ears, small ears,	
And long, long hair.	
Who is it? Who can it be? Who is it? Listen to me!	
He's got brown eyes, brown eyes	
And a small nose, a small nose.	
He's got a big mouth, a big mouth	
And short, short hair.	
Who is it? Who can it be? Who is it? Listen to me!	
She's got green eyes, green eyes	
And a big nose, a big nose.	
She's got big ears, big ears	
And short, short hair.	

Practice

- Describe the characters in Activity 5 to the class. Say *He's got brown eyes*. Pupils guess who you're describing by responding with a different action for each character (e.g. wave for the boy, clap for the girl, and stamp for the witch).

6 **Listen and point. Then play.**

- Explain (L1) that pupils are going to play a guessing game in pairs. One pupil chooses a puppet and describes it to his/her partner. The partner says the number of the puppet described. Play CD2:07 to give pupils an idea of the language they will need to play the game. They then do the activity in pairs.

A She's got a big nose.	**2:07**
B Number 1.	

Practice

- Divide the class into five or six groups. Write five sentences for each group on a sheet of paper, all describing a single boy or girl (e.g. *He's got short hair. He's got brown hair,* etc.) One pupil in the group draws a blank face and the others take it in turns to read a sentence and draw the correct facial features.

AB page 27

4 **Listen and colour.**

- Point to a boy pupil with short hair and say *He's got short hair*. Then point to a girl pupil with long hair and say *He's got long hair*. Elicit what's wrong with the second sentence (we use *she* for girls, not *he*). Continue making sentences about pupils, some with mistakes with *he* or *she*. Pupils say *Right* or *Wrong* and put his/her thumb up or down.
- Play CD2:08. Pupils listen and colour the faces accordingly. Pupils may wish to complete the picture by dictating colours to a partner for the parts of the face not mentioned in the recording.

He's got blue eyes. He's got green ears.	**2:08**
He's got a red mouth. He's got a purple nose.	
She's got brown eyes. She's got a red nose.	
She's got an orange mouth. She's got pink ears.	

5 **Read. Then look and circle.**

- Pupils read the sentences. They then look at the pictures in Activity 4 and circle *Yes* if the sentence is correct or *No* if it isn't.

KEY **2** No, **3** Yes, **4** Yes, **5** No

  **Listen and find. Then sing.**

6  **Listen and point. Then play.**

She's got a big nose.

Number 1.

 1

 2

 3

 4

---

30 **Lesson 3** *He's/She's got (big) (ears). Who is it? big, long, short, small, Colours, Features*

Ending the lesson

- Stick a large sheet of paper on the board and dictate a face for pupils to draw and colour. Say *He's/She's got (green) eyes.*
- Write another verse for the song as a class or in groups, using the drawing of the face on the board. Sing the song again, adding the new verse(s). You could use the karaoke version of the song CD3:45 for this.

OPTIONAL ACTIVITIES
Puppets
Pupils make and display their own sock puppets or masks using old socks, paper plates, wool, buttons, colourful paper, glitter, etc.
Flashcard game
Play Face race see p. 23.

Lesson 4

Starting the lesson

- Play the recording of the song CD2:06 from Lesson 3. Pupils point to the correct parts of his/her own faces as they hear them on the recording.
- If pupils made masks in Lesson 3, they could use these to play a guessing game with the class. Choose a mask to describe and say *He/she's got blue eyes. Who is it?* Pupils answer with the name of the child wearing the mask.

 PB page 31

7 Make a face. Then play (page 75).

- Pupils cut out the eyes, ears, noses and mouths from PB p. 75. Say *It's a (long) (nose)* and pupils show you the correct picture.
- Pupils then work in pairs. One constructs two faces on the outlines in Activity 7, then describes them to a partner (e.g. *He's got green eyes,* etc). The partner listens and positions the features to match. Pupils then check to make sure the pictures match.

Presentation

- Ask pupils to remember which words they learned in the last unit, with the /ɪ/ and /iː/ sounds (*fish, sister, feet, green*). Write some of the words with your finger in the air for pupils to guess.

8 Listen and say.

- Play CD2:09. Pause after the first two lines. Ask pupils which sounds they can hear (/əʊ/ and /eɪ/). Play the first two lines again and pupils repeat.

> oh, oh, ay, ay **2:09**
> oh, ay, oh, ay, oh, ay
> oh ★
> Old. ★ Clothes. ★ Big nose. ★
> Old clothes for a big nose. ★
> ay ★
> Baby. ★ Plays. ★ Shapes. ★
> A baby plays with shapes. ★
> Old clothes for a big nose. ★
> A baby plays with shapes. ★

- Teach the words *clothes* and remind pupils of the words *old* and *nose* by drawing simple pictures on the board or showing homemade flashcards. Say the words several times and pupils repeat. Ask which sound pupils can hear (/əʊ/). Ask pupils which other words they know with this sound (*boat, no*). Now say the words *baby* and *play*. Teach the word *shapes* and ask which sounds pupils can hear (/eɪ/) and which other words they know with the same sound (*wave, face, train, shake*).
- Now play the recording from the beginning to the end. Pupils listen and repeat the words. Play the recording again so pupils are comfortable with these new sounds. Then pupils read the rhymes to a partner.

Practice

- Pupils add the /əʊ/ and /eɪ/ sounds to their Sounds Fun notebooks. Pupils draw pictures of words containing these sounds and label them. Ask pupils to add any new words from this unit to the previously learnt sounds (/ɪ/ big; /ɒ/ long).

 AB page 28

6 Listen and number. Then trace.

- Play CD2:10. Pupils listen and number the words as they hear them. Pupils then trace the words from the Sounds Fun! rhyme.

> oh **2:10**
> ay
> 1 play
> 2 old
> 3 baby
> 4 clothes
> 5 shapes
> 6 nose

---

7 Find and colour. Then say.

- Pupils find the pictures with the /eɪ/ sound and colour them blue, then find the pictures with the /əʊ/ sound and colour them red. Ask pupils *What's (blue)? What colour is the (train)?*

7 Make a face.
Then play (page 75).

SOUNDS FUN!

8 2:09 Listen and say.

Old clothes for a big nose.

A baby plays with shapes.

Lesson 4   clothes, play, shapes, *baby, big, long, old, short, small. Features. He's got... Sounds: /əʊ/ /eɪ/*   **31**

Ending the lesson

- Divide the class into two groups. Give each group a sound from this lesson /əʊ/ or /eɪ/. Say words, some with and some without the new sounds. Pupils stand when they hear their sound, or words beginning with their sound. You could make the game more challenging by dividing the class into more groups and giving them sounds learnt in previous units.

OPTIONAL ACTIVITIES
Game
Each pupil writes a word from the rhyme on his/her partner's back. The partner guesses the word and says another word with the same sound.
Team game
Play Whoops! see p. 25.

Lesson 5

Lesson aims
To consolidate the unit language with a story

Recycled language
big, blue, eyes, head, mouth, nose, red, small.
He's got ...

Materials
Audio CD; Unit 4 Story cards; props for acting out the story, e.g. notepads and pens, a cone of paper to use as a loudspeaker, a crown or tiara

Starting the lesson

- Remind pupils of the story from Unit 3. Ask pupils (L1) which new character was introduced in the story (Frank, the exercise instructor). What were the children doing in the story? (an exercise routine). Who was really calling out the actions? (Pippin).

PB page 32

- Before pupils open their books, show the story cards for Unit 4 in turn and ask the questions from the 'Before reading the story' section written on the back of each card.

  Listen and read. Then act.

- Play the recording of the story CD2:11 and pupils follow along in their books. Play the recording again, pausing after each line for pupils to repeat.
- Call on pupils to read the story. Stop after each frame and check pupils' understanding of the story by asking the questions from the 'After reading the story' section written on the back of each story card. Be sure that pupils understand that the princess was asking for help from the police in finding Pippin.

- After pupils have a clear understanding of the story, invite three or more pupils to the board to act it out. You may wish to play the recording, pause after each line and have them repeat the lines. Alternatively, you could have other pupils read the lines while the pupils act it out or have them say the lines from memory. When acting out, encourage tone of voice and expressions to match those in the pictures. Use props that you've brought to class if you wish.
- Stick the story cards on the board in mixed order. Call a group of four or five pupils to the board to arrange them in the correct order. Challenge several groups to do the same. Make this activity a game by timing each group.

Practice

- Divide the class into five groups. Give each group one word from the story (*eyes, head, mouth, red* and *blue*). Play the story recording and pupils stand and wave his/her arms when his/her word is mentioned. Alternatively, create actions to go with each word, e.g. moving the head for the word *head*; opening and closing the mouth for the word *mouth*, etc. Pupils do the actions in groups or as a class when they hear the words.

AB page 29

8 **Draw and say.**

- Pupils complete the picture of the face by drawing in the features however they want. They then describe their completed drawings to a partner or to the class, e.g. *He's got brown eyes. He's got a small mouth. He's got a long nose*, etc.

9 **Read and match.**

- Pupils read the sentences and match them to the character they best describe. Pupils check his/her answers in pairs. One pupil read a sentence and the other answers with the name of the character.

  **Listen and read. Then act.**

1 He's got big eyes . . .

2 . . . and a big head.

3 He's got a small mouth and a big nose.

4 And he's red and blue.

5 Red and blue?

Eh?

6 WANTED:

PIPPIN THE PARROT
WHERE IS HE??

HE'S MY PARROT!

32 **Lesson 5**   *big, blue, eyes, head, mouth, nose, red, small. He's got…*

Ending the lesson

- Read the text from each frame of the story in mixed order. Pupils find the text and say the number of the frame you're reading from. Pupils can also do this in small groups.

OPTIONAL ACTIVITIES

Hidden text

Cover the sentences inside the speech bubbles on the story cards. Groups have to write the text for each speech bubble without looking at the PB.

Team game

Play Parachute see p. 25.

Lesson 6

Lesson aims
To integrate other areas of the curriculum into the English class; to develop the cross-curricular topic through a short project

Cross-Curricular focus
Maths – Shapes

Target language
circle, rectangle, square, triangle

Recycled language
Features, Numbers. I've got a (triangle). It's a (nose).

Materials
Audio CD; Flashcards (Toys); shapes cut out from coloured card

Optional materials
Cut out shapes of different sizes and colours

Starting the lesson

- Play the chant CD2:03 from Lesson 2. Encourage pupils to touch the part of his/her face as it's mentioned.
- Hand out several flashcards (toys) from Unit 1. Go around the class asking *What have you got?* (*I've got a boat.*) Now ask pupils to hide his/her card. Ask the class to recall which card each pupil has got. Ask *Who's got the (boat)?*

PB page 33

Presentation

- Draw a circle, a triangle, a square and a rectangle on the board. Point to each in turn and say *This is a (circle).* Ask pupils to repeat several times.

10 **Listen and point. Then say.**

- Play the recording CD2:12 about the girl making a face out of shapes. Pupils listen and point to each shape as it's mentioned. Call out the shapes and pupils say the number of the photo it's first found in.

---

1 I've got a big circle.   **2:12**
2 I've got a triangle. One triangle, two triangles. Look. Red eyes!
3 I've got a square. It's a nose!
4 I've got a rectangle. It's a mouth!
5 It's a face!!

Practice

- Write the shape words on the board or make homemade word cards and stick them on the board. Pupils draw the correct shape next to each word. Then say the words and pupils make the correct shape with their fingers.

11 **Count and write.**

- Point to the photo of the pizza. Ask pupils which shape they can see in the photo. Pupils count the shapes in each photo and write the number in the box.

AB page 30

10 **Count and write. Then say.**

- Ask *How many (circles) can you see?* Pupils count the shapes in the shapes man and write the correct number below each shape. They check answers by telling a partner what they have written (*1 square, 7 rectangles, 3 circles, 7 triangles*).

11 **Listen. Then look and circle.**

- Play CD2:13. Pupils listen to the sentences describing the shapes man and circle *Yes* or *No*, depending on whether the sentences are true or false.

---

1 He's got three circles.   **2:13**
2 He's got two squares.
3 He's got eight triangles.
4 He's got seven rectangles.

KEY 1 T, 2 F, 3 F, 4 T

---

12 **Draw. Then write and say.**

- Pupils draw a toy using only shapes. They then complete the sentence by writing what it is they've drawn. Pupils compare the drawings with a partner. Call on some pupils to show their drawings to the class. Ask the class *How many (circles) has it got?* (*It's got six circles.*)

Mini project

12 **Find shapes in your classroom.**

- Allow pupils some time to roam freely around the classroom to find shapes. These could be a rectangular board, square windows, round clocks, etc. Ask them to keep a list (using pictures rather than words) of the things they find. To expand the activity, take the class to the garden and look for shapes in nature.

10 2:12 Listen and point.
Then say.

1 circle

2 triangle

3 square

4 rectangle

5 It's a face.

11 Count and write.

1 ___ circles

2 ___ triangle
___ squares
___ rectangles

3 ___ triangles
___ squares
___ rectangle
___ circle

12 Find shapes in your classroom.

Lesson 6   circle, rectangle, square, triangle. *Features. Numbers. I've got a (triangle). It's a (nose).*   33

Ending the lesson

- Draw the four shapes on the board. Write a number below each shape. You may wish to add a big and a small (circle) or colour them if possible. Ask questions about the shapes. Ask *What's (green)? What's number (4)? What colour is the (square)?*

OPTIONAL ACTIVITIES

Coloured shapes
Hand out different coloured shapes to different pupils. Pupils say what they've got: *I've got a big (circle)* or *I've got a (red) triangle*, etc.

Team game
Play Name the shape see p. 25.

Lesson 7

Lesson aims
To review the unit language with a game

Recycled language
Colours, Features, Shapes. He's got (big) (eyes).
It's a (nose).

Receptive language
Touch your ... Point to a ...

Materials
Audio CD; Flashcards (Face); spinners; Word cards
(Numbers); blank paper for each pupil; Worksheet 4,
cut out shapes

Starting the lesson

- Draw a face on the board with the facial features in
  various sizes. Call on volunteers to label the picture
  with *a long nose, small eyes*, etc.

PB page 34

  Listen and point. Then play.

- Focus on the six children on the game board. Describe
  one of the children. Say *She's got long hair.* Pupils find
  the child and say one more sentence to describe the
  same child. (*She's got brown hair.*) Continue with
  other pictures.
- Ask questions about the shapes on the board. *What
  colour's the circle? (It's red.)* Now point to each of the
  features and ask *What's this? It's (a nose).*
- Divide the class into small groups and give each group
  a spinner. Explain (L1) the rules of the game. Pupils
  begin at START and move around the board following
  the arrows. Pupils say the word when they land on a
  part of the face (*It's an ear*) or a shape (*It's a (blue)
  triangle*). They create a sentence describing the boys/
  girls when they land on a picture of a child (*He's/
  She's got short hair*). Pupils move back one square
  for incorrect answers. The first pupil to land in the
  FINISH square wins the game.
- Play recording CD2:14 to give pupils an idea of the
  language they'll need. They then play the game in
  groups.

A 6!   **2:14**
    1, 2, 3, 4, 5, 6.
    Mmmm ... It's a nose.
B That's right.
A Your turn!
B 2!
    1, 2.
    She's got long hair.
A My turn!

Practice

- Give each pupil a blank sheet of paper. Pupils draw
  his/her favourite cartoon character or create a
  creature. Pupils then label the face and body parts
  in the drawings (e.g. *four arms*). Stronger pupils may
  write complete sentences below the drawings.

14 **Listen and do.**

- Play a quick miming game with the actions from
  Unit 3. Finish by saying *Touch your eyes.*
- If you have some large shapes from the previous
  lesson, stick them around the room. Say *Point to a
  circle.* Pupils continue with the other shapes.
- Play CD 2:15 and pupils do the actions as instructed.
  Play the CD again and make some intentional
  mistakes (e.g. you touch your eyes instead of your
  nose). Pupils clap when you do the action correctly
  and stamp his/her feet when you make a mistake.

Touch your eyes.   **2:15**
Touch your nose.
Touch your face.
Touch your ears.
Touch your hair.
Touch your mouth.

Point to a triangle.
Point to a square.
Point to a circle.
Point to a rectangle.

Practice

- Pupils can now complete Worksheet 4.

1 Say and draw. Then circle and write.

- Pupils choose facial features for the faces and describe
  them to a partner. They choose one of the drawings
  and circle *He's* or *She's* and fill in the blank with
  correct information to complete the sentences.

Pupils find pictures of objects with shapes (e.g.
houses, food, things inside the house). Pupils make
a collage at home and bring it to the next class.
Invite pupils to the board to share their collages.
Choose some of the pupils' pictures and ask the
number of shapes in each. *Ask How many (circles)?*

Pupils can now go online to Tropical Island and
find the chair that Pippin is holding on the Pupil's
Book page. It is next to the desk in the reception
area of the prison. Once pupils click on the chair
they are taken to a supplementary language game
based on the vocabulary in this unit.

13 2:14 🎲 **Listen and point. Then play.**

It's a nose.

She's got long hair.

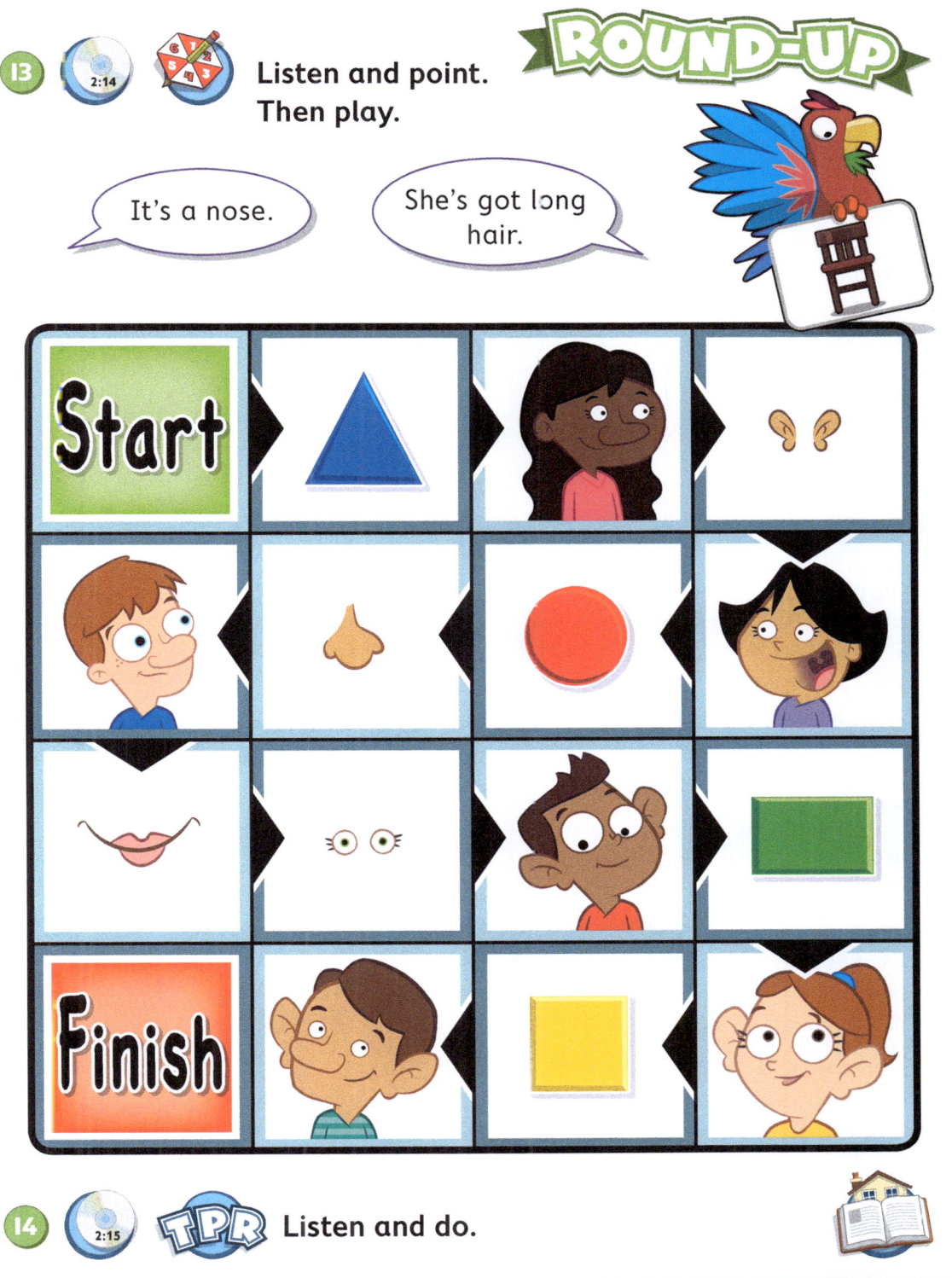

14 2:15 **TPR** **Listen and do.**

34 **Lesson 7** *Colours. Features. Shapes. He's got (big) (eyes). It's a (nose). (Touch your…) (Point to a…)*

Ending the lesson

- Put the flashcards (face) on a pile on a table next to the word cards (numbers 1–5). Draw a large face on the board. Invite a pupil to choose one flashcard and one number card. They draw the number of facial features indicated on the cards (e.g. if a pupil chooses a number 3 and the eyes flashcard, they draw three eyes on the face).

4

Lesson 8

Lesson aims
To personalise the unit language; to provide an opportunity for self-evaluation

Values
Being kind

Recycled language
big, long, short, small, Colours, Features. He's/She's got (green) (eyes).

Materials
Audio CD; Unit 4 Stickers; pictures of cartoon characters; paper to make Project book; DVD; Evaluation sheet 4

Starting the lesson

- Draw a picture on the board focusing on the shapes learnt in this unit. It could be a robot, teddy bear or snowman. Call volunteers to the board and say *Point to the (triangle)*. Ask *How many (circles) has it got?*

PB page 35

15 **Listen, stick, then trace.**

- Pupils point to the appropriate label as you read the words out loud.
- Pupils look at the pictures and find the matching stickers at the back of the Pupil's Book. Play CD2:16. Pupils listen and stick the stickers of each facial feature in place as they are mentioned in the recording. Alternatively, pupils work in pairs, calling out the facial features and sticking the stickers. Finally, they trace over the words.

1 He's got short hair.	**2:16**
2 He's got green eyes.	
3 He's got big ears.	
4 He's got a small nose.	
5 He's got a small mouth.	

16 **Draw a friend. Then write.**

- Pupils draw a picture of a friend in the frame. They then complete the sentences. Invite pupils to the board to share his/her artwork with the class and read out the sentences.

Values

- Talk to pupils (L1) about ways of describing people that are polite and kind and those that are impolite or unkind. Remind pupils that it can hurt people's feelings if friends or strangers laugh about their appearance.

Game

- Stick up four pictures around the classroom, of cartoon characters that pupils are familiar with (two male and two female). Say a sentence about one of the pictures, e.g. *He's got big eyes.* Pupils run to the picture that matches that description. Encourage stronger pupils to make up his/her own sentences to say to the class.

AB page 31

13 **Read. Then look and write.**

- Pupils study the cartoons of the children. They then read the sentences and decide which child each sentence is describing. Pupils write the correct word from the word bank in the gap to complete the sentences.

14 **Find and stick.**

- Pupils find the Unit 4 sticker in the back of his/her Pupil's Book and stick the speech bubble sticker in the correct place to complete the picture. Pupils read the sentences on the sticker to a partner and decide which character each sentence describes.
- Pupils read the three sentences in the Look! Box and tick the ones they can understand and use correctly.
- Explain (L1) that pupils should colour in the stars at the bottom of the page to correspond with how well they think they completed the unit.

AB page 61

- Pupils colour the pictures (my face) in the Picture Dictionary. They then play a game in pairs, taking turns to say a word while his/her partner points to the correct picture
- Choose one of the words in your own PB book and write an X over it, or cover it with a small square of paper. Pupils guess which word it is. Elicit *Is it a (nose)?*

Practice

- Help pupils to make an 8-page booklet as an end of unit project. They write the title *My Unit 4 Project Book* on the cover and draw pictures on each page, of parts of the face or of different people. Pupils write captions below each drawing (e.g. *He's/She's got big eyes*).

 Now watch the DVD.

Evaluation

You can check your pupils' progress using Evaluation sheet 4. See also Teacher's notes p. 176.

Pupils can now go online to Tropical Island and enjoy the fun and games.

15   **Listen, stick, then trace.**

 I CAN DO IT!

He's got …

1

green _eyes_.

short _hair_.

2

4

3

5

big _ears_.

a small _nose_.

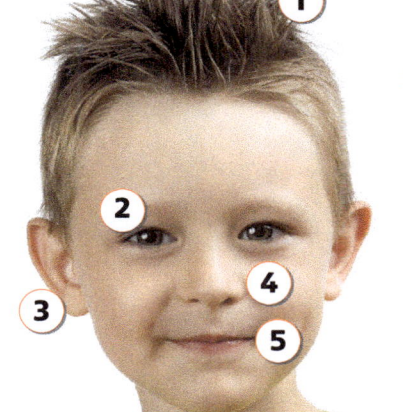

a small _mouth_.

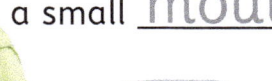 **Stick**

16  **Draw a friend. Then write.**

This is my friend.

He's/She's got _____ eyes

and _____ hair.

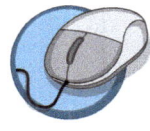 **Now go to Tropical Island.**

Lesson 8   *big, long, short, small. Colours. Features. He's/She's got (green) (eyes).*   **35**

Ending the lesson

- Divide the class into two teams. Call out categories such as face, toys, family, colours and numbers. Team 1 says a word from the category, then Team 2 says another word. They go back and forth until they've run out of words to say. The team that said the last word wins a point.

OPTIONAL ACTIVITIES
Flashcard game
Play Name it see p. 22.
Team game
Play Unscramble see p. 24.

5 Animals

Lesson 1

Lesson aims
To present and practise new vocabulary

Target language
animals, cow, duck, goat, horse, sheep

Recycled language
hen

Receptive language
black, grey, white

Materials
Audio CD; Flashcards (Animals); small pieces of paper and coins

Optional materials
Flashcards (Animals)

Starting the lesson

- Ask pupils to recall what they've learnt so far. Name different categories (e.g. colours, numbers, family, parts of the body and face) and ask them to call out words they know that belong to these categories.

PB pages 36–37

- Remind pupils (L1) of the Quest so far. Where did we last see Lindy and Joe? (They were at a beach party.) Who's now with Lindy and Joe? (Pippin and Grandad). Where are the characters going? (to Princess Emily's castle).
- Ask questions about the main illustration. Remind pupils of the word *hen* and ask *How many (hens)? (3)* Ask pupils what they think is happening in the main illustration. Explain that the farmer is giving Grandad and the children a horse. Ask why they think the farmer is doing this (to help them get to the castle faster).

Presentation

- Give pupils a few minutes to look through Unit 5 and ask what they think they will learn (about animals). Indicate the farm on PB pp. 36–37 and say *This is a farm.* Point to the farmer and say *He's a farmer.*
- Stick the flashcards (animals) on the board. Point to each in turn and say the name of the animal. Now say the animals and pupils find them in their books.

 Listen and say.

- Point to the animals at the bottom of the page and ask for each *What's this?* Play CD2:17. Pupils listen, point to the animals and repeat the words. Then pupils say the missing words in each line until at

the end they are saying all the words. Each word is associated with a sound to indicate when the pupil should say the word. The association of word and sound will also help them to memorise the words. Encourage them to use the pictures at the bottom of PB p. 36 for reference.

> cow ★ horse ★ goat ★ hen ★ sheep ★ duck ★   **2:17**
>
> **Listen and say the missing words.**
> cow, horse, goat, hen, sheep, ★
> cow, horse, goat, hen, ★ ★
> cow, horse, goat, ★ ★ ★
> cow, horse, ★ ★ ★ ★
> cow, ★ ★ ★ ★ ★
> ★ ★ ★ ★ ★ ★

Game

- Pupils use small squares of paper to cover three of the animals in Activity 1. Call out the words in turn. When you say an animal that a pupil covered, they write an X on the paper. A pupil wins when all three animals they covered have been said.

AB page 32

1 What's missing? Write. Then draw and say.

- Pupils read the words in the word bank, find the corresponding animals in the picture and write the words in the boxes next to the correct numbers. They then decide which animal is missing from the picture (a sheep). Pupils draw the sheep into the picture. In pairs, they take turns to say an animal word while his/her partner points to the animal in the picture.

Ending the lesson

- Invite pupils to the board to mime the animals learned in this lesson. If they have difficulty guessing, they can add animal sounds.

OPTIONAL ACTIVITIES

Farm sounds
Show each pupil different animal flashcards (*goat, hen, cow,* etc). Call out the word *cow*. All pupils shown the cow flashcard make a moo sound. Continue with the other animals, encouraging pupils to use the correct sound for each animal. Now tell pupils to imagine they are on a farm. They are all lost and must find the other animals but they aren't allowed to speak; they can only make their animal's sound (e.g. moooo!). Pupils form a chain with the other members of his/her animal group. After all the pupils have found their group, ask them to shout out which animal they are.

Flashcard game
Play Basketball see p. 22, with animal noises.

NOTES

Pairwork

- Divide the class into pairs. One pupil covers an animal with a coin or piece of paper and the other tries to guess which is covered. Pupils then switch roles.

2 Listen and ✓.

- Play CD2:18 and pupils write a tick in the box next to the words as they are mentioned. Play the recording again and pupils join in with the animal noises.

J = JOE L = LINDY P = PIPPIN F = FARMER   **2:18**
G = GRANDAD

J Lindy! It's a farm.
L Look at the animals.
J Look Lindy! It's a cow. It's black and white.
L And look! It's a goat.
J It's a duck.
L Look at the hen.
J Awww, a lovely sheep!!
P What's this?
L It's a grey horse.
F This is MY horse. Here you are. It's for you.
G Oh, thank you.
P Giddiyup! Yippeeeee!

Lesson 2

Lesson aims
To revise the Lesson 1 vocabulary with a chant; to present the new structure

Target language
black, grey, white. Is it a (cow)? Is it (big)? It's (small).

Recycled language
Animals, Colours. It's a (duck).

Materials
Audio CD; Flashcards (Animals); Word cards (Animals)

Optional materials
Paper to draw a farm scene; magazine cut outs of farm animals

Starting the lesson

- Stick the flashcards (animals) in various places around the classroom. Say *Point to the duck.* Continue with the other animals.

PB pages 36–37

Presentation

- Show the flashcard of the hen. Ask *Is it (brown)? (Yes) Is it big? (No, it's small.) Is it a duck? (No, it's a hen.)* Continue with other animals.
- Say the words *black, grey* and *white* several times and ask pupils to repeat. Ask pupils to find things in the room that are black, white and grey. Ask them to find animals with these colours on PB pp. 36–37.

3  **Listen and chant.**

- Play CD2:19. Pause before the answers are given so pupils can answer. Play the chant again and pupils chant along. You might like to stick the flashcards (animals) on the board, and write the colour words and *big* and *small*. Point to them as they are mentioned in the chant, to help pupils say the right words.

Practice

- Give each pupil one of the animals from the chant. Play the chant and ask pupils to stand up when his/her animal is mentioned and make the appropriate animal noise.

L = LINDY J = JOE P = PIPPIN C = CHORUS	2:19

L   What's this? *[neigh]*
J   Is it a sheep?
L   No, it's a horse.
J   Is it white?
L   No, it's grey.
J   Is it small?
L   No, it's big!
P   What's this? *[quack]*
L   Is it a hen?
P   No, it's a duck!
L   Is it big?
P   No, it's small.
L   Is it red?
P   No, it's white.
J   What's this? *[moo]*
P   Is it a goat?
J   No, it's a cow.
P   Is it small?
J   No, it's big.
P   Is it yellow?
J   No, it's black and white.
C   What's this? *[baa]*
    Is it a sheep? Yes!
    Neigh, quack, moo, baa! (x 4)

3 🎵 2:19 🪘 Listen and chant.

horse ☐

hen ☐

4 💿 2:20 ✏️ Listen and number.

Lesson 2   black, grey, white. Is it a (cow)? Is it (big)? It's (small). no, yes, Animals, Colours. It's a (duck).   **37**

---

4  **Listen and number.**

- Play CD2:20. Pupils listen to the questions and number the corresponding animal at the bottom of the page.

> 1 Is it black? Yes.   **2:20**
>   Is it big? No. It's small.
>   Is it a hen? Yes! It's a hen.
> 2 Is it white? No. It's brown.
>   Is it big? Yes!
>   Is it a cow? Yes. It's a cow.
> 3 Is it grey? No. It's white.
>   Is it big? Yes.
>   Is it a horse? Yes! It's a horse!
> 4 Is it yellow? Yes.
>   Is it big? No. It's small.
>   Is it a duck? Yes! It's a duck!

 Quest sticker and song

- Ask pupils (L1) to recall which of Princess Emily's things they found in the first four units (the present, the photo, the key and the sunglasses). Explain that they are now going to find the fifth Quest item. Ask them to look at the main illustration and guess what the item might be. Then play the Quest song CD2:21 so pupils learn the name of the Quest item (a duck).

> Stand up, jump up, come on a quest,   **2:21**
> Come on a quest today.
> Turn around, sit down, come on a quest,
> Look for a duck today.
> A treasure chest, a present, a photo, a key,
> sunglasses and ★ a duck …
> Find a duck today!

- Ask pupils to find the rubber duck sticker at the back of the Pupil's Book and stick it over the grey image of the rubber duck in the pond in the main illustration. Play the recording again and pupils sing along.

AB page 33

2 **Colour. Then say.**

- Pupils colour the animals any colour they wish. They then play a game in pairs. One pupil chooses an animal and describes its colour (*It's yellow*). His/her partner tries to guess the animal (*Is it big? Is it a duck?*)

3 **Look at Activity 2. Then read and write Yes or No.**

- Pupils look at the partial pictures of the animals, then find the animals in Activity 2 that correspond with the partial pictures. Pupils read the questions and write *Yes* or *No*.

Ending the lesson

- Assign each pupil an animal name. Now hold up the animal word cards one by one. Pupils with that animal stand up and make the animal's noise. Continue until you've mentioned all animals.

OPTIONAL ACTIVITIES
Farm scene
In groups, pupils draw a farm scene with a barn, trees, etc. Pupils draw or stick magazine cut outs of farm animals in the scene. Pupils label it *My farm*.
Team Game
Play Reading race see p. 25.

NOTES

5

103

Lesson 3

Lesson aims
To extend the unit vocabulary set; to practise the vocabulary with a song

Target language
cat, dog, fat, thin. It's got (four) (legs).

Recycled language
Animals, Body parts, Colours, Numbers

Materials
Audio CD; Flashcards (Animals)

Starting the lesson

- Call pupils to the board to mime an animal. Stick the flashcards (animals) on the board as each animal is guessed. Then describe one of the animals using *It's big/small. It's (yellow)*, and pupils guess the animal.

PB page 38

Presentation

- Ask pupils which animals they can see in the illustration. Say sentences about the animals (e.g. *It's brown*). Pupils name all the animals which are brown. Do the same with two legs, four legs and different colours.
- Teach the words *dog* and *cat* using the illustration in the book, or by miming and making animal sounds. Then teach *fat* and *thin* by drawing examples on the board using animals or objects.
- Show the horse flashcard and ask *How many legs?* Say *It's got four legs*. Stress the word *It's* when you do so. Do the same with the other animals.

5 Listen and find. Then sing.

- Play CD2:22. Pupils listen and find the animals in the picture that are being described. Play the recording again and pupils sing along. You could also play the karaoke version of the song CD3:46.

MX = MAX   M = MAISIE   B = BOTH   **2:22**

MX I'm Max.
M   And I'm Maisie.
B   We're animal crazy.
M   What's this? What's this?
       It's small and grey. It's got four legs.
MX It's a cat.
MX I'm Max.
M   And I'm Maisie.
B   We're animal crazy.
MX What's this? What's this?
       It's thin and brown It's got four legs.
M   It's a dog.
MX I'm Max.

M   And I'm Maisie.
B   We're animal crazy.
MX What's this? What's this?
       It's small and white. It's got two legs.
M   It's a duck.
MX I'm Max.
M   And I'm Maisie.
B   We're animal crazy.
M   What's this? What's this?
       It's fat and green. It's got four legs.
MX It's a frog.
MX I'm Max.
M   And I'm Maisie.
B   We're animal crazy.

---

6 Listen. Then play.

- Explain (L1) that pupils are going to play a guessing game in pairs. One pupil describes an animal at the bottom of the page and his/her partner guesses which animal it is. Play CD2:23 to give pupils an idea of the language they'll need. They then play the game.

A   It's thin. It's brown. It's got four legs.   **2:23**
B   It's a cat!

AB page 34

4 Look and write. Then listen and colour.

- Pupils write the names of the animals below the pictures. Play CD2:24. Pupils listen and colour the animals.

---

1 It's big and brown. It's got four legs. It's got   **2:24**
   small ears. It's a horse.
2 It's thin and grey. It's got four legs. It's got a
   small nose. It's a cat.
3 It's fat. It's green and brown. It's got two legs.
   It's a duck.
4 It's small and green. It's got four legs. It's got a
   big mouth. It's a frog.

---

5 Read. Then look and write.

- Pupils read the sentences about the animals. They then find the animal each sentence describes and write its name in the gap.

Pupils can now go online to Tropical Island and find the silver bucket that Pippin is holding on the Pupil's Book page. It is next to the barn door, between the hay and the animal wash. Once pupils click on the silver bucket they are taken to a supplementary language game based on the vocabulary in this unit.

5  **Listen and find. Then sing.**

6 **Listen. Then play.**

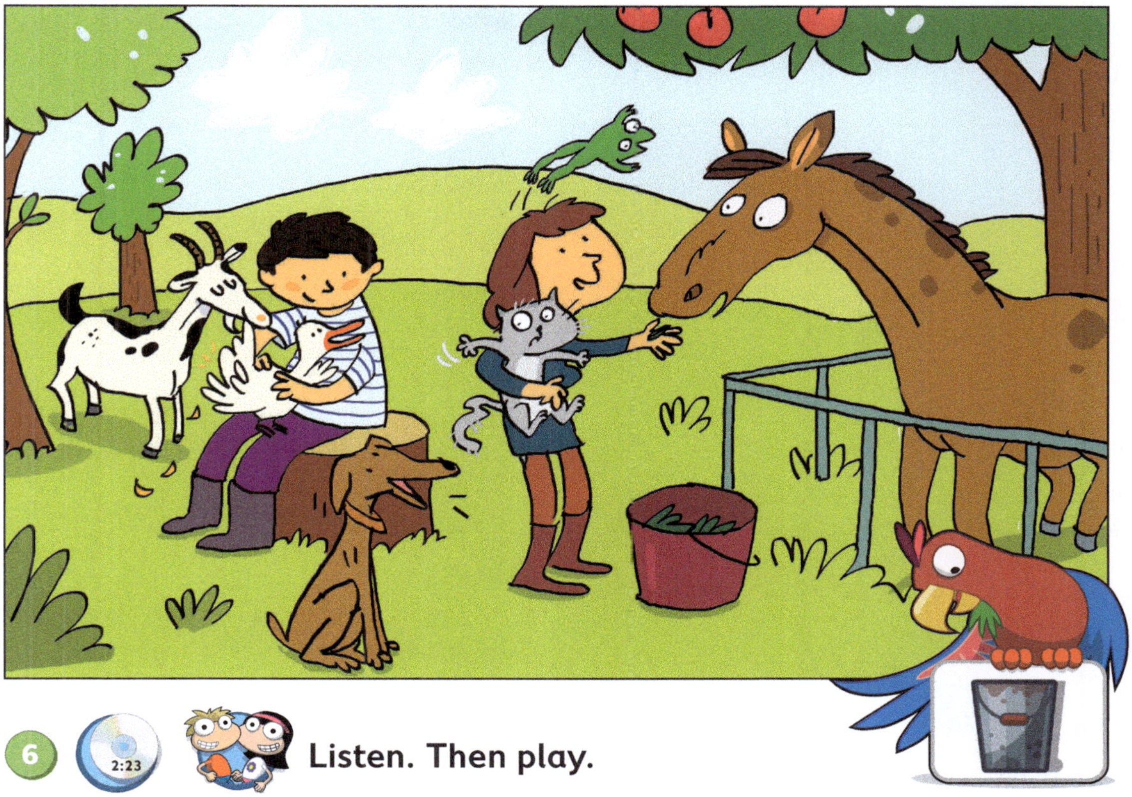

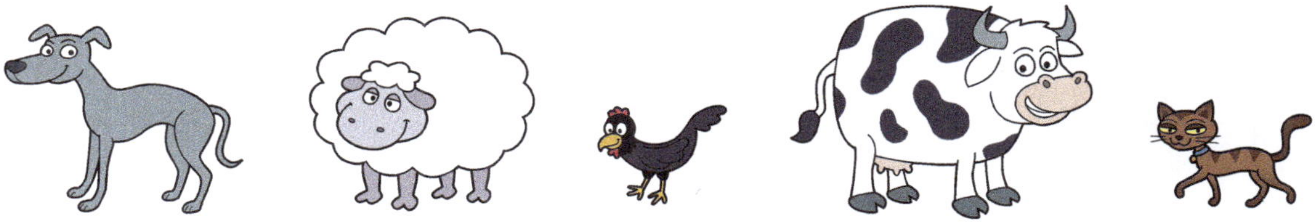

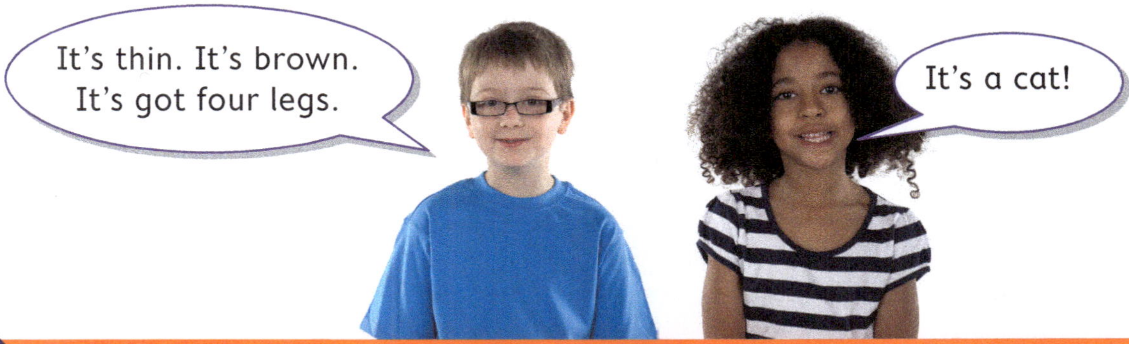

> It's thin. It's brown.
> It's got four legs.

> It's a cat!

Ending the lesson

- Play the recording of the song CD2:22. Write the words *frog*, *cat*, *dog* and *duck* on the board and ask pupils to number them in the order they're mentioned in the song. You could also divide the class into two groups. One group sings while the other group mimes the correct animal for each verse.

OPTIONAL ACTIVITIES
Team game
Play Yes or no? see p. 25.
Flashcard game
Play Pass the flashcards see p. 22.

Lesson 4

> **Lesson aims**
> To develop literacy skills; phonics: /aʊ/ /ɔː/
>
> **Target language**
> crown, torch
>
> **Recycled language**
> yes, no, Animals. Is it a (cow)? Is it (big)? It's got (four) (legs).
>
> **Materials**
> Audio CD; Poster 2; Flashcards (Animals); four small squares of paper for each pupil; Sounds Fun notebooks

Starting the lesson

- Give four pupils a word written on a piece of paper: *frog, dog, duck* and *cat.* Point to a pupil and the rest of the class mimes that animal. Then play the song CD2:22 from Lesson 3. Pupils point to the correct word when that animal is mentioned.

PB page 39

7 Play the game. Ask and answer.

- Play a game of Bingo. Pupils choose four animals on the Bingo game board and write an X over his/her chosen animals. Now give each pupil four small squares of paper. Describe an animal on the game board (e.g. *It's big. It's grey. It's got four legs.)* Pupils guess the animal you've described. (*Is it a horse?*) If you say *yes,* pupils cover that animal with a small square of paper. The winner is the first pupil to cover all the animals with a cross over them.

Presentation

- Review the phonics sounds from the previous units. Draw a boat on the board, label it and ask which animal's got the same sound *(goat).* Write the word *goat* below *boat.* Continue with *hen/pen, feet/sheep, bus/duck, dad/cat, doll/frog/dog.* Ask pupils to think of other words with the same sounds and continue writing them on the board below the correct pictures.

8 Listen and say.

- Play CD2:25. Pause after the first two lines. Ask pupils which sounds they can hear (/aʊ/ and /ɔː/). Play the first two lines again and pupils repeat.
- Teach the word *crown* and remind pupils of the words *cow* and *brown* by drawing simple pictures on the board or showing homemade flashcards. Say the words several times and pupils repeat. Ask which sound pupils can hear *(aʊ/).* Ask pupils which other words they know with these sounds *(house, mouth).*

> ow, ow, or, or,   **2:25**
> ow, or, ow, or, ow, or
> ow ★
> Brown. ★ Cow. ★ Brown cow. ★ Crown. ★
> A brown cow with a crown. ★
> or ★
> Short. ★ Horse. ★ Short horse. ★ Torch. ★
> A short horse with a torch. ★
> A brown cow with a crown. ★
> A short horse with a torch. ★

- Now say the words *short* and *horse.* Teach the word *torch* and ask which sounds pupils can hear (/ɔː/) and which other words they know with the same sound *(four).*
- Now play the recording from the beginning to the end. Pupils listen and repeat the words. Play the recording again so pupils are comfortable with these new sounds. Then pupils read the rhymes to a partner.

Practice

Pupils add the /aʊ/ and /ɔː/ sounds to his/her Sounds Fun notebooks. Pupils draw pictures of words containing these sounds and label them. Ask pupils to add any new words from this unit to the previously learned sounds (/iː/ sheep; /əʊ/ goat; /æ/ cat; /ʌ/ duck; /ɒ/ dog).

AB page 35

6 Listen and match. Then trace.

- Play CD2:26. Pupils listen and match the words with the /aʊ/ sound to the *cow* and the words with the /ɔː/ sound to the *horse.* They then trace the words below the pictures.

> ow   **2:26**
> or
> Cow, crown, house
> Horse, four, torch

7 Listen and circle two words.

- Play CD2:27. Pupils listen and circle two words containing the same sounds. Pupils check his/her answers in pairs.

> 1 Eye, torch, arm, four   **2:27**
> 2 Jump, brown, mouth, orange
> 3 Nose, three, clothes, dad
> 4 Crown, mum, bug, head

- Use Poster 2 see p. 21.

SKILLS

7  **Play the game.**
Ask and answer.

It's small. It's white.
It's got two legs.

Is it a duck?

Yes!

8 2:25 **Listen and say.**

SOUNDS FUN!

A br**ow**n c**ow** with a cr**ow**n.

A sh**or**t h**or**se with a t**or**ch.

Lesson 4 crown, torch, *yes, no. Animals. Is it a (cow)? Is it (big)? It's got (four) (legs).*Sounds: /aʊ/ /ɔː/ **39**

Ending the lesson

- Stick the following flashcards on the board in a horizontal row: a horse, a hen, a duck, a cow and sheep. Pupils write words with the same sound below each flashcard. You could divide the class into teams and award points for correct answers.

OPTIONAL ACTIVITIES
TPR game
Play Grab it see p. 24.
Flashcard game
Play Same sounds see p. 23.

Lesson 5

Lesson aims
To consolidate the unit language with a story

Target language
bad, wings

Recycled language
Animals, cow, duck, parrot, sheep. Is it a ...? It's got ...

Materials
Audio CD; Flashcards (Animals); Unit 5 Story cards; props for acting out the story, e.g. a map, a box, a stick

Starting the lesson

- Choose two to four animals of different colours, numbers of legs, sizes, etc. and write the animal words or stick the flashcards of these animals on the board. Write sentences about the animals on strips of paper (e.g. *It's got two legs*). Be sure that the sentences are true about only one of the animals, otherwise write the same sentence more than once. Show the sentences in turn and pupils stick them below the correct animal.
- Ask questions (L1) about the story from Unit 4. Who were the main characters in the story? (Princess Emily and two police officers). Who did the princess want the police officers to find? (Pippin). Is Princess Emily happy at the end of the story? (No, she's sad.)

PB page 40

- Before pupils open their books, show the story cards for Unit 5 in turn and ask the questions from the 'Before reading the story' section written on the back of each card.
- Teach the word *wings* using mime, and *bad* using a thumbs down gesture and L1 translation.

9 **Listen and read. Then act.**

- Play the recording of the story CD2:28 and pupils follow along in their books. Play the recording again, pausing after each line for pupils to repeat.
- Call on pupils to read the story. Stop after each frame and check pupils' understanding of the story by asking the questions from the 'After reading the story' section written on the back of each story card. Be sure that pupils understand that Pippin was imitating different animals to play a trick on Lindy and Joe.
- After pupils have a clear understanding of the story, invite three pupils to the board to act it out, plus an extra pupil to be a tree for Pippin to hide behind. You may wish to play the recording and pause after each line for pupils to repeat. Alternatively, you could have other pupils read the lines while the pupils act it out or have them say the lines from memory. When acting out, encourage tone of voice and expressions to match those in the pictures. Use props that you've brought to class if you wish.
- Write the transcript of the story inside speech bubbles on the board in random order. Call on pupils to stick the appropriate story card below each speech bubble.

AB page 36

8 **Listen and write. Then draw.**

- Pupils listen to the animal noises on CD2:29 and write the name of the animal in the correct speech bubble. They then draw the correct animal in the boxes.

> 1 Quack.   **2:29**
> 2 Moo.
> 3 Baa.
> 4 Squawk.

9 **Read and match.**

- Pupils read the sentences and match them to the correct animal. Pupils check his/her answers by reading the sentences to a partner, who then says the name of the animal. *It's got wings. It's got big eyes. (It's a parrot.)*

9 Listen and read. Then act. STORY

1
Look! What is it?
It's a **big** animal!
2
Is it a duck?
Quack!
No, it's got four legs.
3
Moo!
Is it a cow?
No. It's got wings.
4
Baa!
Is it a sheep? What is it?
It's a . . .
5
AWK!
parrot!
6
I'm a sheep!
You're a **bad**, **bad** parrot!

40 Lesson 5 *bad, wings, animal, cow, duck, parrot, sheep. Is it a...? It's got...*

Ending the lesson

- Divide the class into six groups and give each group a story card. Read the story from the Pupil's Book. Pupils stand up when you read the lines from their cards. Then call pupils to the board with his/her cards and challenge them to tell the story from memory.

OPTIONAL ACTIVITIES

TPR game

Play Guess the object see p. 24.

Flashcard game

Play Guess the card see p. 22.

5

Lesson 6

Lesson aims
To integrate other areas of the curriculum into the English class; to develop the cross-curricular topic through a short project

Cross-Curricular focus
Science – Nocturnal and diurnal animals

Target language
awake, bat, day, fox, night, owl. It's awake (in the day).

Materials
Audio CD; Flashcards (Animals); pictures of animals that are awake during the day and night

Starting the lesson

- Begin the lesson by playing a game Teacher Says (similar to Simon Says). Use instructions like *touch your (eyes), point to something (red), sit down, clap your hands*, etc. Pupils only follow the instructions if they are preceded by *Teacher says*.

PB page 41

Presentation

- Ask pupils (L1) which animals they have seen or heard at night. Suggest bats, foxes and owls. Show some animal pictures you've brought to class. Sort the animals into groups of day (diurnal) animals and night (nocturnal) animals by drawing a sun and a moon on the board and sticking the pictures below. You can also use flashcards of the animals from this unit.

10 🌐 **Listen and point. Then say.**

- Point to the sun in the first group of pictures and say *It's day*. Ask which animals pupils can see *(a cow, a horse* and *a duck)*. Explain (L1) that these animals are awake during the day. Now point to the moon and say *It's night*. Ask which animals they can see. Teach *bat, owl* and *fox*. Explain (L1) that these animals are awake at night.
- Play CD2:30. Pupils point to the animals as they are mentioned. They then say the new animal names to a partner and the partner points at the animal pictures.

1 It's a cow. It's awake in the day.　　**2:30**
2 It's a horse. It's awake in the day.
3 It's a duck. It's awake in the day.
4 It's a bat. It's awake at night.
5 It's a fox. It's awake at night.
6 It's an owl. It's awake at night.

- Ask pupils why they think nocturnal animals might survive better if they are active at night rather than during the day. Look at pictures of the nocturnal animals you've brought to class and ask (L1) which features they have in common (large eyes/ears, dark fur, etc). Ask why these features help them to stay active at night. Ask why they think a bat has got such large ears. Why does the owl have such large eyes?

11 **Read and find. Then write.**

- Point to the photo of the fox. Say *It's awake at night*. Pupils read the sentences at the bottom of the page, then match them to the correct photos by writing the animal name next to the sentences.

AB page 37

10 **Match. Then trace and say.**

- Pupils match the animal words to the corresponding pictures. They then trace the words and say them to a partner, who points to the correct animal.

11 🌐 **Draw animals from Activity 10. Then listen and check.**

- Pupils draw the animals from Activity 10 in the day or night scene. Then play CD2:31 so pupils can check his/her answers.

The cow is awake in the day.　　**2:31**
The horse is awake in the day.
The duck is awake in the day.
The bat is awake at night.
The fox is awake at night.
The owl is awake at night.

Mini project

12 **Choose an animal. Then describe it.**

- Divide the class into pairs. Pupils choose two animals to describe and compare (e.g. a bat and a fox or a horse and a duck). Pupils make a chart to identify the differences. Use sentences like *It's got two feet/It's got four feet. It's black/It's red and white.* They could also research what their two animals eat, where they live, how they care for their young, etc. and include pictures to represent the information they find out.

10 2:30 **Listen and point. Then say.**

1 cow

4 bat

2 horse

3 duck

5 fox

6 owl

11 **Read and find. Then write.**

What is it?

1
It's red and white.
It's awake at night.
It's a _____.

2
It's got two legs and a big head.
It's awake at night.
It's an _____.

3
It's black and white.
It's awake in the day.
It's a _____.

4
It's got two legs.
It's awake in the day.
It's a _____.

12 **Choose an animal. Then describe it.**

Lesson 6   awake, bat, day, fox, night, owl. It's awake (in the day). *Animals, Body parts, Colours*   41

Ending the lesson

• Mime an animal and pupils guess *Is it a (bat)?* If a pupil guesses correctly, it's his/her turn to mime an animal.

Lesson 7

Lesson aims
To review the unit language with a game

Values
Caring for animals

Recycled language
big, fat, no, small, thin, yes, Animals, Colours. Is it a (hen)?Is it (brown)? It's ...

Materials
Audio CD; Poster 1; Flashcards (Animals) or toy animals; spinners and counters; Worksheet 5

Starting the lesson

- Use Poster 1 see p.20.
- Hide an animal flashcard behind your back and pupils try to guess what it is by asking *Is it big? Is it brown? Is it a horse?* Pupils play the game in small groups.

PB page 42

13 **Listen. Then play.**

- Explain (L1) the rules of the game. Pupils play the game in pairs, with a spinner per pair and a counter for each pupil. Pupils should keep his/her game board secret. One pupil spins the spinner and moves the counter the correct number of spaces along the path. His/Her partner guesses the animal they landed on by asking questions *(Is it brown? Is it fat? Is it a hen?)*. They can ask as many questions as they want if they don't mention an animal but only one question using an animal word. If they guess correctly, they then have a go. If the partner guesses incorrectly, they lose a turn. When pupils land on a question mark, they choose any animal from the board. Pupils must spin the exact number to finish the game.
- Play CD2:32 to give pupils an idea of the language they'll need. They then play the game in pairs.

A Is it brown?	**2:32**
B Yes.	
A Is it fat?	
B Yes.	
A Is it a hen?	
B Yes! 1! 1.	

Practice

- Pupils draw an animal learned in this unit and colour it. Collect the drawings, then hand them out in mixed order so all pupils have a picture drawn by another pupil. Pupils keep his/her drawing secret and choose a partner. Partners guess the animal by asking questions *(Is it big? Is it white? Is it a duck?)*

14 **Listen and do.**

- Play CD2:33. Pupils repeat the sentences, then mime the animals, making animal noises as they do so.

It's a sheep. Baa. It's a sheep.	**2:33**
It's a horse. Neigh. It's a horse.	
It's a cow. Moo. It's a cow.	
It's a duck. Quack. It's a duck.	

Practice

- Pupils can now complete Worksheet 5.

1 **Read and write. Then draw.**

Pupils read the sentences below each box and write an animal word from the word bank in the gap. They then draw the animal in the box.

2 **Write. Then draw.**

Pupils draw an animal of his/her choice in the box and write sentences about the animal.

Game

- Play *What's in the box?* Bring several toy animals to class. Alternatively, use the animal flashcards. Put a toy animal/flashcard in a box, without pupils seeing it. Ask *What's in the box?* Pupils guess by asking *Is it a (horse)?* When a pupil guesses correctly give them the toy/flashcard. Continue with another toy. When all the toys have been handed out, ask pupils to put them back in the box again one by one, saying the name of each animal as they drop it in the box. Play the game again with family flashcards, shapes or face flashcards.

Values

- Ask pupils (L1) how many of them have visited a farm or have pets at home. Discuss ways that we care for animals. Talk about feeding them regularly, grooming and making sure they have enough water to drink. Discuss ways that we benefit from farm animals or things that we get from animals (e.g. milk, eggs, meat).

> Pupils draw an animal at home and tell someone in their family about it. (*It's a goat. It's got four legs. It's thin. It's grey,* etc.) Ask pupils to bring the drawing to class and keep its identity secret. At the next lesson they play a guessing game with a partner. (*Is it big/red/fat? Is it a horse?*)

13 🔘 2:32 🎯 **Listen. Then play.**

14 🔘 2:33 **TPR** **Listen and do.**

42 | **Lesson 7** | *big, fat, no, small, thin, yes. Animals, Colours. Is it a (hen)? Is it (brown)? It's...*

Ending the lesson

- Do a TPR activity. Call out animal names and pupils mime the animal and make the animal's sound. Pupils continue until you say STOP! Pupils freeze his/her positions. Count to ten. Anyone that moves before you say ten must sit down.

OPTIONAL ACTIVITIES

Chain game
Invite pupils to the board. Begin the game by saying *On my farm there's a duck.* The second pupil says the same sentence and adds another animal.

Team game
Play Stop! see p. 24.

Lesson 8

Lesson aims
To personalise the unit language; to provide an opportunity for self-evaluation

Recycled language
Adjectives, Animals, Body parts, Colours, Numbers. It's a (cow). It's (big). It's got (two) (legs).

Materials
Audio CD; Unit 5 Stickers; paper to make Project book; Evaluation sheet 5

Optional materials
Poster 2

Starting the lesson

- Ask pupil to remember the song from Lesson 3. Challenge them to write down the four animals in the order they are mentioned. Play the song CD2:22 so pupils can check his/her answers (*cat, dog, duck* and *frog*).

PB page 43

15 **Listen, stick, then trace.**

- Pupils point to the appropriate label as you read the words out loud.
- Pupils look at the pictures and find the matching stickers at the back of the Pupil's Book. Play CD2:34. Pupils listen and stick the animal stickers in place as they are mentioned in the recording. Alternatively, pupils work in pairs, calling out the animals and sticking the stickers. Finally, they trace over the words.

1 It's got four legs. It's a sheep.	**2:34**
2 It's big. It's a cow.	
3 It's got long legs. It's a horse.	
4 It's got two legs. It's a hen.	
5 It's white. It's a goat.	
6 It's small. It's a duck.	

16 **Draw a farm animal. Then write.**

- Pupils draw a farm animal in the frame. They could draw the animal in a farm scene. They then complete the sentences about the animal they've drawn by writing the correct words. Invite pupils to the board to share their artwork with the class and read out the sentences.

Game

- Write several sentences on the board as headings. Write *It's got two legs. It's got four legs. It's brown. It's white. It's black. It's big. It's small. It's fat. It's thin.* Divide pupils into groups and give each group a sheet of blank paper. Pupils copy the sentence headings onto the paper and list animals below each heading that they describe. Award points for each animal listed and choose a winning group.

AB page 38

12 **Look and write. Then say.**

- Pupils read the sentences below the horse and the duck and fill in the gaps with words from the word bank.

13 **Find and stick. Then colour.**

- Pupils find the Unit 5 sticker in the back of their Pupil's Book and stick the speech bubble sticker in the correct place to complete the picture. They then colour the duck yellow. Pupils read the sentences on the sticker to a partner.
- Pupils read the three sentences in the Look! Box and tick the ones they can understand and use correctly.
- Explain (L1) that pupils should colour in the stars at the bottom of the page to correspond with how well they think they completed the unit.

AB page 61

- Pupils colour the animal pictures in the Picture Dictionary. They then play a game in pairs, taking turns to say a word while his/her partner points to the correct picture. Stronger pupils may wish to cover the written words below each picture and try writing the words themselves.
- Play a phonics games using the words. Say sounds from previous units and pupils find words from the current unit with the same sound.

Practice

- Help pupils to make an 8-page booklet as an end of unit project. They write the title *My Unit 5 Project Book* on the cover and draw or stick pictures of animals on each page. Pupils write captions below each drawing (e.g. *It's big. It's brown. It's a horse*).

Evaluation

You can check your pupils' progress using Evaluation sheet 5. See also Teacher's notes p. 176.

Pupils can now go online to Tropical Island and enjoy the fun and games.

15 2:34 ✏️ **Listen, stick, then trace.**

1 sheep

2 cow

3 horse

4 hen

5 goat

6 duck

Stick

16 ✏️ **Draw a farm animal. Then write.**

It's _____.

It's got _____ legs.

It's a _____.

Now go to Tropical Island.

Lesson 8   *Adjectives, Animals, Body parts, Colours, Numbers. It's a (cow). It's (big). It's got (two) (legs).*   43

Ending the lesson

- Play a game of memory. Stick two flashcards from each unit on the board, face down. Pupils flip over two cards saying the word as the card is turned over. The aim is to match two cards from the same category (e.g. a duck and a horse/mum and dad). Cards that don't match are flipped over again. After all cards are face up, choose different cards and play again.

OPTIONAL ACTIVITIES
Poster activity
See the notes on Poster 2 on p. 21.
Team game
Play Board game see p. 24.

Lesson I

Lesson aims
To present and practise new vocabulary

Target language
apple, banana, chicken, egg, fish, food, pizza, rice, salad

Materials
Audio CD; Flashcards (Food); Word cards (Food); small squares of paper and coins

Optional materials
Blank paper to make food sequences

Starting the lesson

- Revise all vocabulary learnt so far. Say a word (e.g. *dog*). Pupils say as many words as possible from the same category (e.g. *cat, horse, frog*, etc). Do this as a team game and award points for correct answers.

PB pages 44–45

- Ask pupils (L1) what they remember from the Quest so far. Remind them the characters just passed through a farm and are getting ever closer to the castle. Ask which animal the farmer gave Grandad *(a horse)*.
- Ask questions (L1) about the illustration. Where do pupils think the characters are now? (in a café). Which other characters or things can they see in the picture?

Presentation

- Ask (L1) what pupils think they are going to learn in this unit (food). Ask which food they already know in English. For pupils who have studied the Starter Level, they might remember *fruit, meat, honey*, etc. Write these words on the board.
- Teach the new food words. Show each flashcard in turn, then say the word and stick it on the board. Motion to the flashcards on the board and say *food*.

1 🔵 Listen and say.

- Play CD2:35. Pupils listen, point to the food and repeat the words. Then pupils say the missing words in each line until at the end they are saying all the words. Each word is associated with a sound to indicate when the pupil should say the word. The association of word and sound will also help them to memorise the words. Encourage them to use the pictures at the bottom of PB p. 44 for reference.

apple ★ banana ★ pizza ★ chicken ★ egg ★   **2:35**
fish ★ salad ★ rice ★

Listen and say the missing words.
apple, banana, pizza, chicken, egg, fish, salad, ★
apple, banana, pizza, chicken, egg, fish, ★ ★
apple, banana, pizza, chicken, egg, ★ ★ ★
apple, banana, pizza, chicken, ★ ★ ★ ★
apple, banana, pizza, ★ ★ ★ ★ ★
apple, banana, ★ ★ ★ ★ ★ ★
apple, ★ ★ ★ ★ ★ ★ ★
★ ★ ★ ★ ★ ★ ★ ★

Game

- Pupils use small squares of paper to cover three of the foods in Activity 1. Call out the words in turn. When you say a food that a pupil covered, they write an X on the paper. A pupil wins when all three food items they covered have been said.

Pairwork

- Divide the class into pairs. One pupil covers a food item with a coin or piece of paper and the other tries to guess which is covered. Pupils then switch roles.

Practice

- Mime eating different food. Peel a banana, hold a slice of pizza, eat a chicken leg, etc. Pupils guess the food. They then continue in pairs.
- Pupils take turns reading the labels in pairs. One pupil reads and the other mimes eating the food.
- Write the food words on the board, intentionally 'forgetting' a letter from each word. Pupils correct your mistakes.

AB page 39

1 **Look and write. Then draw and say.**

- Pupils write the food words from the word bank next to the pictures of the foods. They then draw the foods with a tick next to them on the plate. Pupils check their answers with a partner.

Ending the lesson

- Stick the word cards (food) on the board. Hand out the flashcards (food) and pupils stick them next to the corresponding word card.

OPTIONAL ACTIVITIES

Food sequences

Pupils create sequences with drawings of food. Draw several examples on the board. Draw a pizza, an apple, two eggs, and a pizza. Point to each food and pupils say the words in turn. Emphasise the plural form of any words. Invite pupils to the board to complete the sequences by drawing the missing items. Pupils create their own sequences on blank paper.

Flashcard game

Play Mix-matched flashcards see p. 23.

NOTES

---

2 **Listen and ✓.**

- Point to the food items in the main illustration in turn and ask for each *What's this? (banana)*. Play CD2:36 and pupils write a tick box next to the words as they are mentioned. Play the recording again. Pause after each line so pupils can repeat.

> **L = LINDY G = GRANDAD J = JOE P = PIPPIN**   **2:36**
> **W = WAITRESS C = CUSTOMER**
> **L** Look at the food!
>   An egg. Mmm, salad. My favourite.
> **G** Mmmm. Mmmmm. I like fish! And I like rice.
> **J** And I like chicken!
> **P** An apple!
> **J** Oh dear! PIPPIN!!
> **W** Aaaah! A banana!
> **C** Ohhhh! My pizza!

- Focus on the labels next to each food. Encourage pupils to read the labels one by one. Sound out the words slowly and ask pupils to repeat. Pupils point to each label and read it to a partner.

Lesson 2

Lesson aims
To revise the Lesson 1 vocabulary with a chant; to present the new structure

Target language
nuts. I like (bananas).

Recycled language
Food

Materials
Audio CD; Flashcards (Food)

Optional materials
Blank paper; magazine pictures of food, animals and toys

Starting the lesson

- Show the flashcards (food) in turn and ask for each *Is it an (apple)?* Then divide the class into groups and give each a food flashcard. Call out a food, then an action (e.g. *Apples – clap your hands! Bananas – touch your toes*). The group with the corresponding food flashcard does the action.

 **PB pages 44–45**

Presentation

- Teach the sentence *I like (bananas)*. Use body language to emphasise the meaning. Show the flashcards (food) in turn. Say *I like (pizza)*. Pupils who like (pizza) stand up and repeat the sentence.

3 🔵 **Listen and chant.**

- Play CD2:37. Create actions to go with the chant. Mime biting into an apple or peeling a banana, etc. When you hear *I like* make a thumbs up motion and rub your stomach. Play it several times until pupils can chant along.

J = JOE L = LINDY P = PIPPIN	2:37
J, L, P	Food, food, food.
L	Tasty, tasty food.
P	I like apples.
J	I like bananas.
L	I like eggs and salad, too.
J, L, P	Food, food, food.
	Tasty, tasty food.
P	I like pizza.
L	I like rice.
J	I like fish and chicken, too.

Practice

- Stick the flashcards (food) on the board. Invite volunteers to the board. Pupils point to the flashcards of the food they like and say *I like (apples). I like (eggs)*, etc.

4 🔵 **Listen and ✓. Then say.**

- Point to the food items in turn and ask *Is it (rice)?*
- Play CD2:38. Joe is talking about food that he likes. Pupils tick the box next to each food that he likes. Ask pupils which three foods were not mentioned in the recording (eggs, salad and rice).

J = JOE	2:38
J	Mmm. I like bananas.
	Yum. I like chicken.
	Ohh. I like fish.

Pairwork

- Pupils look at the images of the food in Activity 4 and say sentences about the foods they like to a partner. *I like (salad)*.

AB page 40

2 Look and write. Then say.

- Pupils write the correct word from the word bank below each picture to complete the sentence. They then read their sentences to a partner.

3 Read and look. Then circle and say.

- Pupils look at the pictures of the food that Joe likes then circle the words that correspond with the pictures. They then read out the words they've circled to a partner.

Ending the lesson

- Stick the flashcards (food) on the board. Write two food words below each flashcard (one correct, the other incorrect). Call pupils to the board to circle the correct word.

OPTIONAL ACTIVITIES

'I like' drawings

Give each pupil a blank sheet of paper. Pupils draw a picture of themselves in the centre of the page with a happy face. Pupils draw pictures of things they like (these may include colours, animals, toys, etc.) or they could stick on pictures cut from magazines if you have any. Pupils share their drawings with the class, saying *I like pink. I like cats.*

Memory game

Play a chain game. Invite eight pupils to the board and arrange them in a single line. The pupil at the front of the line says *I like (apples).* The second repeats the sentence and adds another word *I like apples and bananas.* The third repeats the first two sentences and adds one more word *I like apples, bananas and chicken.* Continue until you reach the end of the line. You may need to offer assistance throughout the game.

NOTES

Quest sticker and song

- Ask pupils to recall which of Emily's things they found in the first five units (the present, the photo, the key, the sunglasses and the rubber duck). Explain that pupils are now going to find the sixth Quest item. Ask them to look at the main illustration and guess what the item might be. Play the Quest Song CD2:39 so pupils learn the name of the Quest item *(nuts).*

Stand up, jump up, come on a quest,   **2:39**
Come on a quest today.
Turn around, sit down, come on a quest,
Look for nuts today.
A treasure chest, a present, a photo, a key,
sunglasses, a duck and ★ nuts …
Find nuts today!

- Ask pupils to find the bag of nuts sticker at the back of the Pupil's Book. Explain that these are Pippin's favourite treat. Pupils stick the sticker over the grey image of the nuts under the table on the left in the main illustration. Play the recording again and pupils sing along.

6

Lesson 3

Starting the lesson

- Play the recording of the chant CD2:37 from Lesson 2. Pupils mime eating the foods as they're mentioned.

 **PB page 46**

Presentation

- Teach the sentence *I don't like (pizza).* Draw two faces on the board, a happy face and a sad face. Hold up the chicken flashcard and say *I like chicken.* Stick it under the happy face. Now show the pizza flashcard, shake your head and make an unhappy face, and say *I don't like pizza.* Stick it under the sad face.
- Teach *How about you?* and *It's very nice,* in L1 if necessary.

5 **Listen and find. Then sing.**

- Focus on the song illustration in the Pupil's Book. Ask *Where are the children? (in the kitchen).* Ask (L1) what they're making. Which foods can they see? Encourage them to say some food in English (*salad, chicken,* etc.) Ask *How many apples/eggs/bananas?*
- Teach the words *bread* and *cheese* by showing the flashcards. Say the words several times and pupils repeat. Point to the fish and ask *What's this? (It's a fish.)* Pretend that you are holding the fish like the boy in the illustration. Make an unhappy face and say *I don't like fish!*
- Play CD2:40. Pupils listen and find the food in the illustration as they hear the words in the song. Then ask pupils to help you stick the food flashcards on the board in the order they are mentioned in the song. Play the song again and ask pupils to sing along. You could also play the karaoke version of the song CD3:47 for pupils to sing along to.

BOTH	I like food, I like food, I like food. How about you? (x2)	2:40
GIRL	I like cheese and chicken, too. I like bananas, how about you? I like pizza, my favourite dish! But I don't like fish.	
BOTH	I like food, I like food, I like food. How about you? (x2)	
BOY	I like bread and apples, too. I like salad, how about you? I like fish, it's very nice, But I don't like rice!	
BOTH	I like food, I like food, I like food. How about you? (x2)	

6 **Listen and point. Then play.**

- Explain (L1) that pupils are going to play a guessing game in pairs, by saying sentences describing the likes/dislikes of the children in the photos. One pupil says *I like fish.* His/Her partner says the number of the correct photo (Number 1).
- Play CD2:41 to give pupils an idea of the language they'll need. They then play the game in pairs.

BOY	I like fish!	2:41
GIRL	Number 1.	

AB page 41

4 **Listen and draw.**

- Pupils listen to CD2:42 of the children's likes and dislikes. They draw a happy/sad face next to each picture as it's mentioned.

1 I like salad! Mmmh!	2:42
2 I don't like cheese! Yuck!	
3 I like apples. Yum.	
4 I don't like fish.	
5 I don't like bread.	
6 I like eggs. Tasty!	

5 **Find and write. Then say.**

- Pupils follow the maze from each child to the food at the opposite side of the activity. Pupils then complete the sentences using the words from the word bank and read their sentences to a partner.

Pupils can now go online to Tropical Island and find the table that Pippin is holding on the Pupil's Book page. It is immediately to the left of the door inside the pizza restaurant. Once pupils click on the table they are taken to a supplementary language game based on the vocabulary in this unit.

 **Listen and find. Then sing.**

   **Listen and point. Then play.**

 I like fish!

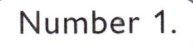 Number 1.

46   **Lesson 3**   bread, cheese. How about you? I don't like (fish). It's very nice. *Food. Numbers. I like (apples).*

Ending the lesson

- Play the song again CD2:40 and encourage pupils to make a 'thumbs up' and rub their tummies, or make a 'thumbs down' and make an unhappy face when they hear *like/don't like*. Now draw a happy and a sad face on the board. Hand out the food flashcards and pupils stick them below the appropriate face according to how they are used in the song.

OPTIONAL ACTIVITIES
Drawing activity
On paper folded in half, pupils draw or stick pictures of food under the headings *I like* and *I dont like*.
Team game
Play Drawing race see p. 24.

Lesson 4

Lesson aims
To develop literacy skills; phonics: /aɪ/

Target language
bike, mice

Recycled language
Food. I don't like (rice). I like (apples).

Materials
Audio CD; Unit 6 Cut outs; Sounds Fun notebooks

Starting the lesson

- Play the recording CD2:40 of the song from Lesson 3. Pupils mime eating the food as they listen.
- Call out colours, food, shapes, animals, etc. Say *I like pink. I don't like dogs.* Pupils stand up and clap if the sentence is true for them and remain seated if it isn't. Call on pupils to take over leading the class.

PB page 47

7 **Play the game (page 77).**

- Pupils cut out the cards from PB p. 77. Say the food in turn and pupils hold up the correct card. Focus on the plates in the photos in the Pupil's Book. Pupils choose four food cards and put them either on the *I like* plate or on the *I don't like* plate. Call out sentences using *I like/I don't like* with food. Say *I like (cheese).* Pupils with the cheese card on the *I like* plate flip over the cheese card. The first pupil to flip over all their cards wins.

Pairwork

- Pupils play a dictation game with the cards. One pupil says *I like (bananas).* Their partner finds the banana card and puts it on the correct plate.

Presentation

- Say some letter sounds learnt in the previous units and pupils say words in Unit 6 containing these sounds. Ask which words have the same sound as *sister* (*fish* and *chicken*), *feet* (*cheese*), *hen* (*egg*) and *dad* (*apple*).

8  **Listen and say.**

- Play CD2:43. Pause after the first two lines. Ask pupils which sound they can hear (/aɪ/). Play the first two lines again and pupils repeat.

---

ai, ai   **2:43**
ai, ai, ai
I. ★ Like. ★ Mice. ★ Bikes. ★
I like mice on bikes. ★
White. ★ Rice. ★ White rice ★
I like mice on bikes with white rice. ★

- Focus on the picture of the mice at the bottom of the page. Indicate the mice and say *Look, two mice!* You may also use this opportunity to teach the word *mouse.* Ask which toy is in the picture (*a bike*). Now ask which food pupils can see (*rice*).
- Now play the recording from the beginning to the end. Pupils listen and repeat the words. Play the recording again so pupils are comfortable with these new sounds. Then pupils read the rhyme to a partner.

Practice

- Pupils add the /aɪ/ sound to their Sounds Fun notebooks. Pupils draw pictures of words containing this sound and label them. Ask pupils to add any new words from this unit to the previously learnt sounds (/iː/ cheese; /æ/ salad, apple; /e/ egg, bread; /ɪ/ fish, chicken).
- Write the word *fish* on the board. Pupils write other words with the same sound below it (*sister, finger, chicken*). Now write the word *rice.* Pupils write other words with the /aɪ/ sound below it (*mice, bike, white, like*). Now compare the /ɪ/ sound with the /aɪ/ sound by saying the words slowly (*rice – sister*) so pupils can hear the difference. Call out a word and pupils say another word containing the same sound.

AB page 42

6 **Find and colour.**

- Pupils read the words in the word bank and find them in the picture. They then colour them in the picture. You could do this as a picture dictation in pairs. One pupil says e.g. *brown mice* and his/her partner colours the picture accordingly.

7 **Listen and match. Then say.**

- Play CD2:44. Pupils listen and draw a line connecting the words with the /ɪ/ sound, then draw a separate line connecting the words with the /aɪ/ sound. Play the recording again and pupils say the words.

---

i   **2:44**
Finger, fish, chicken, sister
ai
White, bike, rice, mice

---

7 Play the game (page 77).

SKILLS

I like …

I don't like …

8 Listen and say.

SOUNDS FUN!

I like mice on bikes with white rice.

Lesson 4   bike, mice. *Food. I don't like (rice). I like (apples).* Sound: /aɪ/   **47**

Ending the lesson

- Hold up a flashcard of a word with a sound pupils have learnt, e.g. *bike*. Explain (L1) that things with the same sound as the flashcard are things that you like, and things with a different sound are things that you don't like. Say *I like white. I don't like green. I like rice. I don't like chicken,* etc. Pupils stamp their feet when you make a mistake (e.g. *I like fish.*)

OPTIONAL ACTIVITIES
Team game
Play Phonics race see p. 24.
Flashcard game
Play Memory see p. 22.

Lesson 5

Lesson aims
To consolidate the unit language with a story

Target language
cake. Happy Birthday!

Recycled language
apples, fish, parrots, pizza. I like/don't like …

Materials
Audio CD, Flashcards (Food); Unit 6 Story cards; props for acting out the story, e.g. a pretend cake, fish and pizza, an apple, a bow tie and jacket, a tray, musical instruments

Optional materials
Blank paper for each pupil

Starting the lesson

- Draw a large happy face and a large sad face on the board. Say four sentences: *I like bananas. I don't like fish. I like cheese. I don't like chicken.* Now hand out the flashcards (food) and pupils put them under the correct face from the sentences you said from memory. Choose pupils to take over as teacher.
- Ask questions (L1) about the story from Unit 5. Which characters were in the story? (Lindy, Joe and Pippin). Who was hiding in the story? (Pippin). Why did Lindy call Pippin a bad parrot? (He was imitating other animals.)

PB page 48

- Before pupils open their books, show the story cards for Unit 6 in turn and ask the questions from the 'Before reading the story' section written on the back of each card.
- Explain the meaning of *Happy Birthday* if pupils are unfamiliar with it and teach *cake* by pointing to the cake in frame 5.

9 **Listen and read. Then act.**

- Play the recording of the story CD2:45 and pupils follow along in their books. Play the recording again, pausing after each line for pupils to repeat.
- Call on pupils to read the story. Stop after each frame and check pupils' understanding of the story by asking the questions from the 'After reading the story' section written on the back of each story card. Be sure that pupils understand that Princess Emily is miserable because she misses Pippin.
- After pupils have a clear understanding of the story, invite seven or eight pupils to the board to act it out. You may wish to play the recording and pause after each line for pupils to repeat. Alternatively, you could have other pupils read the lines while the pupils act it out, or have them say the lines from memory. When acting out, encourage tone of voice and expressions to match those in the pictures. Use props that you've brought to class if you wish.
- Stick the story cards on the board in mixed order and write a number from 1 to 6 below each, in random order. Play the recording of the story or read the transcript from the Pupil's Book, frame by frame. Pause the recording after each frame. Pupils say the number written below the correct frame.

Game

- Create actions for some of the key words in the story (e.g. *apple, fish, pizza* and *parrot*). Ask pupils to close his/her book. Play the story again. Pupils do the actions when they hear the key words.

AB page 43

8 **Read and circle. Then say.**

- Pupils read the sentences below the pictures. They then circle either *like* or *don't like* according to the picture. Pupils then say the sentences.

9 **Read and circle *Yes* or *No*.**

- Pupils read the sentences about the story. They circle *Yes* if the sentence is true and *No* if it's false.

Listen and read. Then act.

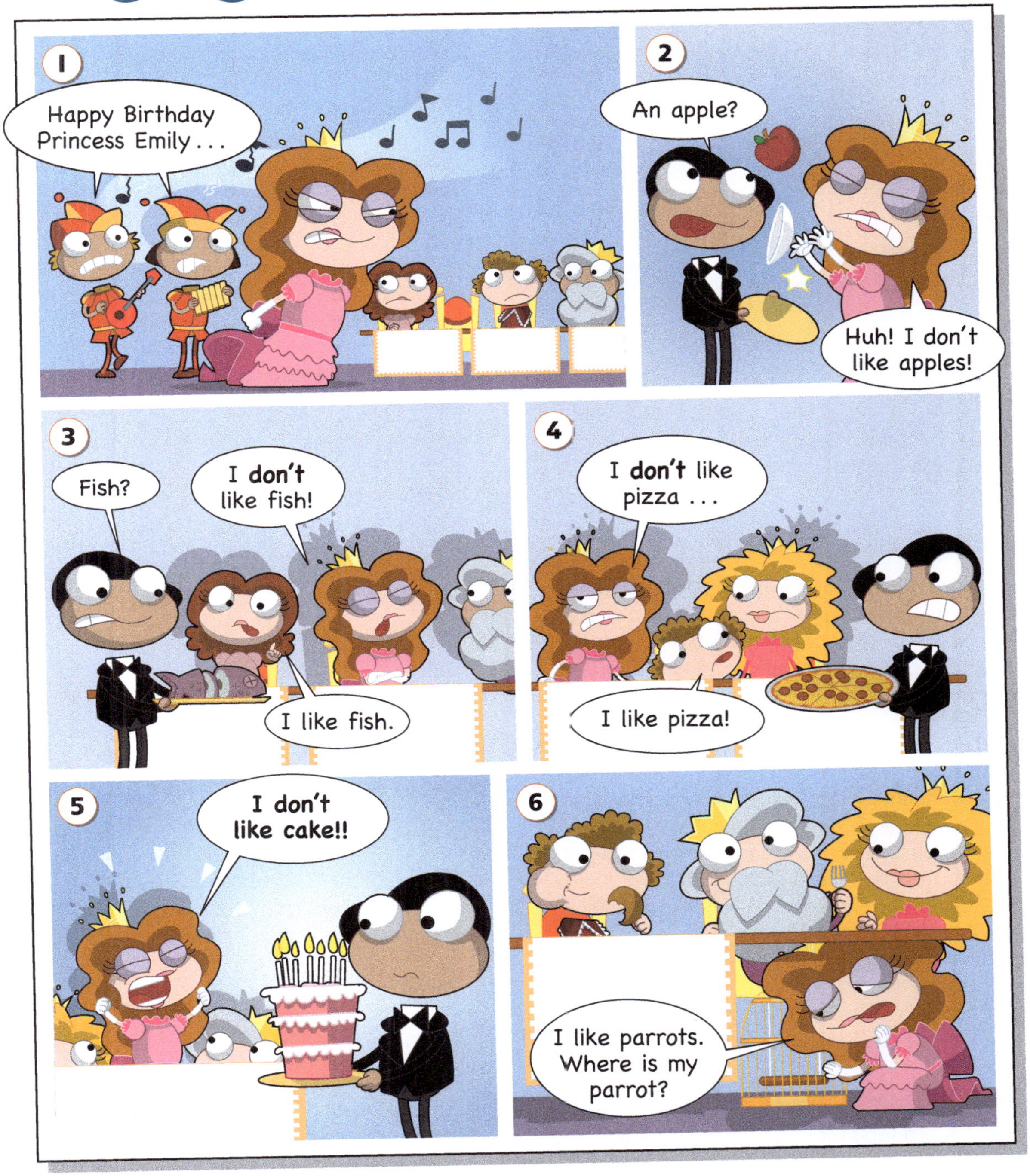

cake, Happy Birthday! apples, fish, parrots, pizza. I like/don't like...

Ending the lesson

- Draw a simple drawing of Princess Emily on the board. Challenge pupils to remember which food she doesn't like in the story. Pupils draw pictures of the food below her picture. Play the story recording again to check pupils' answers.

125

Lesson 6

Starting the lesson

- Cut a hole in a piece of paper and hold it over one of the flashcards (food) so pupils can only see a part of the flashcard. Pupils try to guess which food it is. *(Is it an apple?)* Continue with other food flashcards.

PB page 49

Presentation

- Stick the banana flashcard and homemade flashcards of toast and cereal on the board (or draw these foods on the board). Label each picture. Ask pupils to guess which meal these represent. Say *This is my breakfast* and write the word *Breakfast* above your drawings. Now stick the pizza and apples flashcards on the board (or draw them) and say *This is my lunch*. Write the word *Lunch* above the foods. Finally, draw or stick up flashcards of chicken and rice and say *This is my dinner*. Label the foods *Dinner*.

10 **Listen and point. Then say.**

- Ask pupils which food they can see in each photo. Say *breakfast* and pupils say what food they see in that section. Repeat with the other meals.
- Play CD2:46. Pupils listen and point to each food as they hear it.

BOY 1	Mmmmm! Breakfast! I like cereal for breakfast. And I like toast and bananas, too.	**2:46**
GIRL	It's time for lunch! I like pizza and cheese for lunch. I like apples, too.	
BOY 2	This is my dinner. Fish and salad. I like chicken, too!	

Values

- Have a short discussion about things pupils eat for breakfast, lunch and dinner in your country. Encourage pupils to answer in English but accept answers in L1 and provide the English words when possible. Discuss the importance of eating healthily. Ask which meal pupils think is the most important, and explain that breakfast is important as it helps you concentrate in school and gives you energy for the rest of the day. What are the negative effects of eating foods that aren't healthy? Which foods are the best for us to eat at each meal? What about drinks? Which are healthy/unhealthy? Is it healthier to drink a lot of water every day or only a little?

11 **Listen and draw. Then say.**

- Play CD2:47. Pupils listen and draw the correct food into the pictures.

1 This is my breakfast. I like cereal and bananas for breakfast.	**2:47**
2 This is my lunch. I like pizza and an apple for lunch.	
3 This is my dinner. I like chicken and rice for dinner.	

AB page 44

10 **Read. Then look and number.**

- Pupils read the sentences, decide which meal is described in each, and write the sentence number in the box next to the correct meal.

11 **Find and circle.**

- Pupils find the food words in the puzzle and circle them. Early finishers may label the pictures. Pupils check his/her answers in pairs.

Mini project

12 **Make a menu.**

- Make a menu for a pretend restaurant or café. Pupils choose a name for his/her restaurant and design a cover for the menus. Make three headings inside: Breakfast, Lunch and Dinner. Pupils stick or draw pictures of food under each heading and label the pictures. You might even wish to include prices.

> Pupils create a collage to show his/her favourite meal. Pupils stick or draw pictures on paper and label the food. Pupils title their collages *Breakfast, Lunch* or *Dinner*. Ask pupils to bring their artwork to the next lesson to share with the class.

SOCIAL SCIENCE

10 [2:46] Listen and point. Then say.

eggs

toast

cereal

bananas

breakfast

bread

apples

pizza

cheese

lunch

fish

rice

salad

chicken

dinner

11 [2:47] Listen and draw. Then say.

1

2

3

12 Make a menu.

Lesson 6   breakfast, cereal, dinner, lunch, toast. I like (toast) for (breakfast). *Food. I like (apples)*.   **49**

Ending the lesson

- Hold up the flashcards (food) or pictures of food from magazines one by one. Pupils call out breakfast/lunch/dinner depending when that particular food is usually eaten. Also use local specialities and suggest English names for the dishes when possible.

OPTIONAL ACTIVITIES
Team game
Play Whoops! see p. 25.
Flashcard games
Play Echo see p. 22.

Lesson 7

Lesson aims
To review the unit language with a game

Recycled language
breakfast, dinner, lunch, Food. I don't like (eggs).
I like (apples).

Materials
Audio CD; Flashcards (Food); Word cards (Food);
spinners and markers; half sheet of paper to make
meal cards; large sheets of paper to make a picnic
collage; magazine pictures of picnic food;
Worksheet 6

Optional materials
Poster 1

Starting the lesson

- Write the food words on the board in jumbled form,
  or missing several letters (e.g. *f _ s _*). Pupils stick the
  correct word card (food) next to each jumbled word
  (fish). They then stick the correct flashcard next to the
  words.
- Write the headings *breakfast, lunch* and *dinner* on
  the board. Pupils write words or draw pictures of
  food they eat at each of these meals. Pupils say *I like
  (toast) for (breakfast)* as they do so. Suggest English
  names for local specialities when possible.

PB page 50

13 Listen. Then play.

- Explain (L1) that pupils are going to play a game in
  pairs or small groups. Each group needs a spinner (or
  number cards from 1–5) and a marker for each pupil.
  Each pupil chooses a meal card from the centre of
  the game board. Pupils then travel around the board
  collecting the food shown on his/her meal cards.
  When a pupil lands on a food they need to complete
  their meal, they say *I like (apples)* and cross out the
  food on the card. When a pupil lands on a food not
  shown on his/her meal card, they say *I don't like (fish).*
  The winner is the first pupil in the group to cross out
  all the foods on his/her card. Note: Pupils may need to
  go round the board several times before they are able
  to collect all the food they need.
- Play CD2:48 to give pupils an idea of the language
  they'll need. They then play the game.

GIRL Dinner.	**2:48**
2!	
1, 2 ...	
Fish. I like fish.	
BOY Lunch.	
3!	
1, 2, 3 ...	
Toast. I don't like toast.	

Game

- Give each pupil a half sheet of paper. Pupils create his/
  her own meal cards similar to the ones used in the
  game in Activity 13. They draw three or four foods
  eaten at any particular meal and label the drawing
  Breakfast, Lunch or *Dinner.* Pupils play the game
  again using his/her own cards.

14 Listen and do.

- Mime eating several different foods. Pupils guess the
  food, then say at which meal they eat it. Play CD2:49
  and pupils mime eating the food mentioned.

I like apples.	**2:49**
I don't like pizza.	
I like bananas.	
I don't like cereal.	
I like eggs.	
I don't like bread.	
I like salad.	
I don't like fish.	

- Tell pupils to imagine it's a sunny day and they're
  going on a picnic. Discuss (L1) things they may need
  to take with them (e.g. a blanket, a picnic basket). Ask
  which foods they like eating best at a picnic. Divide
  the class into small groups/pairs and give each a large
  sheet of paper. Pupils draw a picnic scene showing
  themselves and their friends eating their favourite
  foods. They could also stick on food pictures from
  magazines.They label as much of the food as they can.
  Stronger pupils can come to the board and describe
  his/her picnic scene to the class.

Practice

- Pupils can now complete Worksheet 6.

1 Read and draw.

- Pupils read the food words on the girl's card and draw
  the food on the table.

2 Look. Then read and write.

- Pupils look at the food in the thought bubbles and
  complete the sentences below the boy and girl with
  words from the word bank.

 **Listen. Then play.**

I like fish.

I don't like toast.

14    **Listen and do.**

Ending the lesson

- Stick the flashcards (food) on the board. Now divide the class into pairs. Give each pupil a half sheet of blank paper. Pupils draw one of the items from the board but keep it hidden. His/Her partner tries to guess what was drawn by asking questions. *Is it red? Is it an (apple)?*

OPTIONAL ACTIVITIES
Poster activity
See the notes on Poster 1 on p.21.
Flashcard game
Play Tick or cross see p. 23.

Lesson 8

Lesson aims
To personalise the unit language; to provide an opportunity for self-evaluation

Recycled language
Food. I don't like (pizza). I like (apples).

Materials
Audio CD; Unit 6 Stickers; paper to make Project book; DVD; Evaluation Sheet 6

Starting the lesson

- Ask pupils to tell you the new words and sentences from this unit. Ask pupils what they found easy or difficult. Play any of the games from this unit again.

PB page 51

Listen, stick, then trace.

- Pupils point to the appropriate label as you read the words out loud and then trace the words.
- Pupils look at the pictures and find the matching stickers at the back of the Pupil's Book. Play CD2:50. Pupils listen and stick the food stickers in place as they are mentioned in the recording. Alternatively, pupils work in pairs, calling out the food and sticking the stickers. Finally, they trace over the words.

1 I like fish.	2:50
2 I like salad.	
3 I like bananas.	
4 I like eggs.	
5 I don't like apples.	
6 I don't like pizza.	
7 I don't like rice.	
8 I don't like chicken.	

16 Draw two foods you like and don't like. Then write.

- Pupils draw two foods they like and two foods they don't like on the plate. They may wish to divide the plate in half by drawing a line down the middle to do this. They then write the words for the food they've drawn in the sentences next to the picture. Invite pupils to the board to share his/her artwork with the class and read out his/her sentences.

AB page 45

12 Listen and circle. Then write.

- Pupils read the food words in the boxes to a partner. Play CD2:51 of the boy's likes and dislikes. Pupils circle the words in the box as they're mentioned. They then complete the sentences by filling in the gaps with the words they've circled.

1 I like chicken and salad.	2:51
2 I don't like toast or eggs.	

13 Find and stick.

- Pupils find the Unit 6 sticker in the back of their Pupil's Book and stick the speech bubble sticker in the correct place to complete the picture. Pupils read the sentence on the sticker to a partner.
- Pupils read the three sentences in the Look! Box and tick the ones they can understand and use correctly.
- Explain (L1) that pupils should colour in the stars at the bottom of the page to correspond with how well they think they completed the unit.

AB page 61

- Pupils colour the food pictures in the Picture Dictionary. They then play a game in pairs, taking turns to say a word while his/her partner points to the correct picture.
- Write the words on the board in jumbled order or missing some letters. Pupils find the words on the page. Stronger pupils may wish to cover the written words below each picture and try writing the words themselves.

Practice

- Help pupils to make an 8-page booklet as an end of unit project. They write the title *My Unit 6 Project Book* on the cover and draw or stick pictures of food on each page. Pupils write captions below each picture (e.g. *I like pizza. I don't like fish.*).

Now watch the DVD.

Evaluation

You can check your pupils' progress using Evaluation sheet 6. See also Teacher's notes p. 176.

> Pupils can now go online to Tropical Island and enjoy the fun and games.

15 2:50 ✏ **Listen, stick, then trace.**

I CAN DO IT!

1
2
3
4

fish

salad

bananas

eggs

5
6
7
8

apples

pizza

rice

chicken

Stick

16 ✏ **Draw two foods you like and don't like. Then write.**

I like _____

and _____ .

I don't like _____

or _____ .

🖱 **Now go to Tropical Island.**

Lesson 8   *Food. I don't like (pizza). I like (apples).*   51

Ending the lesson

- Divide the class into two teams and have them stand in two straight lines opposite each other. Choose a speaker for each team. Say the name of a food (e.g. *banana*). Teams alternate saying names of other foods. Award points to a team when the opposite team repeats a word or fails to think of another word.

OPTIONAL ACTIVITIES
TPR game
Play Ball throw see p. 24.
Team game
Play Reading race see p. 25.

7 Clothes

Lesson I

Lesson aims
To present and practise new vocabulary

Target language
dress, shoes, skirt, socks, trousers, T-shirt

Recycled language
Colours

Receptive language
I'm wearing …

Materials
Audio CD; Flashcards (Clothes); small squares of paper; coins

Optional materials
Blank paper; envelopes

Starting the lesson

- Revise items and structures learnt in Units 1–6. Point to items or show various flashcards and ask *What's this? It's a (dog). What colour is it? (It's brown.)* Ask *How many (hands) have you got? (I've got two hands.)* Ask pupils to describe his/her friends. *(She's got long hair.)*

> **PB pages 52–53**

- Ask pupils what they remember from the Quest so far. (Our characters have just stopped at a café on the way to the castle).
- Ask questions (L1) about the illustration. Where are the characters? (at the castle). What is different about Princess Emily's clothes in this picture? Explain that she's wearing modern clothes for the first time and she rather likes them. Ask *Where's Princess Emily? (in the bedroom).* Point to the boy and ask *Who's this? (her brother).*

Presentation

- Indicate your clothes and say *my clothes.* Repeat several times. Ask pupils which clothes they already know. Point to the clothes in the illustration and say the word for each, or use the flashcards (clothes) to teach the words.

1 🔵 Listen and say.

- Play CD3:01. Pupils listen, point to the clothes and repeat the words. Then pupils say the missing words in each line until at the end they are saying all the words. Each word is associated with a sound to indicate when the pupil should say the word. The association of word and sound will also help them to memorise the words. Encourage them to use the pictures at the bottom of PB p. 52 for reference.

7 Clothes

52 Lesson I — dress, shoes, skirt, socks, trousers, T-shirt, Colours. (I'm wearing…)

| a T-shirt ★ trousers ★ a dress ★ a skirt ★ | **3:01** |
| shoes ★ socks ★ | |

Listen and say the missing words.
a T-shirt, trousers, a dress, a skirt, shoes, ★
a T-shirt, trousers, a dress, a skirt, ★ ★
a T-shirt, trousers, a dress, ★ ★ ★
a T-shirt, trousers, ★ ★ ★ ★
a T-shirt, ★ ★ ★ ★ ★
★ ★ ★ ★ ★ ★

Game

- Pupils use small squares of paper to cover three of the clothes items in Activity 1. Call out the words in turn. When you say a clothes item that a pupil covered, they write an X on the paper. A pupil wins when all three clothes items they covered have been said.

Pairwork

- Divide the class into pairs. One pupil covers a clothes item with a coin or piece of paper and the other tries to guess which is covered by asking questions. Pupils then switch roles.

Practice

- Say what each character is wearing and pupils find the character. Say *A purple skirt (the princess)*, etc. Pupils continue in pairs.

AB page 46

1 Find and colour. Then write.

- Pupils look at the shapes in the key and find the same shapes on the clothes. They colour the clothes according to the key. Pupils then complete the descriptions with a clothes item which matches the colour in their picture.

> **KEY 1** an orange T-shirt, **2** blue socks, **3** a green skirt, **4** red trousers, **5** a brown shoe, **6** a pink dress

For the next lesson

- Ask pupils to look at home for pictures of people wearing clothes in unusual colours or clothes that are unusual in some other way. They should bring them along to the next lesson.

Ending the lesson

- Write the clothes vocabulary on the board with the letters in jumbled order. Pupils write the words correctly and draw a picture next to the appropriate word.

OPTIONAL ACTIVITIES

What's the word?

Write the letters to form the six clothes words on small pieces of paper. Put each word in a separate envelope. Divide the class into 4–6 groups and give each group several envelopes. Pupils put the letters in order to form words. The first team to complete all their words wins.

Colour dictation

Pupils draw the six items of clothes on blank paper. Now say a *(pink) (skirt)*. Pupils colour the skirt pink. Pupils may also do this in pairs.

NOTES

---

2 Listen and ✓.

- Play CD3:02 and pupils write a tick in the box next to the words in the main illustration as they are mentioned. Play the recording again. Pause after each line in which the clothes items are mentioned, so pupils can repeat.

> E = EMILY BR = BROTHER M = MAID   3:02
> BU = BUTLER
> E   Look at my clothes!
>   I'm wearing a purple skirt and a green T-shirt.
> BR   Very nice. Look at my OLD trousers.
> E   Look at my hands!
> BR   White socks!!
> M   Oh dear! Please princess!!! The dress!
> E   I don't like pink dresses!
>   Look! Black shoes!
> BU   Your shoes ... your SHOE, princess.
> E   WHAT????? WHERE'S MY SHOE!!!
> BU   Oh dear!

- Focus on the labels next to each clothes item. Encourage pupils to read the labels one by one. Sound out the words slowly and ask pupils to repeat. Pupils point to each label and read it to a partner.

Lesson 2

Lesson aims
To revise the Lesson 1 vocabulary with a chant; to present the new structure

Target language
I'm wearing (red) (trousers).

Recycled language
Clothes, Colours

Materials
Audio CD; Flashcards (Clothes, Colours)

Optional materials
Paper; Flashcards (Clothes, Colours); pupils' pictures of people wearing unusual clothes

Starting the lesson

- Show the skirt flashcard and say *a purple skirt*. Then show the dress flashcard and say *a green dress*. Pupils say right or wrong. Continue with the remaining flashcards.
- Call out different items of clothes in different colours (e.g. *blue trousers, white T-shirts*). Pupils stand up when an item is mentioned that they are wearing.

PB pages 52–53

Presentation

- Indicate your clothes and say *I'm wearing a (blue) (shirt). I'm wearing (black) (trousers).* All pupils wearing something you mention repeat the sentence after you. Call other pupils to the board to describe their clothes to the class, using *I'm wearing …* Pupils wearing the same thing repeat their sentence. Note: if pupils are wearing uniform, it might be helpful to bring some different clothes to class (e.g. large coloured T-shirts or socks).

  Listen and chant.

- Focus on the characters' clothes in the main illustration. Ask *Who's wearing a green T-shirt? (Princess Emily).* Continue with other characters and clothes. Play the recording of the chant CD3:03. Pupils listen and find the character being described. Play the recording again and pupils chant along.

B = BROTHER E = EMILY   **3:03**

B I'm wearing red trousers.
Red trousers, red trousers,
I'm wearing red trousers.
How about you?

E I'm wearing a purple skirt.
A purple skirt, a purple skirt,
I'm wearing a purple skirt.
How about you?

dress · socks · T-shirt · skirt

1 3:01 Listen and say.   2 3:02 Listen and ✔.

52 **Lesson 1**   *dress, shoes, skirt, socks, trousers, T-shirt, Colours. (I'm wearing…)*

Practice

- Circulate round the classroom asking *What are you wearing? (I'm wearing (black) trousers.)*

  Listen and colour. Then say.

- Play CD3:04. Pupils listen and colour Lindy, Joe and Grandad's clothes as they hear them.

L = LINDY   J = JOE   G = GRANDAD   **3:04**

L Look at my clothes! I'm wearing a yellow dress and red shoes.

J I'm wearing an orange T-shirt and blue trousers.

G Look at me! I'm wearing green trousers and pink socks!

Pairwork

- Give pupils a few minutes to study the pictures of Lindy, Joe and Grandad's clothes that they have just coloured. Pupils close their books and remember the colours of the characters' clothes. One pupil says a character's name (e.g. *Lindy*) and their partner says what the character is wearing (e.g. *a yellow dress and red shoes*).

Lesson 2

I'm wearing (red) (trousers). Clothes, Colours **53**

2 Read and number. Then colour.

- Pupils read the sentences in the speech bubbles and write the correct number in the box next to the appropriate picture. They then colour the clothes as written in the sentences.

3 Read and colour. Then look and write.

- Pupils colour the pictures of clothes according to the colour written next to each item. They then complete the sentences by writing the colour words in the gaps.

Ending the lesson

- Divide the class into small groups. Each group draws an *Our Discovery Island* character wearing clothes learnt in this lesson and then colours the clothes. Groups then create a new verse for the chant CD3:03 (e.g. *I'm wearing an orange dress,* etc.). Point to each group in turn and they recite their chant. Pupils hold up their drawings while they recite their verses.

OPTIONAL ACTIVITIES

Game

Put the flashcards (colours) in one pile and the flashcards (clothes) in another. Pupils choose one colour card and one clothes card and create a sentence. *(I'm wearing a (blue) T-shirt.)*

Unusual clothes

If pupils have brought in pictures of people wearing unusual clothes, they should show them to the class or to a partner. They pretend to be the person in the picture and say *I'm wearing (green shoes).*

NOTES

Quest sticker and song

- Ask pupils to recall which of Emily's things they have found so far (the present, the photo, the key, the sunglasses, the rubber duck and the nuts). Explain that pupils are now going to find the seventh Quest item. Ask them to look at the main illustration and guess what the item might be. Then play the Quest Song CD3:05 so pupils learn the name of the Quest item *(shoe).*

> Stand up, jump up, come on a quest, **3:05**
> Come on a quest today.
> Turn around, sit down, come on a quest,
> Look for a shoe today.
> A treasure chest, a present, a photo, a key,
> sunglasses, a duck, nuts and ★ a shoe ...
> Find a shoe today!

- Ask pupils (L1) to find the smaller shoe sticker at the back of the Pupil's Book and stick it over the grey image of the shoe, on the butler's tray in the main illustration. Ask pupils why they think there's only one shoe in the picture. Explain (L1) that they'll learn where the other shoe is later in the unit.
- Play the recording again and pupils sing along.

Lesson 3

Lesson aims
To extend the unit vocabulary set; to practise the vocabulary with a song

Target language
bed, boots, jumper, pyjamas, school. It's time for (bed). Put on your (T-shirt). Take off your (shoes).

Recycled language
Clothes

Materials
Audio CD; pictures of clothes; paper; clothes brought from home

Starting the lesson

- Play the chant from Lesson 2 CD3:03. Encourage pupils to chant along.
- Call four pupils to the front of the class. Describe what they're wearing in first person. Say *I'm wearing a (blue) skirt.* Pupils say the name of the child wearing a blue skirt.

PB page 54

Presentation

- Teach *pyjamas, jumper* and *boots* by showing pictures or drawing them on the board. Say the words several times and pupils repeat.
- Mime putting on a T-shirt or trousers. Say *Put on your (T-shirt).* Now mime taking off your T-shirt and say *Take off your (T-shirt).* Continue miming putting on and taking off other clothes. Alternatively, do this with real clothes, asking pupils to put on the clothes over their own clothes and take them off again.

5 **Listen and find. Then sing.**

- Point to picture 1 and ask *What's he wearing? (pyjamas). Where is he? (He's in the bedroom.)* Do this for the other pictures as well.
- Play CD3:06 and pupils listen. Explain the meaning of *It's time for bed* and *It's time for school*, in L1 if necessary. Teach actions to go along with these phrases (e.g. yawning or putting on a rucksack and marching out the door). Play the song again and encourage pupils to perform the actions as they listen.
- With pupils' help, stick or draw pictures of clothes on the board, in the order they are mentioned in the song. Play the song again and pupils join in with the words, using the pictures on the board as prompts. You could also play the karaoke version of the song CD3:48 for pupils to sing along to.

Good morning! Good morning!	3:06

Good morning! Good morning!
Take off your pyjamas.
It's time for school!
Put on your T-shirt. Put on your trousers.
Put on your shoes. Off you go!
It's time for school.
Good night! Good night!
Put on your pyjamas.
It's time for bed!
Take off your jumper. Take off your boots.
Take off your socks. Off you go!
It's time for bed.
Good night! Good night!
Good night! Good night!

- Ask pupils to write the words for the clothes below each picture on the board. Now say *Put on your (boots).* Pupils mime the action. Try several other combinations.

6 **Listen. Then play.**

- Explain (L1) that pupils should choose one of the pictures and describe it to a partner (e.g. *Put on your boots).* Partners say the number written next to the correct picture.
- Play CD3:07 to give pupils an idea of the language they'll need. They then play the game in pairs.

GIRL Take off your shoes. 3:07
BOY Number 3!

Practice

- Have a short discussion in L1 about what pupils wear to school. Ask what they enjoy wearing at the weekend and which their favourite colours are for clothes. Pupils draw their favourite clothes on a blank sheet of paper. Invite them to the board to describe the drawings to the class.

AB page 48

4  **Write. Then listen and check.**

- Explain (L1) that this is a mini story about a boy getting ready for school and a girl getting ready for bed. Pupils fill in the gap in each sentence by choosing a word from the word bank. Play CD3:08 so pupils can check their answers.

1 Take off your pyjamas. 3:08
2 Put on your T-shirt.
3 Put on your shoes.
4 It's time for school!
5 Take off your boots.
6 Take off your jumper.
7 Put on your pyjamas.
8 It's time for bed.

 **Listen and find. Then sing.**

6 3:07 **Listen. Then play.**

Take off your shoes.

Number 3!

Ending the lesson

- Play a TPR game. Divide pupils into small groups and give each group a name (or let them decide on a name for themselves). Call out the group's name and then say an action for them to mime. Say (Birds) – Put on your T-shirt. 'Cats) – Take off your jumper, etc.

OPTIONAL ACTIVITIES
Team game
Play Clothes line see p. 25.
Flashcard game
Play Mixed up flashcards see p. 23.

Lesson 4

Lesson aims
To develop literacy skills; phonics: /ɜː/

Target language
bird, nurse. Put on (a red jumper).

Recycled language
Clothes, Colours.

Materials
Audio CD; Flashcards (Clothes); Sounds Fun notebooks

Starting the lesson

- Begin the lesson by playing and singing the song CD3:06 from Lesson 3. Pupils mime the actions as they sing along.

PB page 55

 7 **Listen. Then colour and say.**

- Point to the drawing of the girl and ask *What's she wearing?* (a T-shirt, a skirt, socks and boots). Now point to the boy and ask *What's he wearing?* (a jumper, trousers, socks and shoes).
- Tell pupils they are going to play a game in pairs, describing the colours of the boy's clothes if his/her partner is a boy or the girl's clothes if his/her partner is a girl. One pupil says e.g. *Put on a (yellow) (T-shirt)* and his/her partner colours the clothes accordingly. Then they swap.
- Play CD3:09 to give pupils an idea of the language they'll need. When pupils finish, they give a description of the clothes they've coloured, e.g. *I'm wearing a (yellow) (T-shirt), a (red) (skirt),* etc.

Put on a red sock.	**3:09**

Presentation

- Ask pupils to remember which words they learnt in the last unit with the /aɪ/ sound (*bike, mice, rice, white*). Draw pictures on the board to help pupils remember.

8 **Listen and say.**

- Play CD3:10. Pause after the first two lines. Ask pupils which sounds they can hear (/ɜː/). Play the first two lines again and pupils repeat.
- Teach the words *nurse* and *bird.* Remind pupils of the word *purple* by pointing to something of that colour, and *skirt* by showing the flashcard. Say all four words several times and pupils repeat. Ask which sound pupils can hear (/ɜː/). Ask pupils which other words they know with these sounds (*T-shirt, thirteen*).

- Now play the recording from the beginning to the end. Pupils listen and repeat the words. Play the recording again so pupils are comfortable with these new sounds. Then pupils read the rhyme to a partner.

ir , ir	**3:10**
ir, ir, ir	
ir ★	
Nurse. ★ Skirt. ★	
A nurse with a skirt. ★	
Purple. ★ Bird. ★ Purple bird. ★	
A nurse with a skirt and a purple bird. ★	

Practice

Pupils add the /ɜː/ sound to their Sounds Fun notebooks. Pupils draw pictures of words containing this sound and label them. Ask pupils to add any new words from this unit to the previously learnt sounds (/ʌ/ jumper; /e/ dress; /aʊ/ trousers).

AB page 49

 5 **Listen and match. Then trace.**

- Play CD3:11. Pupils listen and match each word to the correct picture. Pupils then trace the words and say them to a partner, who points to the correct picture.

ir	**3:11**
Nurse.	
Purple.	
Bird.	
T-shirt.	
Skirt.	

 6 **Match. Then listen and say.**

- Pupils match the two pictures containing the same vowel sound.
- Play CD3:12 and pupils check his/her answers. They then read the pairs of words to a partner.

ir: bird, skirt	**3:12**
or: horse, torch	
ai: mice, bike	
ay: train, baby	

Pupils can now go online to Tropical Island and find the top hat that Pippin is holding on the Pupil's Book page. It is on a coat stand near the entrance to the tent. Once pupils click on the top hat they are taken to a supplementary language game based on the vocabulary in this unit.

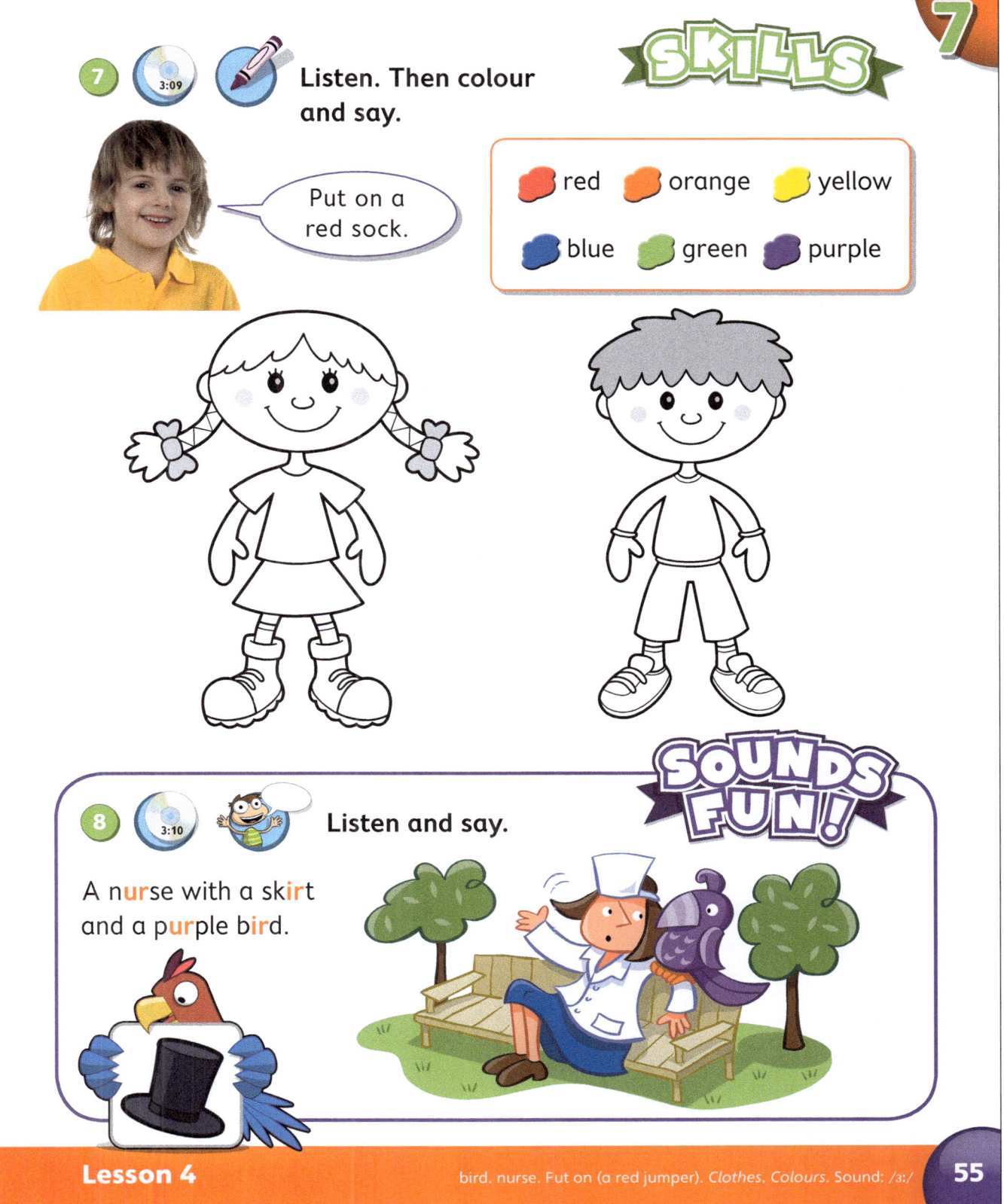

SKILLS

7 🔵3:09 ✏️ **Listen. Then colour and say.**

Put on a red sock.

🔴 red 🟠 orange 🟡 yellow
🔵 blue 🟢 green 🟣 purple

8 🔵3:10 🐝 **Listen and say.**

SOUNDS FUN!

A n**ur**se with a sk**ir**t and a p**ur**ple b**ir**d.

Lesson 4   bird, nurse. Put on (a red jumper). *Clothes. Colours.* Sound: /ɜː/   **55**

Ending the lesson

• Stick up the flashcards for *socks, skirt, trousers, dress* and *shoes* on the board. Ask pupils to write as many words as possible with the same vowel sound below each flashcard. You could divide the class into teams and award points for correct answers.

OPTIONAL ACTIVITIES
Flashcard game
Play Bluff see p. 23.
Team game
Play Phonics race see p. 24.

Lesson 5

Lesson aims
To consolidate the unit language with a story

Target language
shirt. Have you got ...? It's the palace. We're here!

Values
Being polite

Recycled language
shoe. I'm wearing ... I've got ....

Materials
Audio CD; Unit 7 Story cards; props for acting out the story, e.g. a map, a shoe, two policemen's hats

Starting the lesson

- Ask questions (L1) about the story from Unit 6. Whose birthday was it in the story? (Princess Emily's). Was Princess Emily happy? (No.) Did the princess like her birthday cake? (No.) What was the one thing the princess said she liked? (parrots).

PB page 56

- Before pupils open their books, show the story cards for Unit 7 in turn and ask the questions from the 'Before reading the story' section written on the back of each card.
- Explain the meaning of *Have you got ...?* and *We're here*, using L1 if necessary. Teach *shirt* by pointing to one in the classroom or on a story card. Finally teach *palace* by saying *It's a house for a princess* (so far we have seen *castle* but not *palace*).

9 Listen and read. Then act.

- Play the recording of the story CD3:13 and pupils follow along in their books. Play the recording again, pausing after each line for pupils to repeat.
- Call on pupils to read the story. Stop after each frame and check pupils' understanding of the story by asking the questions from the 'After reading the story' section written on the back of each story card. Be sure that pupils understand that Pippin and the princess are finally together again. Ask pupils to remember the Quest item for the unit. Remind them that Princess Emily has found her lost shoe!

- After pupils have a clear understanding of the story, invite five pupils to the board to act it out. You may wish to play the recording and pause after each line for pupils to repeat. Alternatively, you could have other pupils read the lines while the pupils act it out, or have them say the lines from memory. When acting out, encourage tone of voice and expressions to match those in the pictures. Use props that you've brought to class if you wish.

Game

- Stick the story cards for Unit 7 on the board. Number the cards 1–6. Read a sentence from the story and pupils say the number of the card. They could also point to the person who says the line you've read. Play the game in teams and award points for correct answers.

Values

- Ask pupils (L1) what words Princess Emily uses when she gets her shoe back (*thank you*). Discuss why we use this phrase (because it is polite). What other words do pupils use to be polite? (*please, excuse me,* etc). Talk about why is it important to be polite and how pupils feel when someone isn't polite to them.

AB page 50

7 Read. Then match and say.

- Pupils read the speech bubbles written above the characters. They then match these to the character wearing the clothes described. Pupils check his/her answers by saying to a partner *I'm (Lindy). I'm wearing (a jumper).*

8 Draw.

- Point to the frames on the left, which have been taken from the story. Challenge pupils to say the characters' words from memory. Play the recording again to help pupils. Pupils then create the end the story by drawing a picture of Pippin in the heart.

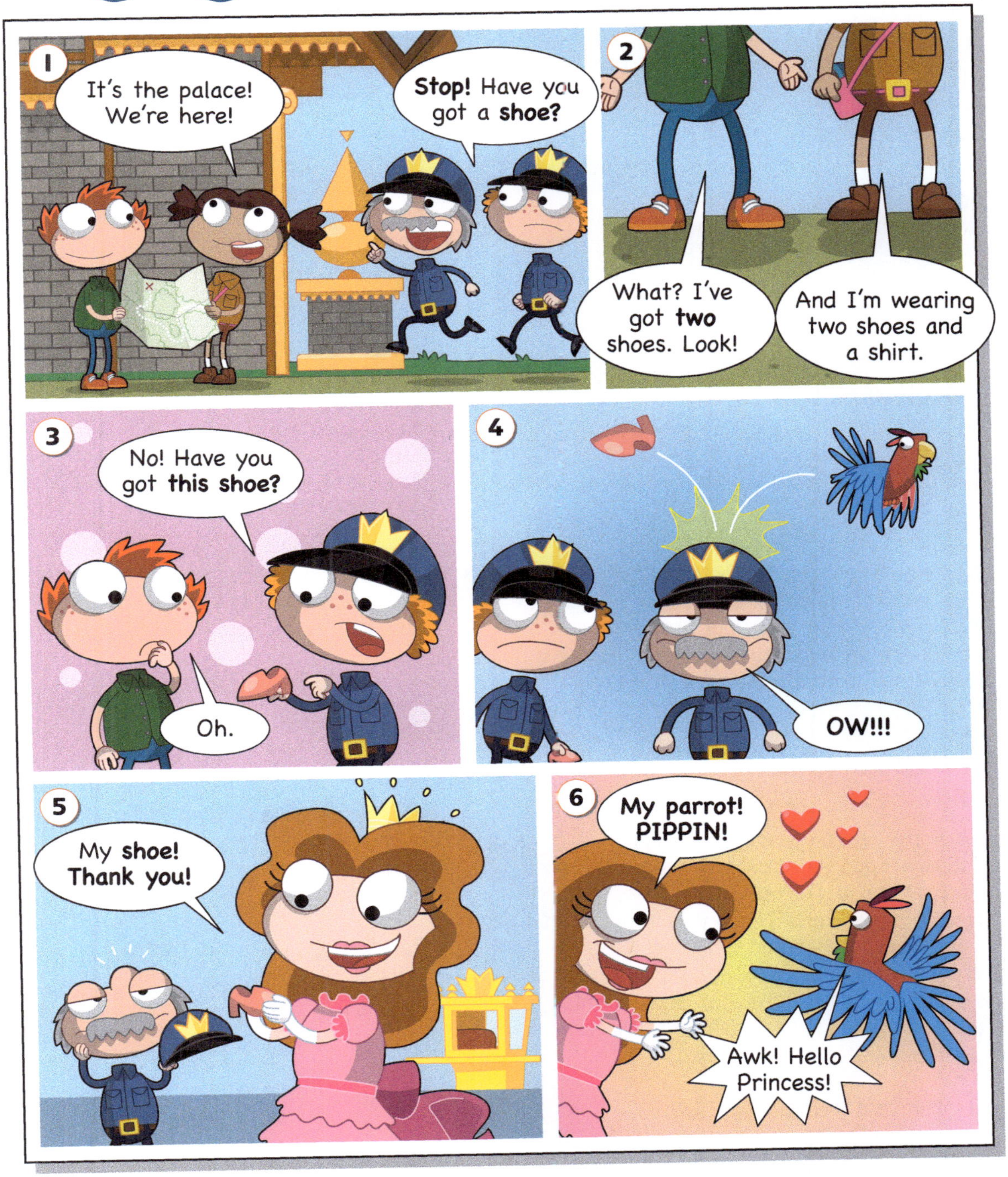

1. It's the palace! We're here!

Stop! Have you got a **shoe**?

2. What? I've got **two** shoes. Look!

And I'm wearing two shoes and a shirt.

3. No! Have you got **this shoe**?

Oh.

4. OW!!!

5. My **shoe**! Thank you!

6. My parrot! PIPPIN!

Awk! Hello Princess!

Ending the lesson

- Round off the lesson by dividing the class into small groups and giving them time to roleplay the story. Call on a few groups to present their plays to the class.

OPTIONAL ACTIVITIES
What happens next?
Ask (L1) what pupils' think might happen in the final part of the story. Give credit for imaginative answers.
Flashcard game
Play Easy or difficult see p. 23.

Lesson 6

Lesson aims
To integrate other areas of the curriculum into the English class; to develop the cross-curricular topic through a short project

Cross-Curricular focus
Social science – Jobs

Target language
chef, coat, firefighter, hat, police officer

Recycled language
nurse, Colours. I'm wearing a ...

Materials
Audio CD; Flashcards (Clothes); Poster 3

Optional materials
Pupils' pictures from magazines of people doing different jobs

Starting the lesson

- Begin the lesson by doing a TPR activity. Include actions like *shake your body, move your arms*, etc.
- Hold a flashcard (clothes) over your head so that pupils can see it but you can't. Try to guess what it is. Ask *Is it a T-shirt?* Invite pupils to the board to do the same.

PB page 57

Presentation

- Teach the words *hat* and *coat* by showing pupils pictures from a magazine, drawing them on the board or pointing to them in the Pupil's Book.
- Remind pupils of the Sounds Fun! rhyme from Lesson 4. Ask (L1) which job they learned in the rhyme *(nurse)*. Now ask pupils to remember the story from Lesson 5. Point to one of the police officers on PB p. 56 and say *This is a police officer.* Explain that pupils will learn about other jobs in this lesson.

10 🔵 Listen and point. Then say.

- Look at the four images at the top of the page. Point to each photo in turn and say the job written below each. Ask pupils which other jobs they know in English. Pupils who have studied Starter Level might remember *doctor, vet, teacher* and *pilot.* Discuss what each person is wearing.
- Play CD3:14 and pupils point to the correct photo and repeat.

> 1 I'm a chef.   **3:14**
> 2 I'm a firefighter.
> 3 I'm a police officer.
> 4 I'm a nurse.

- Have a short discussion (L1) about the jobs people do in your town and the uniforms they wear. If your pupils wear a uniform, ask them to describe it. Ask why they think people wear uniforms.

11 🔵 Listen and number.

- Point to each drawing and pupils say the job (e.g. *a nurse*). Play CD3:15. Pupils listen and number the boxes below the pictures.

> 1 Hello, I'm Jack. Look at my clothes.   **3:15**
>   I'm wearing a black jumper and trousers. I'm wearing black boots, but where's my hat?
> 2 Hello, I'm Sarah. I'm wearing a white dress and white shoes. I help people! But where's my small white hat?
> 3 Hello, I'm Thomas. I like food!! Look at my clothes. I'm wearing white clothes. Where's my big white hat?
> 4 Hello, I'm Marie. I'm wearing a long coat. Where's my yellow hat?

- If you have time, ask pupils to draw the missing hats and cut them out. Play the recording again and pupils put the hats on the people as they listen.

- Use Poster 3 see p.21.

AB page 51

9 Write. Then say.

- Pupils complete the sentences below the people by choosing the correct words from the word bank. They then read out their sentences to a partner to check their answers.

10 Read. Then find and number.

- Pupils read the sentences, then find the person in Activity 9 that each sentence describes. They write the number in the box.

Mini Project

12 Draw your clothes and say.

- If your pupils wear a school uniform, ask them to describe it. Have a short discussion (L1) about uniforms in Britain or in your country. Discuss how the uniforms in the photos from this lesson differ from those in your country. Hand out blank paper and pupils draw and label his/her school uniform or the clothes they normally wear to school. Pupils read the sentence in the speech bubble and create his/her own speech bubbles for their drawing.

10 🔊 3:14 Listen and point.
Then say.

SOCIAL SCIENCE 7

firefighter   chef   nurse   police officer

11 🔊 3:15 ✏️ Listen and number.

12 ✂️ Draw your clothes and say.

I'm wearing a green jumper and black trousers.

Lesson 6   chef, coat, firefighter, hat, police officer, nurse, Colours. I'm wearing a...   **57**

Ending the lesson

● Say sentences like *I'm wearing a white hat.* Pupils guess which job it is. Use examples from the photos in the Pupil's Book so pupils can use them as a guide.

OPTIONAL ACTIVITIES
Group work – Our uniforms collage
Assign each group a job to research. Pupils make a collage with their photos from magazines. They label the clothes. Display all the finished collages.
TPR game
Play Drawing game see p. 24.

7

Lesson 7

Starting the lesson

- Use Poster 1 see p. 21.
- Show the word cards (clothes) one by one. Pupils read the words and stand up and clap if they're wearing that particular item.

PB page 58

  **Listen. Then play.**

- Explain (L1) that pupils are going to play a game in groups of three or more. Focus first on the children in the middle of the game board. Ask what each child is wearing. Explain that each player in the game chooses a child from the game board and has to collect the clothes that that child is wearing. Pupils spin the spinner and move his/her counter around the board. When they land on an item that is part of their outfit, pupils say *Put on your (T-shirt)* and tick the box next to the (T-shirt). Pupils say *Take off your (hat)* when they land on an item they don't need. Pupils go forward one or two squares or go back one square when they land on squares with these instructions. The winner is the first player to collect all his/her clothes. The winning player describes his/her outfit by saying *I'm wearing a jumper, a skirt and socks.*
- Play CD3:16 to give pupils an idea of the language they will need. They then play the game.

BOY	I'm number 2.	**3:16**
	6!	
	1, 2, 3, 4, 5, 6 …	
	T-shirt.	
GIRL	Put on your T-shirt.	
GIRL	I'm number 3.	
	2!	
	1, 2 …	
	Shoes.	
BOY	Take off your shoes.	

  Listen and do.

- Play CD3:17 and pupils mime the actions as they hear them.

Put on your T-shirt.	**3:17**
Take off your shoes.	
Put on your trousers.	
Take off your jumper.	
Put on your hat.	
Take off your coat.	
Put on your dress.	
Take off your socks.	

Game

- Bring several outfits to class. Divide the class into two groups. Write sentences on cards about each of the outfits you brought to class (e.g. *I'm wearing a blue T-shirt, brown trousers and purple socks*). Put all the clothes in a central area. Now give each group one card with a sentence written on it. After pupils read the card, they choose one pupil from the group to find the correct clothes and dress one of their team mates. You may play the game with both teams racing against each other or you may wish to time each team to find a winner.

Practice

- Pupils can now complete Worksheet 7.

1 **Draw and colour. Then write.**

- Pupils draw three items of clothing on the boy and girl. They then complete the sentences by filling in a clothes word in each gap.

2 **Read. Then find and colour.**

- Pupils read the descriptions of the clothes, find them in the picture and colour them the correct colour.

For the next lesson

- Ask pupils to bring clothes for a dressing up party to the next lesson.

Pupils teach his/her family three new words for clothes in English. They draw a picture of the clothes, colour and label them. Ask pupils to show the pictures to his/her family, then bring them into the class. Display the drawings in the classroom.

13 **3:16** Listen. Then play. **ROUND-UP**

Put on your T-shirt.

Take off your shoes.

14 **3:17** TPR Listen and do.

Ending the lesson

- Write a girl's name and a boy's name on the board. These need not be pupils in your class. Below the names, write various items of clothes in different colours (e.g. *brown shoes, a green dress, blue socks*). Pupils draw the two children wearing the correct clothes. Pupils present their drawings to the class. *(I'm wearing ...)*

OPTIONAL ACTIVITIES
Flashcard game
Play Basketball see p. 22.
TPR game
Play Grab it see p. 24.

Lesson 8

Lesson aims
To personalise the unit language; to provide an opportunity for self-evaluation

Recycled language
Clothes, Colours. I'm wearing (blue) (shoes).

Materials
Audio CD; Flashcards (Clothes); Unit 7 Stickers; paper to make Project book; Evaluation sheet 7

Optional materials
Pupils' dressing up clothes brought from home

Starting the lesson

• Play the recording of the song CD3:06 from Lesson 3. Pupils mime the actions as they sing along.

PB page 59

15 **Listen, stick, then trace.**

• Pupils point to the appropriate clothes labels as you read the words out loud.
• Pupils look at the clothes on the clothes line and find the matching stickers at the back of the Pupil's Book. Play CD3:18. Pupils listen and stick the clothes stickers in place as they are mentioned in the recording. Alternatively, pupils work in pairs, calling out the clothes and sticking the stickers. Finally, they trace over the words.

1 A red T-shirt.	3:18
2 Blue trousers.	
3 Black shoes.	
4 Blue and red socks.	
5 A purple dress.	
6 A green skirt.	

16 **Draw yourself wearing clothes you like. Then write.**

• Pupils imagine they are in a play or fashion show and draw a picture of themselves in the frame wearing clothes they like. They then complete the sentences by listing the clothes they're wearing in their drawing. Invite pupils to the board to share his/her artwork with the class and read out his/her sentences.

AB page 52

11 **Read. Then look and write.**

• Pupils read the sentences below each child and fill in the gaps in the sentences according to what each child is wearing. Pupils choose words from the word bank.

12 **Find and stick.**

• Pupils find the Unit 7 sticker in the back of their Pupil's Book and stick the speech bubble sticker in the correct place to complete the picture. Pupils read the sentence on the sticker to a partner and colour Grandad's coat accordingly.
• Pupils read the three sentences in the Look! Box and tick the ones they can understand and use correctly.
• Explain (L1) that pupils should colour in the stars at the bottom of the page to correspond with how well they think they completed the unit.

AB page 61

• Pupils colour the clothes pictures in the Picture Dictionary. They then play a game in pairs, taking turns to say a word while his/her partner points at the correct picture. Stronger pupils may wish to cover the written words below each picture and try writing the words themselves.
• One pupil chooses a word from any unit already learnt but keeps the word secret from the class. Pupils try to guess the word. (*Is it a toy? Is it big/small? Is it an animal?* etc.). Pupils play the game in groups or pairs.

Practice

• Help pupils to make an 8-page booklet as an end of unit project. They write the title *My Unit 7 Project Book* on the cover and draw pictures on each page, of clothes or of people wearing uniforms. Pupils write labels below each drawing e.g. *I'm wearing a purple skirt.*

Evaluation

You can check your pupils' progress using Evaluation sheet 7. See also Teacher's notes p. 176.

Pupils can now go online to Tropical Island and enjoy the fun and games.

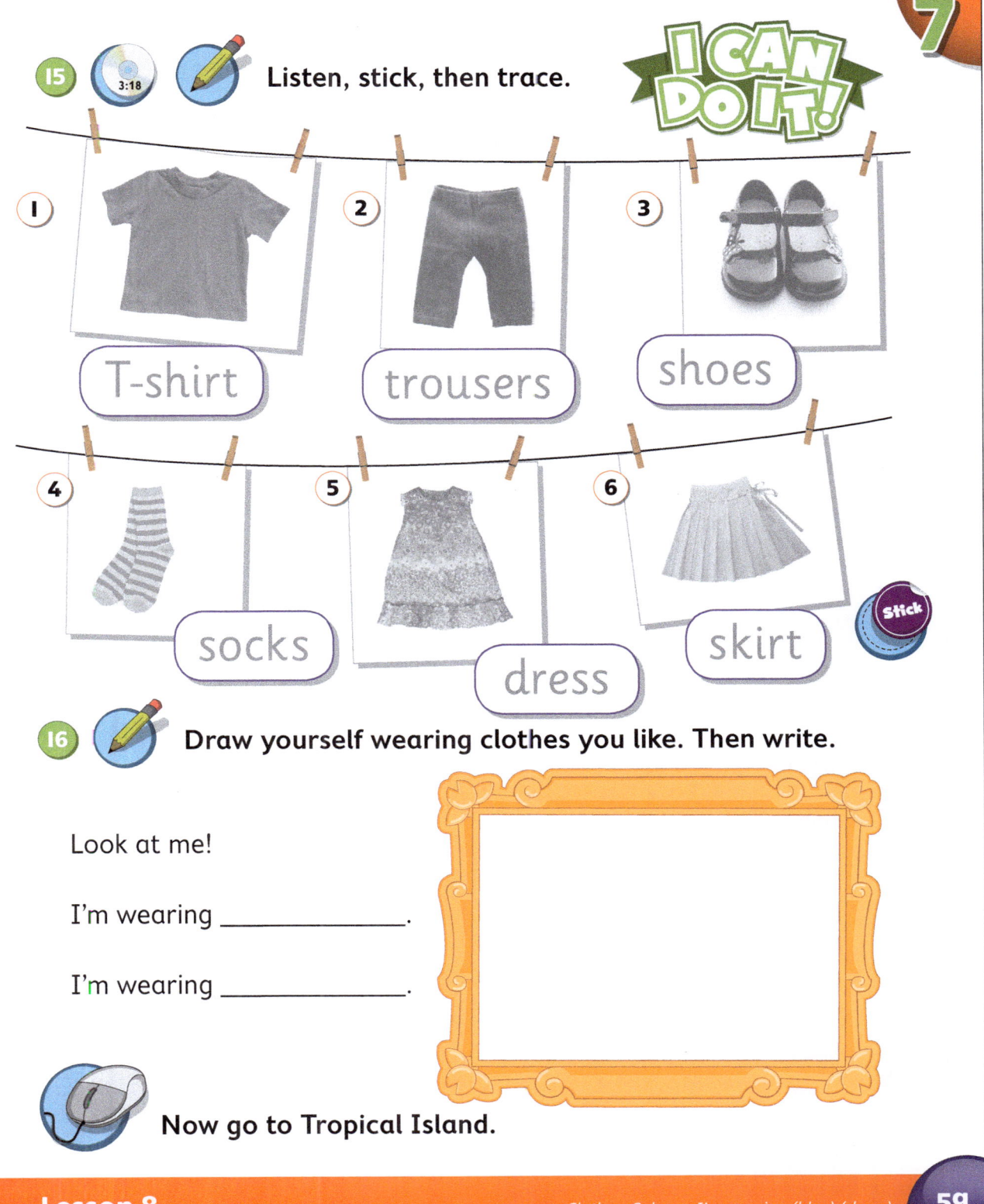

15 3:18 **Listen, stick, then trace.**

I CAN DO IT!

1 **T-shirt**

2 **trousers**

3 **shoes**

4 **socks**

5 **dress**

6 **skirt**

Stick

16 **Draw yourself wearing clothes you like. Then write.**

Look at me!

I'm wearing _____.

I'm wearing _____.

Now go to Tropical Island.

Lesson 8   *Clothes. Colours. I'm wearing (blue) (shoes).* **59**

Ending the lesson

- End the lesson by doing a TPR activity. Include actions from Unit 3 (My body), e.g. *Move your arms, Stamp your feet.* Also include actions from this unit, e.g. *Put on your pyjamas, Take off your boots.*

OPTIONAL ACTIVITIES
Dressing up party
Ask pupils to bring in fun clothes from home and have a dressing up party. Pupils can wear costumes or uniforms. Pupils describe their clothes.
Team game
Play Whoops! see p. 25.

8 Weather

Lesson 1

Lesson aims
To present and practise new vocabulary

Target language
cloudy, rainy, snowy, sunny, weather, windy

Receptive language
Is it (sunny)?

Materials
Audio CD; Flashcards (Weather); small pieces of paper; coins

Optional materials
Blank paper; pictures of people doing things in different types of weather

Starting the lesson

- Revise all vocabulary learnt so far by showing various flashcards and asking *What's this? (It's a duck.)* Divide the class into two teams and award points to pupils giving the correct answers.
- Revise all actions learnt by playing a game of Teacher Says. Say *Teacher says touch your eyes, jump, point to something (blue), wave your arms,* etc. and pupils do the actions. Give the instructions without saying *Teacher says* first and pupils don't do the actions.

> **PB pages 60–61**

- Ask questions (L1) about the main illustration. Where are the characters now? (At the palace/castle). Where's Pippin? (With Princess Emily). Explain that the characters have finally made it to the castle. Lindy, Joe and Grandad are meeting Princess Emily for the first time. They have travelled a long way to bring Pippin and Emily's chest full of belongings to the castle.

Presentation

- Ask pupils what they think they will learn about in this unit. Write the word *Weather* on the board and ask pupils to repeat several times. Stick the flashcards (weather) on the board, point to each in turn and say the word several times.

1 🔘 Listen and say.

- Play CD3:19. Pupils listen, point to the weather symbols and repeat the words. Then pupils say the missing words in each line until at the end they are saying all the words. Each word is associated with a sound to indicate when the pupil should say the word. The association of word and sound will also help them

to memorise the words. Encourage them to use the pictures at the bottom of PB p. 60 for reference.

> sunny ★ cloudy ★ windy ★ rainy ★ snowy ★   3:19
> **Listen and say the missing words.**
> sunny, cloudy, windy, rainy, ★
> sunny, cloudy, windy, ★ ★
> sunny, cloudy, ★ ★ ★
> sunny, ★ ★ ★ ★
> ★ ★ ★ ★ ★

Game

- Pupils use small squares of paper to cover three of the weather conditions in Activity 1. Call out the words in turn. When you say a weather condition that a pupil covered, they write an X on the paper. A pupil wins when all three weather conditions they covered have been said.

Pairwork

- Divide the class into pairs. One pupil covers a weather condition with a coin or piece of paper and the other tries to guess which is covered. Pupils then switch roles.

AB page 53

1 Look and read. Then circle and write.

- Pupils look at the pictures and read the sentence written below each. They then circle *Yes* if the sentence is true and *No* if it's false. Pupils then create sentences by choosing the correct weather condition from the word bank and writing it in the gap.

Ending the lesson

- Create an action for each of the weather conditions (e.g. open your arms wide over your head for *sunny*, make a rainy motion with your hands for *rainy*, sway back and forth for *windy*, etc). Say *It's (sunny)* and pupils mime.

OPTIONAL ACTIVITIES

Sun collage

In groups, pupils draw four or five suns on a large sheet of paper (or hand out cut outs prepared ahead of time). Draw six or seven rays around the sun on which pupils write words. Write a category inside each sun (toys, animals, colours, etc.) and pupils write words belonging to that category on the rays of the sun. Alternatively, give each group one sun/category and stick each group's sun on one large sheet of paper to make a class collage.

Picture perfect weather!

Bring pictures to class of people doing different things in different types of weather (e.g. swimming, sledging, walking with an umbrella, etc). Show the pictures in turn and pupils call out the weather words, e.g. *It's (rainy)*.

NOTES

---

2 Listen and ✓.

- Point to the weather conditions in the main illustration in turn and ask *What's the weather like? (It's sunny.)* Play CD3:20 and pupils write a tick in the box next to the words as they are mentioned. Play the recording again. Pause after each line so pupils can repeat.

> **J = JOE G = GRANDAD L = LINDY E = EMILY   3:20**
> **J** Look! It's the castle! We're here.
> **G** Oh, dear! It's windy. And it's cloudy.
> **J** It's sunny in the picture. I like sunny days.
> **L** Look over there! Is it snowy? I like snowy days.
> **E** Uggghhh! It's rainy!! I don't like rainy days.

- Focus on the labels next to each weather condition. Encourage pupils to read the labels one by one. Sound out the words slowly and ask pupils to repeat. Pupils point to each label and read it to a partner.

Practice

- Give pupils a sheet of blank paper each, folded into four. Ask pupils to choose four weather conditions and draw one in each quarter (ask for things the pupils think of for each type of weather, e.g. snowmen, kites, sunglasses, etc). Pupils write labels e.g. *It's (sunny)* and share the drawings with a partner.

Lesson 2

Lesson aims
To revise the Lesson 1 vocabulary with a chant; to present the new structure

Target language
umbrella. Do you like (cloudy days)?

Recycled language
no, yes, Weather. I like/don't like (rainy days).

Materials
Audio CD; Flashcards (Weather)

Optional materials
Photocopies of survey for each pupil; Word cards (Weather)

Starting the lesson

- Practise the weather vocabulary by hiding one of the flashcards (weather) behind your back. Pupils guess the card by asking *Is it (sunny)?*
- Hold up the *sunny* flashcard and say *I like sunny days.* Now hold up the rainy flashcard and say *I don't like rainy days.* Now show the weather flashcards in turn and ask *Do you like (cloudy) days? (Yes, I do/No, I don't.)*

PB pages 60–61

Presentation

3 **Listen and chant.**

- Play the chant about weather CD3:21. Pupils point to the labels in the main illustration when they hear the word. Play it again several times, until pupils can chant along. Create actions to go along with the chant.

C = CHORUS J = JOE E = EMILY L = LINDY P = PIPPIN	3:21
C Do you like sunny days? Do you like sunny days?	
J Yes, yes, yes, I like sunny days.	
C Do you like rainy days? Do you like rainy days?	
E No, no, no, I don't like rainy days.	
C Do you like snowy days? Do you like snowy days?	
L Yes, yes, yes, I like snowy days.	
C Do you like windy days? Do you like windy days?	
P No, no, no, I don't like windy days.	

cloudy

snowy

WELCOME

sunny

1 3:19 Listen and say.   **2** 3:20 Listen and ✔.

60   Lesson 1

cloudy, rainy, snowy, sunny, weather, windy. (Is it (sunny)?)

4 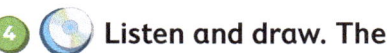 **Listen and draw. Then say.**

- Play CD3:22 about people's likes/dislikes of different weather conditions. Pupils draw a happy or a sad face next to each picture according to the recording. Then, using the pictures as prompts, pupils ask a partner *Do you like (sunny) days? (Yes, I do/No, I don't.)*

G = GRANDAD L = LINDY J = JOE P = PIPPIN	3:22
1 Do you like windy days?	
G No!! I don't like windy days!	
2 Do you like rainy days?	
L Yes! I like rainy days.	
3 Do you like snowy days?	
J Oh yes. I like snowy days.	
4 Do you like sunny days?	
P Yes. I like sunny days.	

 Quest sticker and song

- Ask pupils to recall which of Emily's things they have found so far (the present, the photo, the key, the sunglasses, the rubber duck, the nuts and the shoe). Explain that pupils are now going to find the last Quest item. Ask them to look at the main illustration and guess what the item might be. Then play the Quest Song CD3:23 so pupils learn the name of the Quest item *(the umbrella).*

3 3:21 Listen and chant.

rainy

windy

4 3:22 Listen and draw. Then say.

Lesson 2   umbrella. Do you like (cloudy days)? no, yes. Weather. I like/don't like (rainy days).   **61**

Stand up, jump up, come on a quest,   **3:23**
Come on a quest today.
Turn around, sit down, come on a quest,
Look for an umbrella today.
A treasure chest, a present, a photo, a key,
sunglasses, a duck, nuts, a shoe and ★ an umbrella ...
Find an umbrella today.

- Ask pupils (L1) to find the umbrella sticker at the back of the Pupil's Book and stick it over the grey image of the umbrella next to the castle door in the main illustration.
- Play the recording again and pupils sing along.

AB page 54

2 **Ask and answer. Write *Yes* or *No*.**

- Draw a simple table similar to the one in the Activity Book on the board. Write pupils' names at the top and ask *Do you like (sunny) days?* Write *Yes* or *No* according to each pupil's answer. Pupils complete the survey in the Activity Book in a similar way. They begin by filling out the information for themselves, then write the name of a friend and ask *Do you like (rainy) days?*

- Hold up each flashcard (weather). Pupils say the word and put up his/her hand if they like it. Count the hands, to calculate the class's favourite and least favourite weather condition.

3 **What do you like? Draw, write and say.**

- Pupils choose a weather condition they like and one they don't like and draw an appropriate picture in each box. They then complete the sentences below the boxes with the correct word from the word bank and read his/her completed sentences to a partner.

Ending the lesson

- In pairs, pupils choose a weather condition and act out a scene in that weather to another pair, e.g. one pupil chases a hat to represent a windy day, while his/her partner smiles or frowns. The watching pair makes a sentence about the scene, e.g. *I like/don't like windy days.* Pairs then swap roles.

OPTIONAL ACTIVITIES
Survey
Pupils create surveys asking 'Do you like ...' using toys, colours, food, etc. Give them a photocopied table that you've prepared before class. Pupils create questions by filling in the table with different objects. Give them time to complete their surveys in class or ask them to complete them at home with family or friends.
Word card game
Stick the word cards (weather) on the board. Pupils draw the correct weather conditions next to each card. Now remove the cards and stick them next to the wrong drawings. Pupils correct your mistakes.

NOTES

Lesson 3

Starting the lesson

- Revise the clothes and toys words by playing a flashcard game. Hold a piece of paper over a flashcard and uncover it slowly. The first pupil to guess the flashcard gets to uncover the next one.

 **PB page 62**

Presentation

5 🔵 **Listen and find. Then sing.**

- Ask pupils questions about the song illustrations. Point to various objects and ask *What's this? What colour is it? Is it (sunny)? Which animals can you see? Which toys can you see?*
- Teach the word *mouse* by pointing to the mouse in picture 3.
- Explain (L1) that each verse describes a different picture. Play CD3:24. Pupils listen and point to the picture being described. Play the song again and pupils find the items as they're mentioned. Finally, play the song and pupils sing the words. You might want to draw some pictures or put words on the board to act as prompts. You could also play the karaoke version of the song CD3:49 for pupils to sing along to.

It's a sunny day.	**3:24**
Let's play. Let's play.	
Look at my ball.	
It's red and blue	
And it's small.	
It's a windy day.	
Let's play. Let's play.	
Look at the clothes,	
Socks and jumper,	
Skirt and dress.	

It's a rainy day.
Let's play. Let's play.
I'm in the house
With my cat
and my mouse.
I like sunny days,
I like windy days,
I like rainy days,
Let's play. Let's play. Let's play. (x3) Let's play.

Practice

- Divide the class into five groups. Give each group a weather condition and a large sheet of paper. Pupils stick or draw pictures of things they do or clothes they wear when it's sunny, rainy, etc. Display their artwork in the classroom.

Game

- Play a game of I-Spy as a class using the song illustration. Say *I spy a frog.* Pupils find the frog and say the picture number *(3).* Divide the class into teams and award points to the team who answers first.

6 🔵 **Listen and point. Then play.**

- Describe objects in the pictures in Activity 5 by saying *I'm wearing a skirt.* Pupils say which picture it describes (2). Explain (L1) that pupils are going to continue this activity in pairs, using various structures e.g. *It's a …. It's got … I like … This is …*, etc.
- Play CD3:25 so pupils have an idea of the language they'll need. They then do the activity in pairs.

A I've got a small ball.	**3:25**
B It's Picture 1.	

AB page 55

4 **Look. Then read and number.**

- Look at the two pictures and ask pupils questions. Ask *Where's the chicken?* (Picture 2). *Where's the doll?* (Picture 1). Pupils read the sentences at the bottom of the activity. They then find which picture the sentence describes and write a 1 or 2 in the box after each sentence.

Pupils can now go online to Tropical Island and find the metal cupboard that Pippin is holding on the Pupil's Book page. It is next to the cage halfway up the inside of the volcano. Once pupils click on the metal cupboard they are taken to a supplementary language game based on the vocabulary in this unit.

 **Listen and find. Then sing.**

5

6  **Listen and point. Then play.**

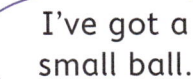

I've got a small ball.

It's Picture 1.

62 **Lesson 3** mouse. It's a (sunny) day. It's (rainy). *Animals, Clothes, Colours, Toys, Weather, I've got a... I like...*

Ending the lesson

- Stick the flashcards (weather) on the board. Divide the class into two teams. Call a pupil from each team to stand a few metres from the board. Say *I like windy days.* Pupils race to the board. The first pupil to touch the *windy* flashcard wins a point for his/her team.

OPTIONAL ACTIVITIES
Make a kite
Give each pupil an outline of a kite to decorate using any materials they wish (paint, sequins, etc). Pupils then write *I like windy days* on their kites.
Flashcard game
Play Spin the spinner see p. 23.

Lesson 4

Lesson aims
To develop literacy skills; phonics: /uː/

Target language
moose, scooter

Recycled language
no, yes, Animals, Clothes, Food, Toys. Do you like (snowy days)?

Materials
Audio CD; Unit 8 Cut outs ; Word cards (Weather); Sounds Fun notebooks

Starting the lesson

- Stick the word cards (Weather) on the board. Pupils draw the correct weather condition next to each card. Then point to each card in turn and ask *Do you like (sunny days)?*

PB page 63

7 Listen. Then play (page 79).

- Pupils read the labels below each photo. They cut out the cards from PB p. 79. Explain (L1) that they are going to play a game in pairs using the cards. Each pupil chooses five of the photos from the Pupil's Book and writes a tick in the box next to it. Pairs put their two sets of cards together in one pile. Pupils then take turns to draw a card and ask his/her partner *Do you like (snowy days)?* If the partner has ticked the box showing the photo of snowy days, they say *Yes* and keep the card. If the snowy days box isn't ticked, they say *No* and the card goes to the bottom of the pile. The first pupil to collect cards for all five of the items they ticked is the winner.
- Play CD3:26 to give pupils an example of the language they can use. They then play the game in pairs.

Do you like sunny days?	**3:26**
Yes.	

Pairwork

- Pupils write his/her own questions to ask a partner using the cards as reference (e.g. *What's this? Is it a bike? Is it blue?*)

Presentation

- Ask pupils to remember words they learnt with the /ɜː/ sound (*nurse, bird, skirt, T-shirt*). Draw simple drawings on the board and pupils write the words next to each drawing.

8 Listen and say.

- Play CD3:27. Pause after the first two lines. Ask pupils which sound they can hear (/uː/). Play the first two lines again and pupils repeat.
- Teach the words *moose* and *scooter* and remind pupils of the words *blue* and *boots* by drawing simple pictures on the board or showing homemade flashcards. Say the words several times and pupils repeat. Ask which sound pupils can hear (/uː/). Ask pupils which other words they know with these sounds (*two, food, shoe*).
- Now play the recording from the beginning to the end. Pupils listen and repeat the words. Play the recording again so pupils are comfortable with these new sounds. Then pupils read the rhymes to a partner.

oo, oo	**3:27**
oo, oo, oo	
oo ★	
Moose. ★ Blue. ★ Blue boots. ★	
A moose with blue boots. ★	
Scooter. ★ On a scooter. ★	
A moose with blue boots on a scooter. ★	

Practice

- Pupils add the /uː/ sound to their Sounds Fun notebooks. Pupils draw pictures of words containing this sound and label them. Ask pupils to add any new words from this unit to the previously learnt sounds (/ʌ/ sunny; /ɪ/ windy; /eɪ/ rainy; /aʊ/ cloudy).

AB page 56

5 Find and colour.

- Pupils find pictures in the bedroom of the words in the word bank containing the /uː/ sound and colour them blue.

6 Listen and circle the odd one out.

- Play CD3:28. Pupils listen and circle the word that doesn't belong in each group. Pause the recording after all four words are said to give pupils a chance to answer.

1 Sock … doll … moose … box.	**3:28**
Moose!	
2 Scooter … cow … shoe … two.	
Cow!	
3 Horse … bird … nurse … skirt.	
Horse!	
4 Boat … goat … nose … dog.	
Dog!	

7 🔵 3:26 👫 Listen. Then play (page 79).

Do you like sunny days?

Yes.

☐ **snowy days**

☐ **bananas**

☐ **horses**

☐ **sunny days**

☐ **salad**

☐ **dolls**

☐ **pink dresses**

☐ **dogs**

☐ **cars**

8 🔵 3:27 👦 Listen and say.

SOUNDS FUN!

A m**oo**se with bl**ue** b**oo**ts on a sc**oo**ter.

Lesson 4   moose, scooter, *no, yes, Animals, Clothes, Food, Toys. Do you like (snowy days)?* Sound: /uː/   **63**

Ending the lesson

- Draw or stick a picture of a box on the board. Write the number 1 above it. Now do the same with a boot and write the number 2 above it. Without saying the words, show pictures/flashcards or draw pictures on the board of words containing the /ɒ/ or /uː/ sound. Pupils call out 1 or 2 depending on which sound the words contain.

OPTIONAL ACTIVITIES
Flashcard game
Play Who's got it? see p. 22.
TPR game
Play Guess the object see p. 24.

Lesson 5

Lesson aims
To consolidate the unit language with a story

Target language
Clothes. Are you hungry? I'm sorry. Thank you.

Recycled language
friend

Materials
Audio CD; Unit 8 Story cards; props for acting out the story, e.g. a crown, some pretend food

Starting the lesson

- Play the recording of the song CD3:24 from Lesson 3. Divide the class into groups and give each group a word or words from the song and create an action to go it (e.g. pupils make a ball with their hands for the word *ball* or make a triangle with their hands over their heads for *house*). Pupils do the actions when they hear his/her word(s).
- Ask pupils (L1) questions about the story from Unit 7. Where did the story take place? (outside the castle). What was the police officer looking for? (Princess Emily's shoe). Who did Princess Emily finally find? (Pippin).

PB page 64

Presentation

- Teach the phrases *Are you hungry? I'm sorry* and *Thank you* by doing quick roleplay with volunteers. Accidently bump into someone and say *I'm sorry*. Then ask for a (pencil) and say *Thank you!* when someone gives one to you. Then pat your stomach and say *I'm hungry*. Ask pupils to repeat the phrases several times.
- Before pupils open their books, show the story cards for Unit 8 in turn and ask the questions from the 'Before reading the story' section written on the back of each card.

9 **Listen and read. Then act.**

- Play the recording of the story CD3:29 and pupils follow along in their books. Play the recording again, pausing after each line for pupils to repeat.
- Call on pupils to read the story. Stop after each frame and check pupils' understanding of the story by asking the questions from the 'After reading the story' section written on the back of each story card. Be sure that pupils understand that Pippin is home again and that Lindy, Joe and Princess Emily are now friends.
- After pupils have a clear understanding of the story, invite four pupils to the board to act it out. You may wish to play the recording and pause after each line for pupils to repeat. Alternatively, you could have other pupils read the lines while the pupils act it out, or have them say the lines from memory. When acting out, encourage tone of voice and expressions to match those in the pictures. Use props that you've brought to class if you wish.

Practice

- Read the story frame by frame in mixed order. Pupils find the correct frame and say the number written in the top left corner.
- Invite six pupils to the board and give them each a story card. Pupils arrange themselves in the correct order. Play the recording of the story to check they did this correctly.

AB page 57

7 **Read and match.**

- Pupils read the sentences at the top of the activity. They match the sentences to the correct pictures from the story. Pupils check his/her answers by reading the story together in pairs.

8 **Draw and write. Then say.**

- Pupils draw a picture of themselves between Joe and the princess. They then complete the sentence by writing his/her own name in the gap. With a partner, they read out the speech bubbles.

1
Oh Pippin.

Awk! Emily!!

2
Oh. I'm sorry! Thank you. My name's Princess Emily.

Wow! **You're** the princess!

3
Yes, I am! I like **your** clothes.

Oh! Thank you!

4
My **new** friends. Joe and Lindy.

But Pippin's **my** friend.

5
New friends. Oh! Are you hungry?

Yes, we are!

6
WELCOME HOME, PIPPIN!

Now I've got **three** friends.

64   Lesson 5

clothes. Are you hungry? I'm sorry. Thank you. *friend*

Ending the lesson

• Read the story to the class again. Change some words while you're reading (e.g. in frame 2 say *My name's Alex* instead of *My name's Princess Emily*). Pupils stand up when they hear a mistake and say the correct word

OPTIONAL ACTIVITIES
Favourite story
Divide pupils into 8 groups. Each group chooses one of the stories from Units 1–8. Give them time to act out their roles and perform their stories.
Team game
Play Number spin see p. 25.

157

Lesson 6

Starting the lesson

- Give each pupil a strip of paper and instruct them to draw three weather symbols on it (e.g. a sun, a cloud, a raindrop, a snowflake, or a leaf falling for *windy*). Say *I like (sunny) days*. Pupils who drew a sun cross it out. The first pupil to cross out all of his/her symbols wins.

PB page 65

Presentation

- Ask questions (L1) about the days of the week. Ask how many days there are in a week. Which are pupils' favourite days? Bring an English calendar to class if possible and point to the days as you say them. Ask pupils *What day is it today? It's (Monday)*.
- Write the days of the week on the board. Point to each in turn and say the day. Pupils repeat.

10 **Listen and say.**

- Play the recording of the days of the week CD3:30. Pupils point to the days as they are said. Call on several pupils to recite the days from memory.

Monday.	**3:30**
Tuesday.	
Wednesday.	
Thursday.	
Friday.	
Saturday.	
Sunday.	
What day is it today?	

11 **Read and write. Then say.**

- Have a discussion (L1) about the weather and how it affects our daily lives. Ask why rain clouds are black. What makes it rain and snow? What do we use to measure the temperature?
- Focus on the photos. Pupils write any day of the week from the word bank beneath each photo. Then they say to a partner *It's (Monday)* while miming the weather condition (e.g. blowing around in the wind). His/Her partner guesses the weather.

AB page 58

9 **Look and write. Then listen and check.**

- Pupils write the missing days in the calendar, in the correct order. Play the recording so pupils can check his/her answers.

Monday.	Friday.	**3:31**
Tuesday.	Saturday	
Wednesday.	Sunday.	
Thursday.		

10 **Read. Then look and ✓ or ✗.**

- Pupils read the sentences below the weather chart and write a tick if the statement is true and a cross if it isn't.

Mini project

12 **Make a weather chart.**

- Pupils create their own weather charts by writing the days of the week and recording the weather for one week. They may use the example in Activity 10 of the Activity Book for reference.
- You could put a large outdoor thermometer near the classroom. Pupils check the temperature every day at the same time.
- Pupils could also make weather streamers to find out about the wind. Give each pupil a craft stick or a straw and some party streamers cut in 1 to 1.5 metre strips. Glue the streamer to the stick. Take the streamers outside to check the direction and strength of the wind. Do this every day for a week and note your findings.

Pupils watch a weather report on TV or find a weather report on the internet with their parents' help. They make a weather prediction chart for a week by drawing a weather symbol next to each day of the week. If pupils don't have access to TV or the internet, they could make their own predictions. Pupils bring their charts to the next lesson. Display them in the classroom and compare their predictions with the weather each day.

10 🔵 3:30 Listen and say.

SCIENCE

Monday	Tuesday	Wednesday
Thursday	Friday	Saturday	Sunday

11 ✏️ Read and write. Then say.

Wednesday   Monday   Thursday   Friday   Tuesday

1
It's _____.
It's sunny.

2
It's _____.
It's windy.

3
It's _____.
It's cloudy.

4
It's _____.
It's snowy.

5
It's _____.
It's rainy.

12 Make a weather chart.

Lesson 6   Monday, Tuesday, Wednesday, Thursday, Friday, Saturday, Sunday. It's (Thursday). *Weather*   **65**

Ending the lesson

• Create your own TV weather programme. Pupils write short dialogues as a class. (A *Hello. It's Tuesday.* B *Is it windy?* A *Yes, and it's cloudy.* B *Oh dear! I like sunny days.* etc.) You could bring a large box to class cut out to look like a television and put it on a table. Pupils sit behind the box and present their weather forecast to the class.

OPTIONAL ACTIVITIES
Weather game
Write the days of the week on the board. Say *It's Wednesday. It's sunny.* Pupils stick the sunny flashcard below the correct day.
Flashcard game
Play Guess the card see p. 22.

Lesson 7

Lesson aims
To review the unit language with a game

Recycled language
Actions, Animals, Body parts, Clothes, Family, Features, Food, Numbers, Toys, Weather

Materials
Audio CD; pictures of seasonal clothes; blank paper; Word cards and Flashcards (Units 1–8); Worksheet 8

Starting the lesson

- Bring in some pictures of seasonal clothes (e.g. winter jackets, sunglasses, flip flops, raincoats, etc.) from home, or draw some on the board. Point to each in turn and pupils say in which weather conditions they might wear these clothes.

PB page 66

 Listen and follow. Then say.

- Pupils put a marker or a finger on START. Play CD3:32 while pupils follow the pictures. They can move one square at a time either left, right, up or down. Pupils will be directed towards one of the presents at the bottom of the page. When they hear STOP they say which number is below the last image they are currently on (e.g. if they land on the sun, they say Number 1).

Start …   **3:32**
a cow …
a banana …
a hat …
a train …
pyjamas …
feet …
a duck …
a boat …
snowy …
STOP! What number is it?
It's number 4.
Start …
hands …
a train …
pyjamas …
a granny …
ears …
sunny …
STOP! What number is it?
It's number 1.

- Play the recording again to give pupils an idea of the language they'll need to play the game.

- Pupils play the game in pairs or small groups. One pupil is chosen to be the speaker and creates a path for the other pupils to follow.

Game

Divide the class into two teams. Combine the flashcards from Units 1–8 together and put them in a pile. Invite a pupil from each team in turn to choose a card. The team must say a sentence using the picture on the card or pupils say another word with the same vowel sound (e.g. If the card is a doll, the correct answer could be *It's a (doll), I like (dolls), It's (pink), or frog*). Award points for correct answers.

 Listen and do.

- Revise parts of the body and face. Say *Touch your (arms). Touch your (eyes).* Pupils continue in pairs for a few rounds. Then play CD3:33 and pupils do the actions as instructed.

Stand up.   **3:33**
Touch your eyes.
Point to something blue.
Jump!
Turn around!
Touch your ears.
Dance!
Move your arms.
Point to something red.
Shake your body.
Sit down.

Game

- As revision, write four headings on the board (e.g. My Toys, My Face, My Family and Animals). Stick four or five sheets of paper below each heading. Write a question or draw a picture on the back of each paper (e.g. draw/stick a picture of a horse and ask *Is it a cow?* Write the word *boot* and pupils must say three more words with the same sound, etc.). Now divide the class into two teams. Pupils choose a category and answer one of the questions. Award points for each correct answer. You may wish to give more difficult questions a higher point value to make the game more interesting.

Practice

- Pupils can now complete Worksheet 8.

1 Read and write. Then play.

- Pupils complete the sentences by choosing words from the word bank at the top of the activity. Pupils then play a guessing game in pairs by saying sentences about one of the pictures (*It's sunny*). (Picture 1).

 **Listen and follow. Then say.**

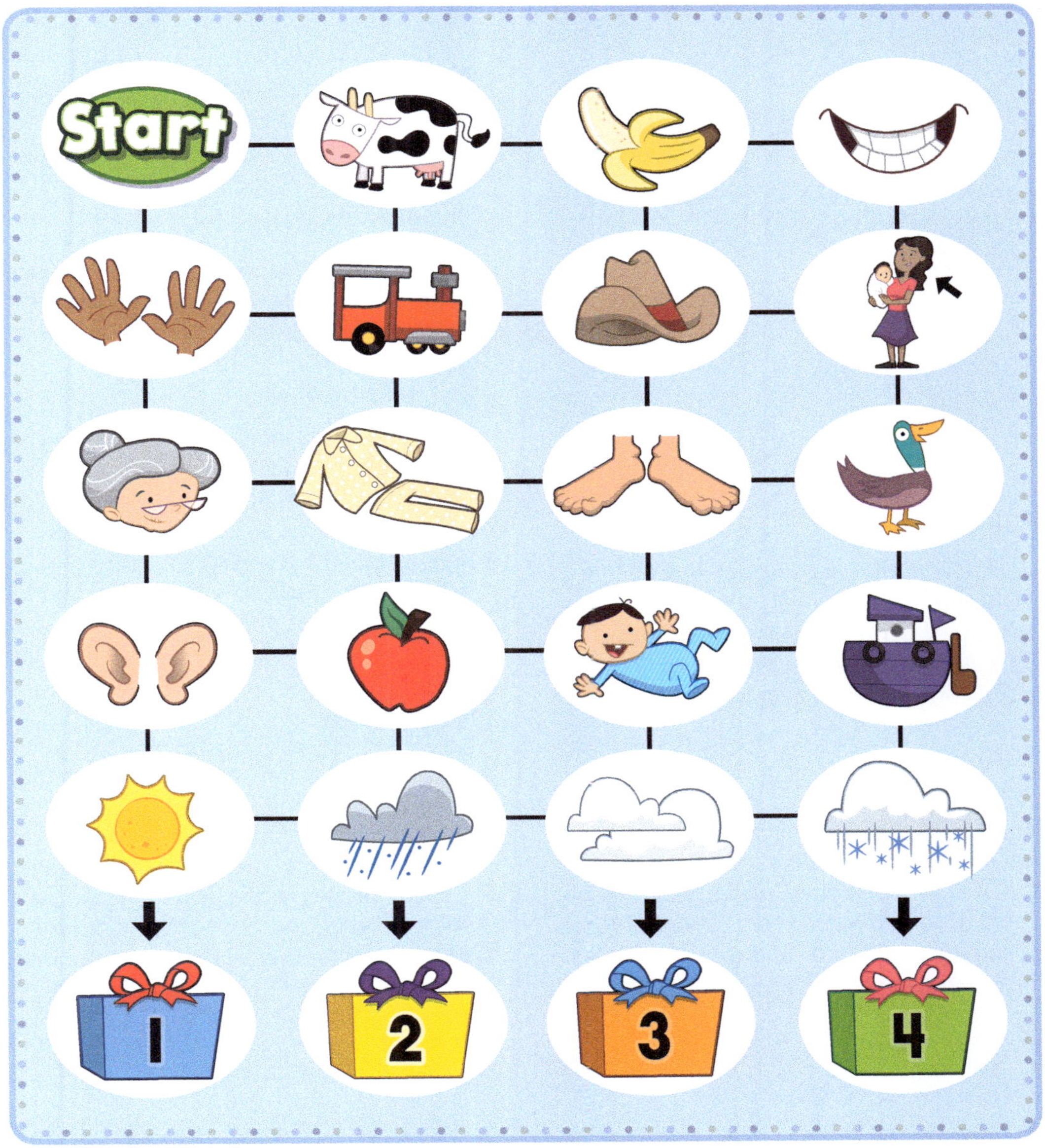

   **Listen and do.**

Ending the lesson

- Choose ten word cards from various units. Give each pupil a blank sheet of paper and ask them to write the numbers 1–10 down the left side. Show the word cards in turn and pupils draw a picture for each. For stronger classes, you may do this activity using flashcards and have pupils write the words rather than draw pictures.

OPTIONAL ACTIVITIES

Write a letter
Pupils write a letter to a friend using all sentence structures learnt in Units 1–8. Write an example letter on the board to help pupils with ideas.

Flashcard game
Play Easy or difficult see p. 23.

Lesson 8

Starting the lesson

- Do a TPR activity with the weather words. Divide the class into groups and give each group a weather word. Say a weather word in a sentence, then an action (e.g. *It's sunny. Dance! It's rainy. Jump!)* Only the pupils in the corresponding group do the action.

Values

- Discuss (L1) what you should do to stay safe in different weather, e.g. on hot sunny days, put on suncream, wear a sunhat and sunglasses, drink lots of water, stay in the shade during the hottest part of the day; on cold days, wear a hat and gloves, etc. You might like to show a photo of a child with bad sunburn and discuss the dangers of overexposure to the sun.

PB page 67

15 **Listen, stick, then trace.**

- Pupils point to the appropriate weather words as you read them out loud.
- Pupils look at the weather photos and find the matching stickers at the back of the Pupil's Book. Play CD3:34. Pupils listen and stick the weather stickers in place as they are mentioned in the recording. Alternatively, pupils work in pairs, calling out the weather conditions and sticking the stickers. Finally, they trace over the words.

1 It's snowy.	**3:34**
2 It's cloudy.	
3 It's sunny.	
4 It's rainy.	
5 It's windy.	

16 **Draw yourself on your favourite day. Then write.**

- Pupils draw themselves and the weather condition they like best in the frame and complete the sentences next to the picture by writing his/her favourite day and weather condition, e.g. *It's Saturday. It's sunny. I like sunny days.*

AB page 59

11 **Read. Then find and write.**

- Pupils read the sentences and decide which picture it best describes. They then choose a weather word from the word bank to complete each sentence.

12 **Find and stick.**

- Pupils find the Unit 8 stickers in the back of their Pupil's Book and stick the speech bubble stickers in the correct place to complete the picture. Pupils read the sentences on the stickers to a partner.
- Pupils read the three sentences in the Look! Box and tick the ones they can understand and use correctly.
- Explain (L1) that pupils should colour in the stars at the bottom of the page to correspond with how well they think they completed the unit.

AB page 61

- Pupils colour the weather pictures in the Picture Dictionary.
- Write the vowel sounds learnt in each unit on the board. Pupils find the words on the page with the same sounds and make lists in groups or as a class. Alternatively, give each group a different sound and each group finds words with the same sound. Write the words below each sound on the board when they are finished.

Practice

- Help pupils to make an 8-page booklet as an end of unit project. They write the title *My Unit 8 Project Book* on the cover and draw pictures of different weather on each page. Pupils write captions below each drawing (e.g. *It's sunny. I like sunny days.*).

 Now watch the DVD.

Evaluation

You can check your pupils' progress using Evaluation sheet 8 and give them the End of year evaluation sheet. See also Teacher's notes p. 176.

> Pupils can now go online to Tropical Island and enjoy the fun and games.

8

15 3:34 **Listen, stick, then trace.**

I CAN DO IT!

1

2

3

snowy

cloudy

sunny

4

5

Stick

rainy

windy

16 **Draw yourself on your favourite day. Then write.**

It's _____.

It's _____.

I like _____ days.

Now go to Tropical Island.

Lesson 8   *Days of the week, Weather. It's (Monday). I like (sunny days). It's (snowy).*   **67**

Ending the lesson

• Divide the class into groups. Each group chooses a favourite game from the course. Give each group the opportunity to play the game with their group and then lead the class in playing the game.

OPTIONAL ACTIVITIES
Poster activity
See the notes on Poster 3 on p. 21.
Flashcard game
Play Collect the cards see p. 22.

Goodbye

Lesson aims
To consolidate the vocabulary of the Quest items; to revise vocabulary from Units 1–8

Target language
Goodbye.

Recycled language
duck, key, nuts, photo, present, shoe, sunglasses, treasure chest, umbrella. Where's the photo?

Materials
Audio CD; Flashcards (Units 1–8); Word cards (Units 1–8); blank paper; glitter, sequins, stickers, etc. to decorate a certificate

Optional materials
Snacks for a party

Starting the lesson

- Revise different structures learnt throughout the course. Show different flashcards and ask *What's this?* Ask *What are you wearing? What colour is this?* etc.
- Play the Quest song CD3:23 from Unit 8 to remind pupils of all the Quest items they collected throughout the course. Pupils sing along.

PB pages 68–69

1 Listen and find.

- Talk about the characters and what's happening in the picture. (The characters are having a party. Princess Emily and Pippin have been reunited. Princess Emily is now friends with Lindy and Joe. She's very happy.) Ask questions (L1) about the picture. *Who's this? What food is on the table? What colour are the (bananas)?* etc.
- Ask pupils which Quest items they found in Units 1–8 (a treasure chest, a present with a doll inside, a photo, a key, sunglasses, a duck, nuts, a shoe and an umbrella). Explain (L1) that all the Quest items are hidden in the picture. Play CD3:35 and pupils find them in the picture as they are mentioned. Pause the recording to give pupils more time to find the items if necessary.

> Hi! Let's find Princess Emily's things. **3.35**
> Where's the photo?
> Where's the duck?
> Where are the sunglasses?
> Where's the treasure chest?
> Where's the shoe?
> Where's the present?
> Where's the key?
> Where's the umbrella?
> Where are the nuts?

Practice

- Revise some phonics sounds. Say words and ask pupils to find things in the picture with the same sound. Say *mum*. Pupils find other things containing the /ʌ/ sound (*duck, nuts*). Continue with *crown/brown; blue/shoe, green/key; frog/doll, big/fish*, etc.

2 Listen and number. Then play.

- Look at the Quest items shown in the treasure chest. Say a word and pupils find it. Play CD3:36 and pupils number the boxes as the items are mentioned. Pupils check their answers in pairs. One pupil says a number and their partner says the Quest item.

> 1 I've got the photo! **3:36**
> 2 I've got the duck!
> 3 I've got the umbrella!
> 4 I've got the key!
> 5 I've got the sunglasses!
> 6 I've got the treasure chest!
> 7 I've got the shoe!
> 8 I've got the present!
> 9 I've got the nuts!
>   We've got them all!

Stand up, jump up, come on a quest,   **3:37**
Come on a quest today.
Turn around, sit down, come on a quest,
Come on a quest today.
A treasure chest, a present, a photo, a key,
sunglasses, a duck, nuts, a shoe and an umbrella.
We've got them all today!
Princess Emily's got new friends
And Pippin's home again – Hurray!
Princess Emily's got new friends
And Pippin's home again – Hurray!
Hurray! Hurray! Hurray!
Hurray! Hurray! Hurray!

4 Trace. Then draw yourself.

- Point to the speech bubble in the picture at the bottom of PB p. 69. Say *Goodbye!* Wave your hand to help with the meaning. Pupils trace the word 'Goodbye!', then draw themselves as a prince/princess under the crown.

End of year project

- Pupils make a book from blank paper to show things they've learnt throughout the year. Pupils write a unit number on each page and draw pictures of words they learnt in that unit. They could also write sentences to show the structures from that unit. Allow pupils to use their Pupil's Book as reference.

Ending the lesson

- Photocopy the certificate see p. 173. Give each pupil a copy to colour and congratulate them for completing the course. Pupils write their names on their certificates. Pupils may use glitter, sequins, etc. to decorate their certificates.

> **OPTIONAL ACTIVITIES**
> **Quiz**
> Divide the class into groups. Give each group one unit from the Pupil's Book. Each group creates a quiz for their classmates. They could include words with a box for pupils to draw the object; they could write colouring instructions or puzzles. Encourage pupils to use the Activity Book for ideas. Photocopy the quizzes for each pupil.
> **Party!**
> Hold a celebration party in the classroom. Bring snacks and ask pupils to dress up. Play the songs from the course and hold a dance competition. End the party with some favourite games.

Game

- Play a game of noughts and crosses on the board. Draw a large grid of nine squares and stick a word card from any unit at the top of each square, face down. Divide the class into two teams. One team is Xs and the other is Os. The first team chooses a square and flips over the word card. Pupils read the card and choose one member of the team to draw a picture of the word on the card. Pupils write an X or an O in the square if they draw the correct object. Teams take turns until one team is able to write three Xs or Os in a row or diagonally.

3 Listen and sing.

- Challenge pupils to sing the Quest song from memory. Now play CD3:37 of the final Quest song and pupils point to the items and characters mentioned. Play it several times until pupils can sing along. You could then ask them to sing to the karaoke version of the song CD3:50.

Christmas

Starting the lesson

- Draw a Christmas tree or a Christmas stocking on the board. Ask which festival the item represents. Teach the phrase *Happy Christmas!* Discuss (L1) when Christmas is celebrated and how or if it is celebrated in the pupils' country. Talk about Christmas traditions and things pupils like doing at Christmas time. Explain that in Britain, Christmas is a time for giving. Point to Santa and ask *Who's this?* If your pupils are unfamiliar with Santa, explain that children believe he brings gifts on Christmas Eve. Explain the difference between Christmas and Christmas Eve.

PB page 70

Presentation

- Teach the words *stocking, star, Christmas tree, present* and *card* by drawing pictures on the board and writing the words below each. Alternatively, use homemade flashcards or pictures you brought to class.
- Ask questions about the picture. *How many (presents)? What colour's the (star)? Who's this? What's this?* Ask which room pupils can see in the picture *(the living room)*.

1  Listen and sing. Then find and say.

- Play the recording of the song CD3:38. Pupils listen and point to the *stocking, Christmas tree, Santa* and *presents* when they hear those words in the song. Elicit the Christmas words they heard and write them on the board in the correct order. Play the song again several times and pupils try to join in with the words.

- You might also like to invent some actions with the class (hanging up stockings, carrying a sack of presents, gesturing a long beard and a big nose, etc.), which they do as they listen and sing. You could also play the karaoke version of the song CD3:51 for pupils to sing along to.

> Hang up your stockings   **3:38**
> By the Christmas tree.
> Hang up your stockings,
> It's Christmas Eve. (x 2)
> Who's this with a brown sack
> In the living room?
> With a long white beard
> And a big red nose
> And he laughs with a Ho, ho, ho!
> Is it true? Can it be?
> Yes, it's Santa! Come and see.
> With a long white beard
> And a big red nose
> And presents for you and me.
> Hang up your stockings
> By the Christmas tree.
> Hang up your stockings,
> It's Christmas Eve. (x 2)

Project

2 Make. Then give and say.

- Photocopy the Christmas cut outs at the back of the book. Pupils cut out and colour the front of their present, star, etc. as they wish. On the back, they draw a picture of a toy or something they would like to give a friend as a gift for Christmas. You can either use the drawings to decorate the classroom for Christmas or pupils may give their 'gifts' at the end of the lesson, saying *Happy Christmas* as they do so.

AB page 62

1 Match. Then trace and say.

- Point to each of the pictures in turn and ask *What/Who's this?* Pupils match the words to the correct picture and then trace the words. Pupils check their answers in pairs by saying the words to a partner, who points to the correct picture.

2 Look and colour.

- Say a number and pupils read the colour word written next to the number. Pupils colour the picture according to the number key at the top of the activity.

Christmas

1 🔊 3:38 🎵 Listen and sing. Then find and say.

star

Christmas tree

stocking

present

Santa

2 ✂️ Make. Then give and say.

Happy Christmas!

Ending the lesson

- Play a game of Pass the Christmas ornament with ornaments that won't break easily. Play some Christmas music. Pupils sit in a large circle and pass the ornament around the circle. When you stop the music, the pupil holding the ornament says something he/she would like for Christmas, then returns to their seat. Continue until there's only one child remaining.

OPTIONAL ACTIVITIES

Decorate a tree
Draw a large Christmas tree on sturdy green card. Pupils make ornaments to decorate the tree and stick the presents they have made below it.

Flashcard game
Play Flashcard mime see p. 23.

Valentine's Day

Starting the lesson

- Draw a large heart on the board or bring a Valentine's Day card to class. Ask which festival the heart represents. Say *Happy Valentine's Day!* Discuss (L1) when Valentine's Day is celebrated and how or if it is celebrated in the pupils' country. Talk about Valentine's Day traditions in Britain, especially giving a card or present to a person you love.

PB page 71

Presentation

- Teach the words *heart, balloon, chocolates, flower* and *card* by drawing pictures on the board and writing the words below each. Alternatively, use homemade flashcards or pictures you brought to class.
- Ask questions about the picture. *What's this? What colour is it? How many (flowers)?* Point to the family members in turn and ask *Who's this?*

1. Listen and sing. Then find and say.

- Play the recording of the song CD3:39 and pupils point to the words labelled in the picture as they are mentioned. Elicit the words they heard and write them in a column on the board in the correct order. Then write *dad, mum, grandad* and *granny* in a second column. Play the song a second time and afterwards pupils match the two columns on the board.
- Play the song again several times and pupils try to join in with the words. You could also play the karaoke version of the song CD3:52 for pupils to sing along to.

I'm so happy!   3:39
Let's sing and play.
I'm so happy!
It's Valentine's Day!
Here's a flower for my mum.
Some chocolates for my dad.
Here's a heart for Granny
And a card for Grandad.
I'm so happy!
Let's sing and play.
I'm so happy!
It's Valentine's Day!

Game

- Draw simple pictures on the board of a balloon, a heart, a flower, a card and some chocolates. Write the Valentine words on small strips of paper and put them in a bag or small box. Ask pupils to sit in a large circle. Play the recording of the song and pupils pass the bag or box round the circle. Stop the music. The pupil holding the box or bag chooses a strip of paper from inside it, reads it and sticks it on the board below the correct picture. Continue until all the words have been used.

Project

2. Make and play.

- Give each pupil a photocopy of the cards at the back of the book. Pupils colour the cards and cut them out. Divide the class into pairs. Pupils play a game of memory by spreading out both their sets of cards face down on their desks and choosing two cards to make a match. Pupils keep the cards when they find two of the same card and put them face down again if they aren't the same. The pupil with the most cards at the end of the game wins.

AB page 63

1. Write the words.

- Point to the pictures in turn and ask *What's this?* Now call out a word (e.g. *chocolate*) and pupils say the number written next to it (1). Pupils complete the crossword puzzle by writing the correct words in the puzzle. Pupils check answers in pairs by comparing their puzzles.

2. Draw a present for a friend.

- Ask pupils to remember who received which present in the song in PB Activity 1. Ask (L1) which present they would like to receive. In the frame, pupils draw a Valentine's Day present they'd like to give to a friend. They then complete the sentence next to his/her drawing by writing his/her friend's name in the gap.

Valentine's Day

1  **Listen and sing. Then find and say.**

balloon

flowers

heart

card

chocolates

2   **Make and play.**

Two hearts!

Ending the lesson

- Play a game of Bingo with the cards from PB Activity 2. Pupils choose three cards and put them face up on their desks. Call out the words in turn. Pupils turn the cards over as they are called. The first pupil to turn over all the cards wins the game.

OPTIONAL ACTIVITIES
Make a Valentine card
Pupils make a Valentine's Day card, using coloured paper, glitter, etc. Then they write *Happy Valentine's Day* inside and give it to someone in their family.
Team game
Play Yes or no? see p. 25.

Lesson aims
To learn vocabulary relating to Easter

Target language
chick, Easter bunny, egg, flower, rabbit. How are you?

Recycled language
jump, turn around, wake up

Materials
Audio CD; Easter Bunny cut out; sticky tape or glue; several eggs cut out of coloured card

Optional materials
Hard-boiled eggs for pupils to decorate

Starting the lesson

- Ask pupils which special days or festivals they remember from previous lessons. Sing the songs for Christmas CD3:38 or Valentine's Day CD3:39.
- Draw some Easter eggs in a basket on the board. Ask (L1) which festival they represent. Talk about how Easter is celebrated in the pupils' country and in other countries. Talk about things people in Britain do at Easter (e.g. paint eggs, have egg hunts, eat chocolate bunnies and chocolate eggs, etc). Explain that *bunny* is another word for *rabbit*.

 **PB page 72**

Presentation

- Teach the words *egg, basket, rabbit, flower* and *chick* by drawing pictures on the board and writing the words below each. Alternatively, use homemade flashcards or pictures you brought to class.
- Ask questions about the pictures in PB Activity 2. *What's this? What colour is it?*

1 **Make. Then listen and sing.**

- Make a photocopy of the Easter Bunny cut out at the back of the book for each pupil. Pupils cut out and colour the Easter Bunny as they wish. Pupils then attach a craft stick or pencil to their bunnies with tape or glue.
- Teach/revise the actions in the song (*jump, turn around, wake up* and *fall down*) by miming them. Then say *Hello! How are you today?* Explain any unknown words in L1 if necessary.

- Play the recording of the song CD3:40. Pupils listen and use their bunnies to do the actions as they hear them. Play the song again several times, until pupils are able to sing along to the words. You could also play the karaoke version of the song CD3:53 for pupils to sing along to.

> Hello Easter Bunny. **3:40**
> How are you today?
> Wake up, wake up,
> Come and play.
> Jump, jump, jump,
> Easter Bunny jump.
> Turn around, turn around,
> Fall down with a thump.
> Hello Easter Bunny.
> How are you today?
> Wake up, wake up,
> Come and play.
> Jump, jump, jump,
> Easter Bunny jump.
> Turn around, turn around,
> Fall down with a thump.

2 **Play the game.**

- This is a game of 'battleships' played in pairs. Explain (L1) that the grid on the left is a pupil's own card and the grid on the right is for recording their partner's card. Each pupil draws a rabbit, egg, chick and flower into their own grid, using four of the six squares. Pupil A picks a square (e.g. *1 Blue*) and if Pupil B has an object in that square they say *Hit! The (rabbit)!* If there isn't anything in the square that Pupil A chose, Pupil B says *Miss!* Pupil A then puts a tick or cross in that square of the grid on the right and Pupil B has a turn. The winner is the first player to hit all four of his/her partner's drawings.

AB page 64

1 **Match. Then trace and say.**

- Point to each of the pictures in turn and ask *What's this?* Pupils match the words to the correct picture and then trace the words. Pupils check answers in pairs by saying the words to a partner, who points to the correct picture.

2 **Read. Then count and write.**

- Pupils study the picture. They then read the sentences below the picture and count the items. Pupils write the correct number in the box after each sentence, then compare answers in pairs.

> **KEY 5** chicks, **9** eggs, **4** flowers, **2** rabbits

Easter

1 Make. Then listen and sing.

2 Play the game.

rabbit

egg

chick

flower

1		
1		
2		
3		

2		
1		
2		
3		

chick, Easter bunny, egg, flower, rabbit. How are you? *jump, turn around, wake up*

Ending the lesson

- Divide the class into groups. Each group is given a set of different coloured eggs that you've cut out from coloured card. Choose one or two children from each group to wait in the corridor while each group hides their eggs in the classroom. Call the pupils back into the classroom and they find their group's coloured eggs.

OPTIONAL ACTIVITIES

Egg decorating
Bring hard-boiled eggs into class for pupils to paint. Use markers or crayons to decorate the eggs.

TPR game
Play Guess the object see p. 24.

Word cards

eleven
twelve
thirteen
fourteen
fifteen
sixteen
seventeen
eighteen
nineteen
twenty

boat
bike
ball
train
doll
car

granny
grandad
mum
dad
sister
brother
baby
house
garden

head
body
arms
hands
fingers
legs
feet
toes

face
eyes
ears
nose
mouth
hair

fat
thin
short
long
hot
cold

cow
horse
goat
sheep
duck
hen

chicken
fish
pizza
rice
salad
apple
banana
egg
bread
cheese

T-shirt
dress
trousers
skirt
shoes
socks

cloudy
rainy
snowy
sunny
windy

Flash cards

boat
bike
ball
train
doll
car

granny
grandad
mum
dad
sister
brother
baby
house
garden

head
body
arms
hands
fingers
legs
feet
toes

face
eyes
ears
nose
mouth
hair

fat
thin
short
long
hot
cold

cow
horse
goat
sheep
duck
hen

chicken
fish
pizza
rice
salad
apple
banana
egg
bread
cheese

T-shirt
dress
trousers
skirt
shoes
socks

cloudy
rainy
snowy
sunny
windy

Well Done!

Tropical Island

Evaluation

Evaluation can be described as an attempt to analyse the learning that a child has achieved over a period of time as a result of the classroom teaching/learning situation. It plays an integral part in the teaching and learning process.

The evaluation material included in *Our Discovery Island* has been designed to analyse pupils' progress with the aim of reinforcing the positive aspects and identifying areas for improvement.

There are five main reasons for evaluation:

Formative – to increase motivation by making evaluation a part of the continuous learning process.

Summative – to give pupils feedback on their progress or achievement at a particular point in time, often formally through tests.

Informative – to give pupils and parents feedback on progress or achievements.

Diagnostic – to monitor individual pupils' needs and help identify pupils who need special support.

Evaluative – to identify pupils' level of achievement and select or order pupils according to merit, to check effectiveness of teaching methods, teaching materials and teachers.

Our Discovery Island provides eight photocopiable evaluations for use at the end of each unit and a further end of year evaluation. A photocopiable evaluation chart to record pupils' progress can be found on p. 175 and a photocopiable certificate can be found on p. 173 for the children to take home to their parents.

Our Discovery Island also encourages self-evaluation at the end of each unit in the Activity Books, giving the pupils an important opportunity to express their own opinion of their progress.

PUPIL'S NAME	EVALUATION CHART								
	1	2	3	4	5	6	7	8	E-o-Y

MARKING CRITERIA   ★ 1 – 3 = Still developing   ★★ 4 – 6 = Progressing well   ★★★ 7 – 10 = Excellent

Evaluation teaching notes

Evaluation sheet I

 Listen and colour.

- Read the script. Pupils listen and colour the toys on the page accordingly.

> **Teacher script**
> It's a ball. It's black.
> It's a car. It's yellow.
> It's a doll. It's green.
> It's a bike. It's purple.
> It's a boat. It's red.
> It's a train. It's blue.

> **KEY: 2** green **3** purple **4** yellow **5** blue **6** red
> (5 points)

 **Read. Then write.**

- Pupils read the written number on the right and write in the correct number on the left.

> **KEY: 2** 17 **3** 13 **4** 19 **5** 12 **6** 15
> (5 points)

Evaluation sheet 2

 Listen. Then write a ✓ or a ✗.

- Read the script. Pupils find the people and mark the boxes with a ✓ or ✗ accordingly.

> **Teacher script**
> 1 **LINDY:** Where's my granny?
>   **CHILD:** She's in the kitchen.
> 2 **LINDY:** Where's my brother?
>   **CHILD:** He's in the bathroom.
> 3 **LINDY:** Where's my grandad?
>   **CHILD:** He's in the living room.
> 4 **LINDY:** Where's my sister?
>   **CHILD:** She's in the bedroom.
> 5 **LINDY:** Where's my dad?
>   **CHILD:** He's in the living room.
> 6 **LINDY:** Where's my mum?
>   **CHILD:** She's in the bathroom.

> **KEY: 2** ✓ **3** ✗ **4** ✓ **5** ✓ **6** ✗
> (5 points)

 Write.

- Pupils look at the pictures of the girl's family and write in the correct answers.

> **KEY: 2** grandad **3** sister **4** dad **5** granny
> **6** brother
> (5 points)

Evaluation sheet 3

  Listen and number.

- Read the script. Pupils listen and write the correct number of the monster 1-3 in the boxes.

Teacher script
1 I've got four legs.
2 I've got six toes.
3 I've got four feet and twelve toes.
4 I've got two arms.
5 I've got eight fingers.
6 I've got three hands.

KEY: b 3 **c** 1 **d** 3 **e** 1 **f** 2
(5 points)

   Look. Then read and write.

- Pupils complete the sentences by looking at the pictures and writing the correct word from the word bank into the gap.

KEY: 2 hands **3** feet **4** toes **5** arms/hands
6 body
(5 points)

Evaluation sheet 4

  Listen and number.

- Read the script. Pupils listen and number the faces in the order they are described.

Teacher script
1 He's got small eyes.
2 She's got a small nose.
3 She's got long hair.
4 He's got a small mouth.
5 He's got small ears.

KEY: b 4 **c** 5 **d** 2 **e** 1
(4 points)

   Read. Then look and write.

- Pupils look at the faces and read the sentences. Then they complete the sentences by writing the correct word from the word bank into the gap.

KEY: 2 short **3** big **4** small **5** big **6** long **7** big
(6 points)

Evaluation teaching notes

Evaluation sheet 5

  Listen. Then circle.

- Read the script. Pupils listen and circle the animal being described.

> **Teacher script**
> 1 It's small. It's got two legs. It's got a big head.
> 2 It's big. It's got four legs. It's thin.
> 3 It's big. It's got short legs. It's fat.
> 4 It's got four legs. It's got long ears.

> **KEY:** 2 a goat 3 a cow 4 a dog
> (3 points)

  Listen and write.

- Read the script. Pupils listen and write the animal whose sound they hear.

> **Teacher script**
> 1 Quack. What is it?
> 2 Moo! What is it?
> 3 Ribbit. What is it?
> 4 Baaa! What is it?
> 5 Meow! What is it?
> 6 Neigh! What is it?
> 7 Kluk! What is it?
> 8 Woof! What is it?

> **KEY:** 2 cow 3 frog 4 sheep 5 cat 6 horse 7 hen
> 8 dog
> (7 points)

Evaluation sheet 6

  Listen and match.

- Read the script. Pupils listen and draw a line to the happy or sad face accordingly.

> **Teacher script**
> 1 I like salad.
> 2 I don't like bread.
> 3 I like rice.
> 4 I like apples.
> 5 I don't like fish.
> 6 I like eggs.
> 7 I don't like chicken.

> **KEY: like:** rice, apples, eggs; **don't like:** bread, fish, chicken
> (6 points)

  **Read, then draw.**

- Pupils look at the shopping list. They then draw the food with the ✓ on a plate.

> **KEY:** ✓ banana, fish, apple, pizza
> (4 points)

Evaluation sheet 7

  Listen and write a or b.

- Read the script. Pupils listen and write *a* or *b* according to whether they hear information about the girl (*a*) or the boy (*b*).

Teacher script
1 I'm wearing socks.
2 I'm wearing shoes.
3 I'm wearing trousers.
4 I'm wearing boots.
5 I'm wearing a T-shirt.
6 I'm wearing a dress.

KEY: 2 b 3 b 4 a 5 b 6 a
(5 points)

   Read and write.

- Pupils complete the sentences by writing the correct word from the word bank into the gap.

KEY: 1 jumper 2 pyjamas 3 dress 4 skirt, T-shirt
(5 points)

Evaluation sheet 8

  **Listen and draw.**

- Read the script. Pupils listen and draw the correct weather condition under the correct day of the week.

Teacher script
1 It's Monday. It's snowy.
2 It's Saturday. It's cloudy.
3 It's Friday. It's sunny.
4 It's Sunday. It's rainy.
5 It's Thursday. It's cloudy.
6 It's Tuesday. It's sunny.
7 It's Wednesday. It's rainy.

KEY: Tuesday – sunny **Wednesday** – rainy
Thursday – cloudy **Friday** – sunny **Saturday** –
cloudy **Sunday** – rainy
(6 points)

  Write.

- Pupils look at the characters and the weather conditions. They then complete the sentences by writing the correct word into the gap.

KEY: 2 cloudy 3 windy 4 rainy 5 snowy
(4 points)

Evaluation teaching notes

End of year evaluation sheet

  Listen and write *a* or *b*.

- Read the script. Pupils listen and write *a* or *b* in the boxes according to which picture is being described.

Teacher script
1 It's sunny.
2 I've got a car.
3 I like apples.
4 I've got a ball.
5 I'm wearing a jumper.
6 I'm wearing a T-shirt.

KEY 2 a 3 a 4 b 5 a 6 b
(5 points)

   Read, then write.

- Pupils complete the sentences about Picture b from Activity 1 with the correct word from the word bank.

KEY 2 skirt 3 garden 4 sunny 5 ball 6 salad
(5 points)

Evaluation sheet I

Name: .... Class: ....

1  **Listen and colour.**

1

2

3

4

5

6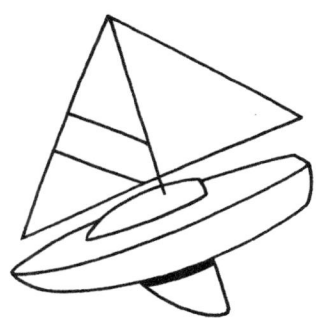

2   **Read. Then write.**

1	II	eleven	2	☐	seventeen	3	☐	thirteen
4	☐	nineteen	5	☐	twelve	6	☐	fifteen

Evaluation sheet 2

Name: .... Class: ....

1 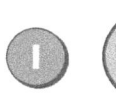  Listen. Then write a ✔ or a ✗.

1 ☒ 2 ☐ 3 ☐ 4 ☐ 5 ☐ 6 ☐

2  Write.

1 This is my __mum__. **2** This is my _____. **3** This is my _____.

4 This is my _____. **5** This is my _____. **6** This is my _____.

1 5 points   2 5 points   Total

Evaluation sheet 3

Name: .... Class: ....

 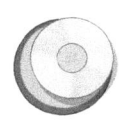  **Listen and number.**

a 2   **b** ☐   **c** ☐   **d** ☐   **e** ☐   **f** ☐

 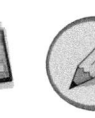 **Look. Then read and write.**

body	feet	arms
~~legs~~	toes	hands

1 Move your __legs__ .

2 Clap your _____ .

3 Stamp your _____ .

4 Touch your _____ .

5 Wave your _____ .

6 Shake your _____ .

1 5 points   2 5 points   Total

4 My face

Evaluation sheet 4

Name: .... Class: ....

  **1** **Listen and number.**

a  **3**

b  ☐

c  ☐

d  ☐

e  ☐

   **2** **Read. Then look and write.**

short	small	big	long
big	big	small	

1 He's got **small** ears.

2 He's got _____ hair.

3 She's got _____ eyes.

4 He's got a _____ mouth.

5 He's got a _____ nose.

6 She's got _____ hair.

7 She's got a _____ mouth.

① 4 points   ② 6 points   Total

5 Animals

Evaluation sheet 5

Name: .... Class: ....

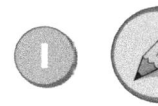  **1** **Listen. Then circle.**

1

2

3

4

2  **Listen and write.**

| horse | hen | ~~duck~~ | sheep | cat | dog | cow | frog |

1 __duck__   2 _____   3 _____

4 _____   5 _____   6 _____

7 _____   8 _____

6 Food

Evaluation sheet 6

Name: .... Class: ....

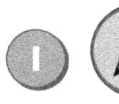  **1** Listen and match.

  **2** Read, then draw.

| 1 6 points | 2 4 points | Total |

Evaluation sheet 7

Name: .... Class: ....

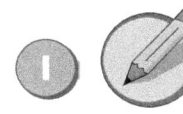  **1** Listen and write *a* or *b*.

a   b

1	a	**2**	
3		**4**	
5		**6**	

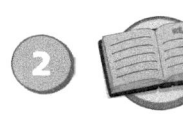  **2** Read and write.

~~trousers~~   dress   pyjamas   T-shirt   jumper   skirt

1

I'm wearing __trousers__
and a _____ .

2

I'm wearing _____ .

3

I'm wearing a _____ .

4

I'm wearing _____
and a _____ .

1 5 points   **2** 5 points   Total

8 Weather

Evaluation sheet 8

Name: .... Class: ....

  **1** **Listen and draw.**

Monday	Tuesday	Wednesday	Thursday	Friday	Saturday	Sunday
❄️						

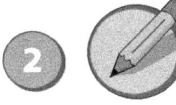 **2** **Write.**

1 It's ___sunny___ .

2 It's _____ .

3 It's _____ .

4 It's _____ .

5 It's _____ .

1 6 points   **2** 4 points   Total

End of year evaluation sheet

Name: .... Class: ....

1 🖍️ **Listen and write *a* or *b*.**

a

b

1 `b` **2** ☐ **3** ☐ **4** ☐ **5** ☐ **6** ☐

2 📖 🖍️ **Read, then write.**

| garden | skirt | salad | ~~dog~~ | sunny | ball |

I've got a __dog__ . It's got four legs.

I'm wearing a T-shirt and a _____ .

Where's the girl? She's in the _____ .

It isn't snowy. It's _____ .

I've got a toy. It's a _____ .

I like _____ .

1 5 points   2 5 points   Total

Worksheet 1

Name: .... **Class:** ....

1  **Read. Then find and colour.**

It's a boat. It's orange.

It's a bike. It's blue.

It's a ball. It's red.

It's a doll. It's purple.

2 **Draw. Then write.**

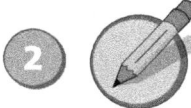

1 It's a _____ .

2 It's a _____ .

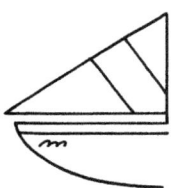

3 It's a _____ .

4 It's a _____ .

car   boat   train   doll

Worksheet 2

Name: .... Class: ....

1  **Write.**

sister   brother   dad   mum   grandad   granny

1 _____   2 _____   3 _____   4 _____   5 _____   6 _____

2  **Draw and write.**

1 Where's my mum?
She's in the _____ .

2 Where's my brother?
He's in the _____ .

3 Where's my granny?
She's in the _____ .

4 Where's my dad.
He's in the _____ .

5 Where's my sister?
She's in the _____ .

6 Where's my grandad?
He's in the _____ .

Worksheet 3

Name: .... Class: ....

1 📖 ✏️ **Read and draw.**

1 *I've got four arms.*

2 *I've got six legs.*

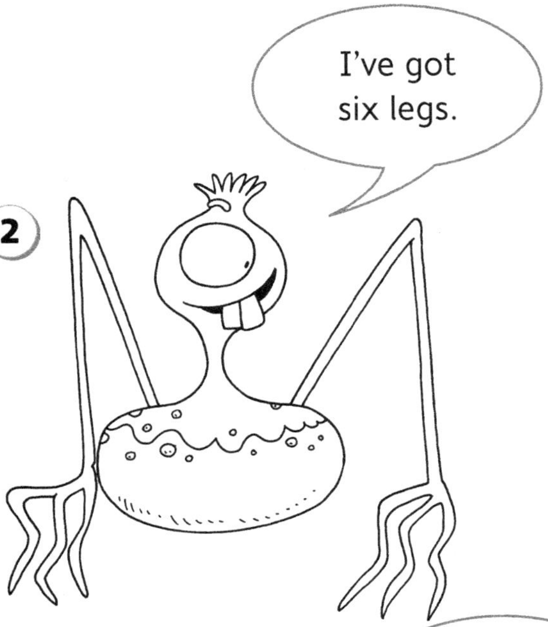

3 *I've got four hands and four feet.*

4 *I've got one head.*

2 📖 ✏️ **Read and ✓ or ✗.**

1 I've got seven toes. ✗

2 I've got two long arms. ☐

3 I've got two heads. ☐

4 I've got three legs. ☐

Worksheet 4

Name: .... **Class:** ....

   **Say and draw. Then circle and write.**

 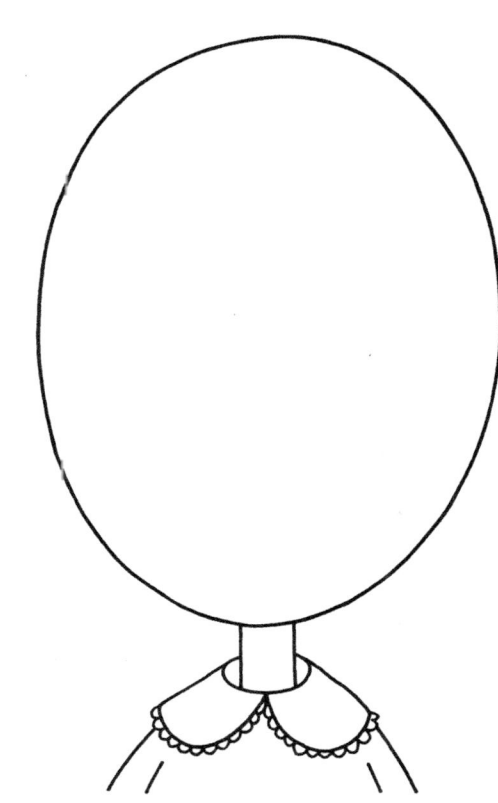

1 He's / She's got _____ eyes.

2 He's / She's got _____ hair.

3 He's / She's got a _____ nose.

4 He's / She's got a _____ mouth.

5 He's / She's got _____ ears.

5 Animals

Worksheet 5

Name: .... Class: ....

 **Read and write. Then draw.**

duck   horse   sheep

1

2

3

It's big.

It's got four legs.

It's got long legs.

It's a _____ .

It's small.

It's got two legs.

It's got short legs.

It's a _____ .

It's big.

It's got four legs.

It's got short legs.

It's a _____ .

  **Write. Then draw.**

It's _____ .

It's got _____ .

_____ .

_____ .

Worksheet 6

Name: .... Class: ....

   **Read and draw.**

    **Look. Then read and write.**

fish   pizza   eggs   rice

I like _____ and _____ .   I don't like _____ and _____ .

Worksheet 7

Name: .... Class: ....

   **Draw and colour. Then write.**

a jumper   shoes   a T-shirt   trousers   a skirt   boots

1 I'm wearing _____ , _____ and _____ .

2 I'm wearing _____ , _____ and _____ .

   **Read. Then find and colour.**

a blue dress

a purple skirt

black shoes

a yellow T-shirt

orange trousers

a green jumper

8 Weather

Worksheet 8

Name: .... Class: ....

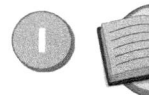  **Read and write. Then play.**

| T-shirt | sunny | living room | boat | dress | rainy | garden | train |

1

It's _____ .

He's in the _____ .

He's got a _____ .

I'm wearing a _____ .

2

It's _____ .

She's in the _____ .

She's got a _____ .

I'm wearing a _____ .

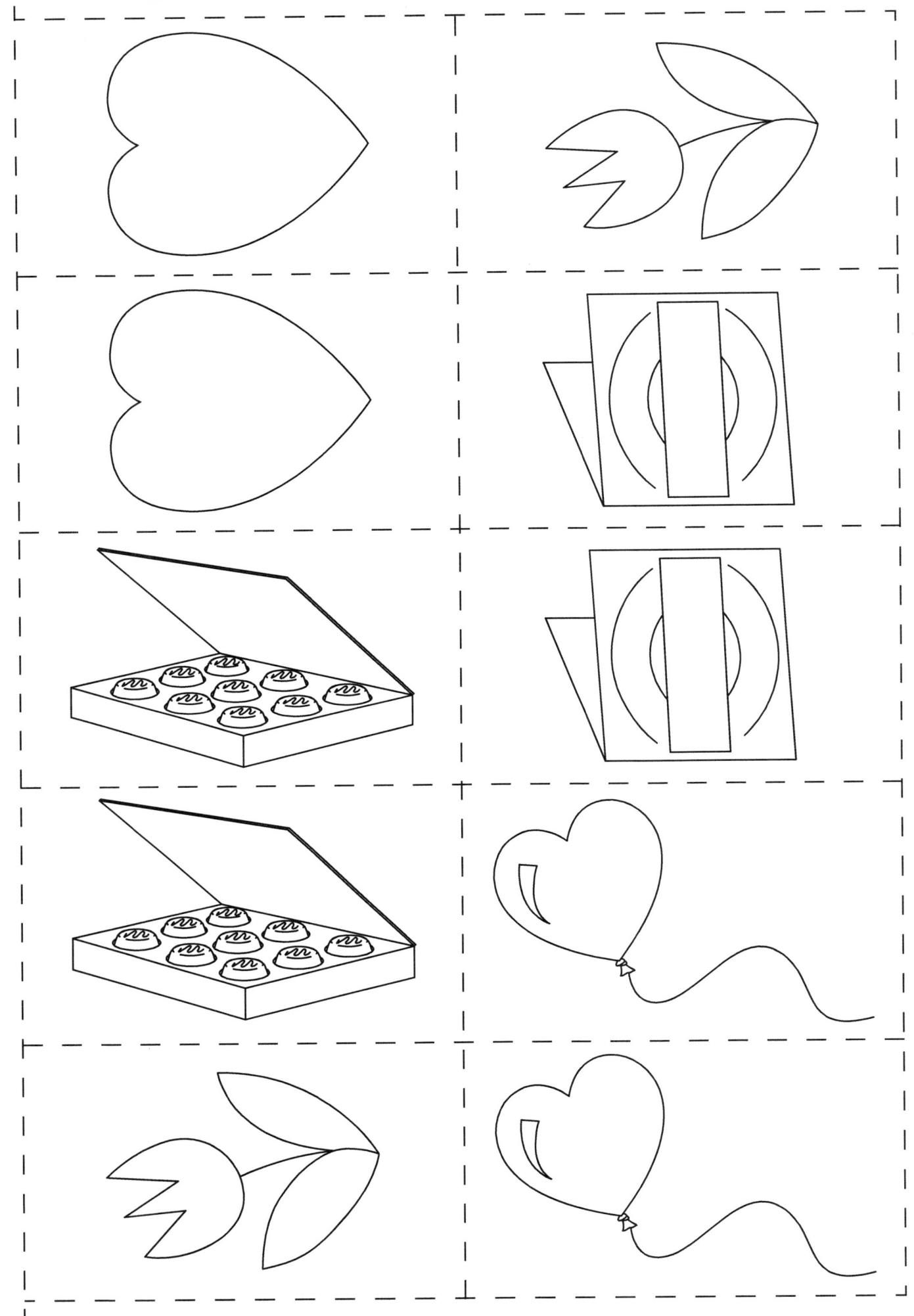

thirteen

sixteen

nineteen

twelve

fifteen

eighteen

eleven

fourteen

seventeen

bike	doll	granny
boat	train	grandad
twenty	ball	car

sister

house

body

dad

baby

head

mum

brother

garden

fingers	hands	arms
toes	feet	legs
ears	eyes	face

hair

short

cold

mouth

thin

hot

nose

fat

long

goat	horse	cow
hen	duck	sheep
pizza	fish	chicken

apple

bread

dress

salad

egg

T-shirt

rice

banana

cheese

shoes	skirt	trousers
rainy	cloudy	socks
windy	sunny	snowy